# Confessions of a Tomboy Grandma

## On the Eternal Destiny of the Human Race

Diane Perkins Castro

Cover Design by Christine M. Castro
The cover image looks like a fiery inferno but is actually a brilliant sunrise. God's purposes may appear to be destructive but actually lead to a glorious new beginning.

Reviewed by Bruce E. Foster

ID Publishing House
IMAGO DEI
Beverly, MA

## DEDICATION

Dedicated to all those who have ever feared that they or someone they love will suffer eternal torment in hell.

But now thus says the Lord, he who created you,
"Fear not, for I have redeemed you;
I have called you by name, you are mine."
(Isaiah 43:1)

# Also by Diane Perkins Castro

*Reflections of a Tomboy Grandma: On the Immeasurable Worth of Every Human Being*

# PREFACE
# BY THOMAS TALBOTT

In these compelling reflections, Diane Perkins Castro pursues a set of questions that too few scholars and pastors in her own evangelical community have had the courage to address openly and honestly. Her most basic question, under which many related questions fall, is as simple as it is profound. How, she asks, can the Christian gospel be truly good news, as the word itself implies, if this gospel includes the supposed teaching that some of our dearest loved ones (perhaps even some of our own children) might be separated from us and tormented forever in that torture chamber known as hell? Related questions include such questions as these: Is there really, as so many assume, a clear and obvious biblical warrant for the traditional understanding of hell as a place of unending punishment and misery? Is there not a much stronger biblical warrant for the teaching that God will eventually reconcile the entire human race to himself through his Son? And where does the Bible even hint that God's love might have a built-in time limit for the lost, usually understood as the moment of one's physical death?

Although Diane Perkins Castro describes herself as a "tomboy grandma," don't let that fool you. She is sharp as a tack, tenacious in debating a point, and fully capable of exposing the scholarly pretensions of those who think they find a clear and obvious doctrine of unending punishment in the Bible. Are not these the same scholars who try to persuade us that such texts as Romans 5:18 and 11:32 do not really mean what they in fact say? According to Romans 5:18, "one righteous act resulted in justification and life for all people"; and according to Romans 11:32, "God has bound everyone over to disobedience so that he may have mercy on them all."

Where do such texts as these leave any room at all for the traditional understanding of hell? (See Chapters 19 and 25 of her book.) In a three-part discussion of limited atonement, this "tomboy grandma" also tackles such formidable Reformed theologians as W. G. T. Shedd (19th century) and Wayne Grudem, whose *Systematic Theology* was published in 1994. She successfully shows, in my opinion, that Shedd's defense of limited atonement rests upon some rather silly word games and that Grudem's argument against universalism is weak because it can be reversed so easily (Chapters 35 and 36). She may not have an advanced degree in theology, but she has read widely, has spent a lifetime studying and leading Bible studies, and was a member of a Presbyterian church for 25 years. Perhaps that is why she disposes so easily (in Chapter 5 and elsewhere) with so many of the hackneyed comments in the NIV Study Bible—comments that try to persuade its readers that a text does not really mean what it in fact says. In any case, I doubt that many credentialed theologians in the evangelical community could provide anything remotely like a plausible answer to her penetrating questions.

Still, the author of this book is indeed a kind and loving grandmother; and as such, she fully appreciates the following hard truth: the more you are filled with love for someone, the more any source of misery for your beloved becomes a source of misery for you as well. She thus recounts in her opening chapter the shock and grief that she and her then 14-year-old son experienced in the year 2000 when one of his friends tragically committed suicide. "Few people," she observes, "would come right out and tell grieving parents that their son is now burning in hell." But isn't that precisely what the preaching in many churches clearly implies? What possible solace could grieving parents receive from such preaching? And as the author makes ever so clear, such preaching leaves grief-stricken people with the following unacceptable alternative: either (a) God's redemptive love is limited in its scope, as the Calvinists believe, and he has never loved some of our own loved ones, whom Jesus commanded us to love, or (b)

God's loving will suffers an ultimate defeat, as the Arminians believe. So which is it? Are we to believe that God is limited in love, or that his loving will suffers an ultimate defeat? For Diane Perkins Castro, the true God of the Bible loves each of us equally and unconditionally, and his loving will for us, though no doubt resistible for a while, cannot be defeated forever (see, for example, Chapter 43).

This book also has some unusual characteristics. Many of its short chapters can stand alone as individual reflections; its author thus explains in her introduction that a few chapters "are consecutive and sometimes the essays on a specific theme are grouped together, but otherwise there is no linear order." In that respect the book is similar to a handbook, whose chapter headings, indexes, and appendixes permit one to skip around according to one's particular interests. One helpful appendix entitled "Quick Questions" provides brief answers to commonly posed questions concerning Christian universalism. A chapter entitled "In What Way Are God's Ways Higher Than Our Ways?" one entitled "I Wish It Were True, But …," and one entitled "Heretic!" address common responses to the author's rejection of an everlasting hell. And three chapters on limited atonement plus a four-part series entitled "What Is Hellfire?" deal with critical exegetical and theological issues related to that rejection.

Some chapters and one appendix feature outside sources included for the purpose of making an important point. One of the appendixes features Robin Parry's essay "Bell's Hells: seven myths about universalism," in which he corrects several misunderstandings that many people, including a number of scholars who should know better, seem to have about Christian universalism. In addition to that appendix, one chapter features a letter written by a woman, now in her thirties, who describes the anxiety, depression, and sheer terror that standard "Christian" preaching instilled in her as a young child: the fear in particular that some of her closest friends might be separated from her forever in a place of everlasting torment. This reminded me of the time my own mother, herself an earnest and loving Christian, confessed to me late in life that she never would have sent her children to Sunday school had she known how hard that can be on the psyche of a child. Another chapter features Lewis Carroll's beautifully written essay on eternal punishment, and still another features excerpts from a chapter on religious cruelty in Thomas B. Thayer's book *The Origin and History of the Doctrine of Endless Punishment* (1855). But perhaps most intriguing of all to me is a chapter that features Anne Brontë's wonderful poem entitled "A Word to the 'Elect.'" Although I had never seen this poem before, it includes one powerful verse after another, including this one:

> And, wherefore should you love your God the more,
> Because to you alone his smiles are given;
> Because he chose to pass the many o'er,
> And only bring the favored few to Heaven?

Finally, one can find a good many interesting stories and anecdotes sprinkled throughout this book, such as the fact that its author was present near the finish line when the bombs exploded at the 2013 Boston Marathon. More humorous, even hilarious, are the accusations that some of her online critics have made against her. I counted 34 accusations of the following kind: "You are a child of Satan" and "You were long ago designated for this condemnation" (see note 1 of Chapter 58). The hilarious point is that such accusations are inevitably a sign that the accuser has already lost an argument. But more seriously, why do so many consider it heretical to reject the idea that some are destined to be lost forever and do not consider it heretical to limit the scope of God's redemptive love, as the Calvinists do, or alternatively, to limit the scope of his ultimate victory over sin and death, as the Arminians do? Fortunately, Diane Perkins Castro opposes every attempt to twist the "good news" of the gospel into a message of fear, and *Confessions of a Tomboy Grandma: On the Eternal Destiny of the Human Race* is a most valuable fruit of that opposition.

Thomas Talbott

# FOREWORD
# BY GEORGE W. SARRIS

My wife and I have known Diane Castro and her husband, Tony, for over 35 years as people we dearly love and deeply respect. When our children were young, we would often get together with a few other families for picnics and birthdays and special events and not-so-special events. When we did, our children would play and the adults would talk. Our conversations often touched on theological issues where we discussed, and sometimes argued, a wide array of topics, ranging from the age of the earth to the subtleties of Reformed or Arminian theologies.

Interestingly, one issue that was close to my heart never came up until many years into our friendship.

As a third-year seminary student some years before I met Diane and Tony, I wrestled with the idea of how a good God could allow anyone to suffer consciously forever. When I was in college, God's love had captured my heart and transformed my life. I wanted to tell others about this wonderful Being who had done such marvelous things in my life. But there was something deep inside of me that kept saying something was wrong with the prevailing teaching about hell within the Christian community. It just didn't seem consistent with what I knew about God's character.

For one of my theology courses at the seminary, I decided to address the issue in a straightforward manner as the subject of a research paper. I had previously written a paper on the reliability of the Bible and concluded that a deep confidence in the trustworthiness of God's Word was the foundational doctrine upon which all the other doctrines of the Christian faith must be built. I wanted to find out for sure what the Bible actually taught about Hell.

What I discovered was something I had never heard before. For the first 500 years after Christ, a prominent view—and according to some scholars the dominant view—of the leadership and the laity was that God would ultimately redeem *all* of His creation. And they based their views on Scripture. For them, hell was real, but it didn't last forever. Its purpose was to transform sinners, not torture them for all eternity.

I was excited by this discovery! It filled my heart with joy and great peace. It also gave fresh boldness and strength to my faith. I wrote the paper and received an A– grade. Because of how important I thought this was, I passed along copies of the paper to some of the seminary professors and others whom I thought were well equipped as scholars to delve into the issue further. I was hoping that my preliminary study would motivate them to address the question, as I had, in an honest way. I was surprised and saddened to learn that none of them thought it was worth studying. They all assumed that the issue had been settled by theologians centuries ago and was not worth pursuing in any serious manner.

It was obviously a controversial subject, so I kept the belief as a private hope for many years and rarely talked about it to others, even close friends. Then, 29 years after I wrote my paper, I decided it was time to study the issue in more depth.

Right around that time, we were attending an event with friends, and Diane was there. Toward the end of the evening, she came up to me and said she had heard that I held some kind of strange view about heaven and hell, and wondered what it was. I briefly explained what I believed and offered to send her a copy of the paper I had written in seminary. Not long after that, I sent her a book I had just come across that laid out in much more detail a Biblical case for ultimate restoration. Diane emailed me to say,

> I just wanted to let you know that I read the book and it has, in fact, given me more hope than I have ever felt. It not only gives me permission to entertain the idea that maybe God will restore all (without worrying

that I am indulging in wishful thinking or slipping into unorthodoxy), but it gives strong biblical support for the idea. Why shouldn't we believe that Jesus' redemptive work is more powerful and effective than Satan's destructive work?

From that point on, Diane began looking...and thinking...and writing essays about God's unlimited power and amazing grace. She carefully thought through issues as they came up to make sure that her conclusions were correct and in line with the actual Biblical teaching.

The book you are now holding in your hands is the fruit of years of thoughtful reflection and careful study by Diane. There are essays—some short, some longer, all interesting— on a wide variety of subjects relating to what the Scriptures actually teach about who God is and what His ultimate plan is for all of His creation.

At the heart of it all is a deep confidence in the goodness of God. As you read, your faith will be strengthened as you grow in your knowledge and understanding of the God of heaven whose love is unconditional, whose power is irresistible, and who never gives up!

George W. Sarris

# FOREWORD
# BY JOHN DAVID KOOB

"Which commandment is the first of all?" Jesus answered, "The first is 'Hear O Israel: the Lord our God, the Lord is one; you shall love the Lord your God with all your heart, and with all your soul, and with all your mind, and with all your strength.' The second is this, 'You shall love your neighbor as yourself.' On these two commandments hang all the law and the prophets." —Mark 12:28–31, Matthew 22:40
(New Revised Standard Version)

> Who can find a virtuous woman?
> for her price is far above rubies.
> She stretcheth out her hand to the poor;
> yea, she reacheth forth her hands to the needy.
> Strength and honor are her clothing;
> and she shall rejoice in time to come.
> She openeth her mouth with wisdom;
> and in her tongue is the law of kindness.
> —From Proverbs 31 (King James Version)

Diane was one of the first to welcome me to the new Anglican church that opened near my home in the fall of 2009. She has served as a greeter, an usher, a Scripture reader, and an active participant in many areas of church life, from home study groups to kitchen crew. Diane believes that God loves and values every single human being, and she reflects the same kindness and respect toward others, ministering to them in a multitude of ways, such as reaching out to those in distress, taking them into her home, praying for them, and giving practical aid such as meals and transportation.

And gladly wolde she lerne, and gladly teche.
—After Geoffrey Chaucer's *The Canterbury Tales*

Diane has also taught small study groups in her home. She is always well-prepared, and she encourages all participants to express their thoughts, while she maintains a friendly environment characterized by mutual respect. As a teacher myself, I think she is among the best I have seen at leading a small group. Her ability to explain differing word meanings in the Scriptures and their subsequent translations is extraordinary. In the class she taught on "Ultimate Restoration" (which is the central focus of this her second book), she showed how the theme of redemption runs strong throughout the Bible and ties together the ideas revealed there.

> Verily I say unto you, Inasmuch as ye have done it
> unto one of the least of these my brethren,
> ye have done it unto me.
> —Matthew 25:40 (King James Version)

In short, she excels in faith and works. I believe Diane to be as close to a saint as this church has. I know something of saints, as my grandfather's cousin, a Franciscan Sister known as Mother Marianne of Molokai for her ministry to the lepers of Hawaii, has recently been elevated to sainthood. As God's will would have it, she and Diane share the same birthday, are from the same area—Syracuse, New York—and share the same love of humanity, even the least of these.

> For it was you who formed my inward parts.
> You knit me together in my mother's womb.
> I praise you, for I am fearfully and wonderfully made.
> —Psalm 139:13–14 (New Revised Standard Version)

As a biologist who has taught courses on human life from conception to birth and as a teacher of special-needs students, I have a profound appreciation for the worth of every human being. Through her respect and kindness toward all people, Diane lives out her belief that God created and knows and values each person, and that none are expendable to him.

I am now over eighty and my time grows short. I appreciate Diane's great hope for "the resurrection of the dead and the life of the world to come." I have asked her if at my death she will conduct the burial service, and she has consented.

Over the years I have read some of Diane's writings, and I have encouraged her to publish them so that others might benefit. I hope that through reading this book you will come to share Diane's unshakable belief in the love of God for all his creation and in the ultimate restoration of all his people.

When the evening of this life comes,
you will be judged on love.
—From St. John of the Cross,
a 16th-century founder of the Discalced Carmelites
and confessor to St. Teresa of Avila

John David Koob

# CONTENTS

# INTRODUCTION

In my first book, *Reflections of a Tomboy Grandma,* there were only whispers of the grand truth that has under-girded and energized my life for the last decade. In this present book, I openly confess that I believe that Jesus Christ is the Savior of the world and will *actually* save the whole world. Not only will I offend many evangelicals for believing that Jesus will save *all*; I will also offend others by saying that Jesus is the *only* way to salvation. But no matter what religion you profess (if any) or where you might be on the spiritual spectrum—from confirmed fundamentalist to hard-core atheist—I encourage you to keep reading. Don't be afraid to question what you have been taught or to re-examine your most cherished beliefs.

This book is a collection of essays looking at the whole topic of eternal destinies from many different angles. The pieces in a series are consecutive and sometimes the essays on a specific theme are grouped together, but otherwise there is no linear order. The whole subject is so immense and the ideas so interwoven that it is impossible to speak on one particular issue without touching on others, so you will find recurring ideas appearing in different contexts.

You can read the book straight through or use the Table of Contents, the Index, or the Scripture Index to find topics or Bible passages that interest you. Some of the pieces are devotional, some are philosophical, and others are exegetical—there's something for everyone! If you want something that speaks to your heart, read the devotional pieces (e.g., "Come What May" or "Paradise Regained"). If you like to wrestle with ideas, try the philosophical essays (e.g., "Pick Two" or the "Unified Field" series). If you want to dig in to Scripture, choose the exegetical pieces, some of which look at the original Greek of the New Testament (e.g., "Reconciliation: The Heart of God's Grand Plan for Creation" or "By the Righteousness of One"). To get the whole picture, read the whole book! If you are looking for short answers to questions about the salvation of all, go to Appendix A, "Quick Questions," where you will find brief answers to the most common questions and objections. Don't take my word for anything; use your Bible and your brain, and decide for yourself!

Although I hesitate to label myself, some explanation of terms might be helpful. The word *Universalism* accurately conveys the idea that the entire universe will be restored and reconciled to God, but I'm reluctant to use it to refer to my belief because it is often considered to be outside of historic Christianity and different from it. Since the word *universal* speaks to the limitless extent of God's work to include every human being He has ever created, I do use it, usually in combination with other terms. The word *ultimate* reflects the idea that the complete fulfilling of God's purposes will come *in the end,* so it too is useful. The abbreviation UR can stand for any combination of Universal or Ultimate with Redemption, Restoration, or Reconciliation. An Evangelical Universalist is a Bible-believing, Trinitarian Christ-follower who holds to the commonly accepted tenets of the orthodox Christian faith and also believes that God will redeem all of humanity through Jesus Christ. For a concise explanation of Evangelical Universalism, read Robin Parry's article in Appendix B. Belief in the salvation of all is sometimes called The Larger Hope. The Greek word *apokatastasis,* meaning "restoration," is often used to refer to the final restoration of all things.

If I had to give a three-word summary of the theme of my first book, it would be "Love one another." The underlying theme of the book you now hold is "God is love." As you read, put this proposition to the test to see if it is true, and if so, what it might mean for your life.

Diane Perkins Castro

# 1

# TRUE HOPE

Easter morning 2000 started out with the anticipation of joyously celebrating the resurrection and new life, but death intruded and the mood abruptly turned tragic. We were just about to leave for church when my 14-year-old son Andy got a phone call with the news that one of his friends had committed suicide during the night. Despite the glorious music around me and powerful preaching from the pulpit, I sat through the service under a great cloud, feeling a weight of grief for the boy's family and friends and wondering where the hope in the Easter message was. Figuratively speaking, if only this kid had waited to see the light of resurrection morning! But he was trapped in the darkness and despair of night.

Few people would come right out and tell grieving parents that their dead son is now burning in hell. But if the parents have heard "gospel" preaching that says those who die without Christ are destined for an eternity of suffering, what else are they to conclude, if their son was not a Christian? What hope could be offered to the parents of this young man, whom I'll call Joseph, beyond vague assurances that God is good and will take care of him? A well-intentioned person might cheerily offer the thought that we never know what might have happened in the last moments of a person's life; maybe Joseph repented and cried out to God before the noose tightened around his neck and choked the life out of him. Can there be any comfort in such a wish so fraught with uncertainty? And what do you tell his friends? Use it as a morality tale that they should ask Jesus into their hearts before it's too late and they end up in hell? My son branded Joseph's initials into his arm, the scars a reminder to this day of a friend who was lost—forever, if the standard Christian view of eternal damnation is true.

Back in those days I used to sit in church, even on Easter Sunday, and wonder how I could ever be fully joyful and contented knowing that people I cared about would suffer forever. Preachers promised perfect personal bliss for me and everybody else in the Christian club, but the majority of human beings are not in the club. Not that they would be unwelcome in it, but most of them either haven't heard of it or have misconceptions of what it is or don't like the people in it or haven't been chosen to be part of it or don't want to do what it takes to get in, so for all practical purposes, they are excluded. I just couldn't get excited about going to heaven if it was only for the select ones who met the rather narrow (and unclear) conditions for entrance.

Now, with the understanding that Jesus' work on the cross not only is offered to all but ultimately will be effective for all, I can truly see the hope of the resurrection! Some say that speaking of the final salvation of all offers false hope, but it really is **true hope,** as contrasted with the false terror and despair offered by the view that many are eternally damned. Now I don't have to grit my teeth and force myself to trust God even though His ways seem unjust; I can truly worship the God who formed the wonderful plan of full redemption and will bring it to pass. I still grieve alongside people like Joseph's parents—death is an enemy that brings heartache and anguish—but I can gently yet confidently offer the assurance that God will bind up their broken hearts and reunite them with their loved ones.

4

Will you allow yourself to explore the possibility that Jesus might actually save the world? I challenge you to re-examine your assumptions and question what you have been taught. Dare to contemplate that Jesus' death on the cross might fully accomplish the purpose for which He died and rose again: "When I am lifted up from the earth, *I will draw all people to myself*" (John 12:32). If you feel a stirring of hope that one day this sin-ravaged world will be restored and all the broken people in it will be redeemed, then come with me on this journey to search the Scriptures and discover the riches of God's gracious purposes.

> Put your **hope** in the LORD, for with the LORD is **unfailing love** and with him is **full redemption** (Ps. 130:7).

# 2

# HEAVEN: WE HAVE A PROBLEM

As I was talking with my husband about heaven and hell and who goes where and why, he told me, "You have a big problem with your idea that God will restore everything and everybody. There are verses in the Bible that clearly teach that some people will never be restored to God." I agreed; I *do* have a problem. But I said, "We *both* have a problem. My problem is that some verses do seem to teach that some people will be eternally condemned. Your problem is that some verses seem to teach that ultimately God will redeem and restore His entire creation."

So we have two competing ideas:

1) Some people will never be redeemed.
2) God will eventually redeem all people.

Two contradictory ideas, both with biblical warrant but mutually exclusive. They cannot both be true; what is a Christian to do? Those who hold to the traditional view of hell accept statement 1 and consider statement 2 to be erroneous if not heretical. Others would say that God's plan to redeem and restore His entire creation is clearly taught in Scripture, and any passages that seem to teach otherwise need to be re-evaluated. A variant of these positions is Annihilationism— that the wicked are punished and eventually are destroyed and cease to exist. According to this doctrine, like the traditional position, statement 1 is true and statement 2 is false.

Thoughtful people on all sides will recognize that we *do* have a dilemma. Since it is impossible for both ideas to be true, one idea must be more fundamental, and verses that seem to teach the other must be interpreted in light of the foundational idea. In the traditional view, the belief that the wicked are eternally separated from God is a non-negotiable. Passages like Isaiah 66:24 and Daniel 12:2 in the Old Testament, and Matthew 25:46, Luke 16:19–31, 2 Thessalonians 1:8–9, Jude 14–15, Revelation 20:11–15, Revelation 21:7–8, and Revelation 22:14–15 in the New Testament are cited as proof that the wicked are condemned to everlasting torment from which there is no hope of escape. Any verses that seem to teach that God will ultimately redeem all mankind are subordinated to the doctrine of eternal condemnation.

Conversely, those who hold that God's love, as expressed by Christ on the cross, is foundational will interpret the eternal damnation verses in light of the ultimate purpose of God to reconcile all to Himself. They appeal to the character of God as revealed throughout Scripture and to the many passages that speak of His plans for restoration, such as John 12:32, Romans 5:12–19, Romans 11:32, 1 Corinthians 15:22, Philippians 2:9–11, Colossians 1:15–20, 1 Timothy 2:3–6, 2 Peter 3:9, and 1 John 4:14.

Furthermore, the very notion of "going to heaven" when you die as the final destiny of the Christian is thoroughly ingrained in our common understanding but is far from the New Testament picture of God's final purpose. As N. T. Wright[1] so capably shows, God is not going to discard this world but rather renew it and bring the kingdom of heaven to earth and resurrect and transform us to live in it.

So when it comes to the question of heaven, we *do* have a problem: we have befuddled ideas about what it is and the Bible seems to give contradictory messages about who will inhabit it. This book challenges readers to take a hard look at their own beliefs. If you have the courage to question common assumptions and go against the grain, please read on.

---

[1]N. T. Wright, *Surprised by Hope: Rethinking Heaven, the Resurrection, and the Mission of the Church*. HarperOne, 2008.

# 3

# BURNING WITH FIRE

On a chilly night after Christmas, we built a fire in the fireplace with used wrapping paper and dry logs. It was pleasant sitting around the fire drinking hot chocolate, but as I watched the paper blazing up and then the logs burning with a steady flame, I couldn't help thinking what it would be like to be *in* the fire. I couldn't imagine having even one hand in even such a little fire for even one minute. And yet standard Christian theology says that all unbelievers will be in a blazing furnace for all eternity with no hope of relief! Their whole body will be engulfed in flames and yet never consumed. They will experience conscious torment forever and ever. Any pleas for mercy will be ignored.

Is that what you teach your children and preach to your neighbors? Are you absolutely certain that the God you know will treat His fallen creatures that way? Has this belief been so drilled into you that you think you *have* to accept it in order to be a good, Bible-believing Christian? Or does the still, small voice of your conscience tell you that something is horribly wrong with this idea? Do you see any inconsistency between the picture of eternal conscious torment (ECT) and the character of the God you have put your trust in?[1]

You may feel it is dangerous to draw analogies between human thoughts and God's thoughts, but Jesus Himself urges us to do so! In Luke 11 He asks,

> *What father among you,* if his son asks for a fish, will instead of a fish give him a serpent; or if he asks for an egg, will give him a scorpion? (Luke 11:11–12).

Like God, a good father gives his child what is *best* for him!

Jesus' parables in Luke 15 also compare God's actions to those of good people. In the parable of the lost sheep, He asks,

> *What man of you,* having a hundred sheep, if he has lost one of them, does not leave the ninety-nine in the open country, and go after the one that is lost, until he finds it?" (Luke 15:4)

Similarly, in the parable of the lost coin, He asks,

> *What woman,* having ten silver coins, if she loses one coin, does not light a lamp and sweep the house and seek diligently until she finds it? (Luke 15:8).

An ordinary man or woman will keep seeking something precious that is lost until it is found and made safe. How much *more* so with a father and a precious child! The father of the prodigal was desperate for his wayward son to return home and welcomed him with lavish love:

> But while he was still a long way off, his father saw him and felt compassion, and ran and embraced him and kissed him (Luke 15:20).

Jesus' point is that God is even *better* than the best human father. It most certainly is appropriate to question whether God would do something that we would consider heinous if it were done by a human father.

If you want to be faithful to Scripture and yet struggle with the idea of eternal damnation, take heart! You can be a sound, Bible-believing Christian without accepting a literalist understanding of a fiery torture pit. If your heart cries out for the lost, know that God actually has a far better plan for them. His judgment is *real,* but it is purposeful and redemptive. He will not leave anyone to suffer endlessly and pointlessly. He sent His Son to save the world, and He will accomplish it!

---

[1]George MacDonald speaks of the cognitive dissonance of believing that a loving God will abandon billions to eternal suffering: "To accept that as the will of our Lord which to us is inconsistent with what we have learned to worship in him already, is to introduce discord into that harmony whose end is to unite our hearts and make them whole" (*Unspoken Sermons*).

# 4

# I WISH IT WERE TRUE, BUT…

When presented with the idea that all people might eventually be saved, most Christians will say, "I wish it were true." You long for assurance that all those you love will be in heaven. You may find joy in the thought of even terrible sinners being redeemed. You have heard testimonies of murderers, rapists, addicts, and abusers who have been pardoned and transformed, and each one is a testament to God's grace and a source of joy to us and to the angels. You long to hear more of those stories.

But then you are brought back to reality when someone says that believing everyone will be saved is just wishful thinking: You're trying to impose your own desires on God's Word, which makes it clear that some people will be forever separated from God. You're just making an accommodation to the present age; the Universalist Jesus fits in very well with the tolerant, pluralistic spirit of postmodern culture. You reject the idea of eternal damnation because it doesn't make sense or because it offends your "enlightened" moral intuitions. The great majority of godly and learned Christians over the ages have rejected Universalism; you are foolish to question the consensus of the Church. Telling yourself that a loving God can't possibly torment people for all eternity helps to ease the psychic pain caused by worry over unbelieving loved ones, but that view cannot be supported from Scripture.

Obviously, wishing that something were true does not make it so. But the fact that you wish for something that seems too good to be true does not mean that it is untrue either, especially not when it comes to the purposes of God.

The argument from "emotion"—that there is a universal *longing* for the restoration of all things—proves nothing, but I don't think it should be entirely discounted. Let me explain.

Everyone knows that something is desperately wrong with the world. We all long for something better, and most religions offer hope of a better life after we die. In most belief systems, including the traditional Christian view, the rewards (whatever they are) belong to the "believers" (whoever they are), while the punishments are for unbelievers (infidels, the wicked, the ungodly).

Throughout most of church history,[1] this paradigm has been taught—that unbelievers will suffer eternal condemnation, while believers will experience eternal bliss. This doctrine has been maintained for centuries, despite the fact that many feel a nagging uneasiness with the standard explanations. Most treatments of the topic acknowledge that the idea of people suffering everlasting hellfire is disturbing. Francis Chan, author of *Erasing Hell* (a defense of the traditional position), describes the anguish he experienced:

> The saddest day of my life was the day I watched my grandmother die.... According to what I knew of the Bible, she was headed for a life of never-ending suffering. I thought I would go crazy. I have never cried harder, and I don't ever want to feel like that again. Since that day, I have tried not to think about it. It has been over twenty years.[2] [My note: Can we expect all grieving people who agonize over lost loved ones to "try not to think about it"? Do we have nothing better to offer to those who "don't ever want to feel like that again"?]

In *The Problem of Pain*,[3] C. S. Lewis said of hell, "There is no doctrine which I would more willingly remove from Christianity than this, if it lay in my power." One Christian friend told me, "Hell has ruined my life." Sinclair B. Ferguson, a contributor to *Hell Under Fire*[4] (which identifies both Universalism and Annihilationism[5] as aberrations) admits,

…[E]very right-minded Christian should surely have a deep sympathy with John R. W. Stott's comment on everlasting punishment: "Emotionally, I find the concept intolerable." There is, surely, a profound sense in which this ought to be the reaction of all of us…. That such creatures [humans made for fellowship with God] should be banished forever into the outer darkness, with no escape exit, should fill us with a sense of horror.

Grady Brown likens the doctrine of endless punishment to the "'crazy uncle' that the Church, with justifiable embarrassment, has kept locked in the back bedroom" (in the foreword to Gerry Beauchemin's *Hope Beyond Hell*.[6]) Even the title of a recent book about hell acknowledges the repugnance we feel to the idea of never-ending suffering: *Hell is Real (But I Hate to Admit It)*, by Brian Jones.[7]

Does this resistance stem from bleeding-heart liberalism or rebellion against God and unwillingness to accept what He has revealed? Perhaps it's a desire to create and peddle one's own religion and scam the church. It has been suggested that people just want their ears to be tickled with pleasant ideas, so opportunists promote myths like Universalism that ignorant people latch onto.

**OR** could it be that our feelings are telling us that something truly is terribly wrong with the idea that a loving God could torment people for all eternity or cast them out of His presence forever? When I was a younger Christian I struggled with this idea, but I believed that as I matured and developed a deeper sense of man's sinfulness and God's holiness and became more in tune with His heart and His justice, I would be better able to accept the idea of eternal punishment for our offenses against God. It didn't happen. As I grew in my understanding of God's character and my compassion for people, the distress only increased, and I saw that God would no more torment His creatures forever than a good human father would cause his children permanent harm.

God gave us a mind, a conscience, and a heart—that is, a sense of reason, justice, and compassion—and He expects us to use them. There are many mysteries that we will never be able to fully comprehend with our mind, but we can use our **mind** to take all that God has revealed and try to put it together into a clear picture of God's character, work, and purposes. In fact, that is precisely what we all do when we formulate the theology by which we live. We are not to follow our sinful human logic but be transformed by the renewing of our mind, so that we can understand God's good, pleasing, and perfect will (Rom. 12:2).

God planted in us a **conscience** that enables us to discern right from wrong. Unless their conscience is completely seared, even those who do not know God have a basic understanding of good and evil (Rom. 2). And those who do know Christ and have the Holy Spirit develop a sanctified conscience that is even more sensitive to God's standards of right and wrong. They know, for example, that it is right to forgive others and it is wrong to harm others. If something seems terribly wrong to someone with a sanctified conscience, it probably is.

And as we get to know God better, our **heart** will be more and more in tune with His heart for people. Any love, compassion, and kindness that we show toward others is only a pale reflection of His enduring mercy and lovingkindness. We are loved by Him, so we can love others:

> As God's chosen people, holy and dearly loved, clothe yourselves with compassion, kindness, humility, gentleness and patience. Bear with each other and forgive whatever grievances you may have against one another. Forgive as the Lord forgave you. And over all these virtues put on love, which binds them all together in perfect unity" (Col. 3:12–14).

So if you feel even a twinge of resistance to the idea that billions of people will suffer in hell forever, consider whether that resistance may spring from a sanctified understanding of

God's true heart. Don't ignore that still, small voice. Or if the voice is screaming to you that never-ending torture is wrong, don't try to suppress that megaphone roar!

It's true that we find seemingly conflicting and confusing pictures of God's character in Scripture. But if you want to know what God is really like, *look at Jesus.*[8] John said that Jesus, "the only God" or "the only Son," has made God known (Jn. 1:18). Jesus Himself said, "Whoever has seen me has seen the Father" (Jn. 14:9) and "Whoever sees me sees him who sent me" (Jn. 12:45). Jesus is "the image of the invisible God" (Col. 1:15). He is "the radiance of God's glory and the exact representation of his being" (Heb. 1:3).

How can we know God and see His glory? God "has shone in our hearts to give the light of the knowledge of the glory of God *in the face of Jesus Christ*" (2 Cor. 4:6). So keep looking at Jesus to know what God is like. Think of Jesus' heart and His promises. Go ahead and picture the most glorious vision of God's purposes you can possibly imagine; your vision will still fall short of what He will actually do. Would He be displeased if we, by faith, picture Him drawing countless multitudes to Himself? Even the most hardened sinners drawn by His love? What if we were to believe that none will be left behind? Is it possible that our imagination could go beyond what He will actually do? No! His Word says He is able to do immeasurably *more* than all we ask or imagine!

---

[1]Tracing beliefs about heaven and hell throughout church history is a massive topic in itself, one that I do not tackle in this book. I refer you to other writers who have written about this subject in depth, particularly Ilaria Ramelli, who wrote the 900-page volume *The Christian Doctrine of Apokatastasis*. Steven Nemes of Fuller Theological Seminary calls her book "a labor of manifest erudition and capability" (Journal of Analytic Theology, Vol. 3, May 2015). Using primary sources, Ramelli traces the belief in *apokatastasis* (restoration) from the New Testament to John Scotus Eriugena in the ninth century and shows that it was widely held in the early centuries of the Church. As Nemes says of her work, "The evidence brought forth is compelling; the conclusion is the doctrine of *apokatastasis* is a Christian doctrine and is grounded in Christ,…regularly espoused in defense of orthodoxy against the heresies of the times."

The era of the Church Fathers was a confusing time, as the fundamentals of this new faith were being sorted out, orthodoxy was being defined, and heresy was being identified. But there were some Church Fathers who, although they may not have sorted out everything to our satisfaction, were recognized for their sound doctrine and godly lives. My favorite is St. Gregory, Bishop of Nyssa (c. 335–395). Gregory, his brother Basil the Great, and their friend Gregory of Nazianzus were known as the Cappadocian Fathers. Gregory of Nyssa was particularly recognized for his contributions to the doctrine of the Trinity and the Nicene Creed, as well as for his godly life. Although some of his statements seem contradictory, Ramelli and others have shown that he clearly holds the hope that God will become "all in all" as all people are reconciled to Him. On a personal note, St. Gregory's feast day in the Orthodox Church is also my birthday. ☺

[2]Chan, Francis, *Erasing Hell: What God Said about Eternity, and the Things We've Made Up.* 2011. pp. 13-14. It is worth noting than Chan's co-author, Preston Sprinkle, has more recently edged away from eternal damnation toward Annihilationism, and he is respectful of biblical Universalism.

[3]Lewis, C. S., *The Problem of Pain.* 1940. C. S. Lewis also wrote *The Great Divorce,* about an imaginary journey to hell. See Chapter 49 in this book.

[4]Morgan, Christopher W. and Robert A. Peterson, ed., *Hell Under Fire: Modern Scholarship Reinvents Eternal Punishment.* 2004. p. 220. This book is a defense of the traditional view, with contributions by nine prominent contemporary scholars. See description in Other Resources at the back of this book.

[5]Those who believe the wicked will be annihilated and will cease to exist often prefer the term "Conditional Immortality" to indicate that people are not innately immortal but are granted immortality when they trust in Christ.

[6]Beauchemin, Gerry. *Hope Beyond Hell.* 2007. p. 4.

[7]In an effort to underscore the urgency of warning unbelievers about the horrible fate in store for them, Jones paints a very ugly picture of the God who supposedly ordains hell. In response to atheist Richard Dawkins' scathing assessment of the God of the Old Testament, Jones says, "Dawkins is dead wrong, not because he paints God with too cruel of a brushstroke, but because he's too flattering. The God of the Bible is *far* more vengeful than Dawkins could ever dream. The real God…is infinitely more bloodthirsty, vindictive, genocidal, pestilential, sadomasochistic, and capriciously malevolent than human language could begin to express." If Dawkins is guilty of blasphemy, how much more so is Jones.

[8]I had in mind to write a piece on the theme "If you want to know what God is like, look at Jesus," but Brian Zahnd has already done it far better and in more depth. See the description of his book *Sinners in the Hands of a Loving God* in Other Resources.

# 5

# PRESUPPOSITIONS AND
# INTERPRETATIONS

Throughout most of church history, the doctrine of eternal condemnation has been accepted by the majority of Christians as a fact taught in Scripture. However they describe the nature of hell and whoever they define as the inhabitants of hell, most Christians believe that some people are eternally separated from God. The separation may entail everlasting conscious torment or a long period of punishment followed by annihilation or the state of being away from the presence of God, but there is agreement that the wicked will be sentenced to a place or a condition from which there is no escape.

This essay is a call to re-examine our presuppositions regarding the doctrine of hell and to consider how they have influenced our interpretation of Scripture. We will look at a number of verses that seem to present a different picture of God's ultimate purposes and man's final destiny, suggesting that there may be an alternate paradigm that better accounts for the truths that have been revealed in Scripture. The challenge is to step back and scrutinize our basic assumptions to make sure they are correct, so that the interpretations built upon them will also be true. So settle in for a long chapter, or better yet, read it little by little, with open Bible, open mind, and open heart.

Many years ago I was in a crowded grocery store on a busy Saturday afternoon. I was making my way toward the checkout area, where dozens of people were jostling for a place in one of the long, amorphous lines. A rather large woman with bulgy eyes and a grim, mean-looking face was pushing her carriage in my direction. Suddenly she crashed right into another carriage, and I thought, "What a jerk, trying to force her way into the line!" But a second later I regretted the thought. In a very kind voice, the woman apologized profusely to the other person. "Oh, I'm *so* sorry. I just had an operation on my eyes, and I can't see very well."

My assumption that she was mean and was trying to butt in line was dead wrong; the bulgy eyes, the determined look on her face, and the collision with another customer had an entirely different explanation—that she had had an operation on her eyes and could not see well and was trying to focus. Although it happened a long time ago, I have never forgotten that incident; it reminds me that the assumptions I make about a situation can lead to a completely wrong interpretation of it. If I stop to check my assumptions, I may end up looking at the situation through an entirely different lens.

A much more powerful example of such a paradigm shift is recounted by Stephen Covey in his book *The 7 Habits of Highly Effective People*. He was on a subway in New York when a man and his children boarded. The children were loud and annoying, but the father closed his eyes and did nothing. The irritation of the other passengers was mounting, and Covey finally asked the man if he might control his children a bit. The father lifted his gaze and said, "Oh, you're right. I guess I should do something about it. We just came from the hospital where their mother died about an hour ago. I don't know what to think, and I guess they don't know how to handle it either."[1] As Covey learned the true nature of the situation, he experienced an instant shift in his attitude. He realized that his presuppositions had been wrong—he was seeing not bratty children with a negligent father, but rather a grieving family. The way he viewed the situation changed because his framework for understanding it had changed.

We all bring presuppositions into every area of our belief systems. We view the world through the grid of a lifetime of accumulated experiences and teachings, from the time we were little children to the present. Whether we're aware of it or not, we interpret what we see and hear and read according to the framework we have developed; in other words, we tend to form our interpretations on the basis of what we already believe.

With respect to our Christian faith, it is good to have strong convictions about what we believe, but we also must be willing to take a hard look at our assumptions and to change if we have been wrong. It is a healthy exercise to allow our presuppositions to be challenged—if we are wrong, we want to bring our beliefs more in line with the truth; if we are right, then answering a challenge will strengthen our convictions.

An example of interpretations being influenced by pre-suppositions is the New International Version Study Bible, which I was using as my principal translation for Bible study. The annotators believe in eternal damnation, and I started noticing that their exegesis (and sometimes even the trans-lation itself) reflects that belief. There are several passages where the notes say, in effect, "this verse doesn't really mean what it seems to say, because the apparent meaning contradicts the doctrine of eternal punishment, which we already know is true."

To illustrate, one such verse is 1 Timothy 2:4 (Passage 1), which says that God our Savior "wants all men to be saved and to come to a knowledge of the truth." The NIV note says, "God desires the salvation of all people. On the other hand, the Bible indicates that God chooses some (not all) people to be saved." In support of this statement, 1 Peter 1:2 is cited: Peter is writing to "God's elect...who have been chosen according to the foreknowledge of God the Father, through the sanctifying work of the Spirit, for obedience to Jesus Christ." (Note that this verse does not say that the "elect" go to heaven and the rest do not; it says that the elect are chosen "for obedience to Jesus Christ.")

The note goes on to give two interpretations of the Timothy passage: "Some interpreters understand the passage to teach that God has chosen those whom he, in his foreknowledge, knew would believe when confronted with the gospel and enabled to believe. Other interpreters hold that, though human reasoning cannot resolve the seeming inconsistency, the Bible teaches both truths and thus there can be no actual contradiction. Certainly there is none in the mind of God." The note does not even mention the possibility that God not only *wishes* that all men would be saved but will actually make it happen.

The passage continues, "For there is one God and one mediator between God and men, the man Christ Jesus, who gave himself as a ransom for all men—the testimony given in its proper time" (vv. 5–6). Again Paul indicates that the work Jesus did on the cross was for *all* men. You could make a case that the phrase "a ransom for all men" means that the ransom works for *anybody* who comes to Christ, regardless of rank, race, or nationality. However, the plain sense of the verse is that Jesus' sacrifice was intended for all human beings and fulfills God's desire that all be saved.

Later in the same book, Paul says "we have put our hope in the living God, who is the Savior of all men, and especially of those who believe" (1 Tim. 4:10, Passage 2). Here the note says of the phrase *Savior of all,* "Obviously this does not mean that God saves every person from eternal punishment, for such universalism would contradict the clear testimony of Scripture. God is, however, the Savior of all in that he offers salvation to all and saves all who come to him." Only if you have already concluded that God does *not* save everyone from eternal punishment is it "obvious" that the verse means that He does not save everyone from eternal punishment. Otherwise, the verse *does* seem to say that He saves all.

In the NIV, Titus 2:11 (Passage 3) reads, "For the grace of God that brings salvation has appeared to all men." The verse actually says, *Epephanē gar hē charis tou theou hē sōterios pasin anthrōpois* (Ἐπεφάνη γὰρ ἡ χάρις τοῦ θεοῦ σωτήριος πᾶσιν ἀνθρώποις). Other translations properly put "to all men" (*pasin anthrōpois*) with "bringing salvation" (*hē sōterios*). For example, the New American Standard reads, "The grace of

God has appeared, *bringing salvation to all men*." By translating the verse as it does, the NIV has no need to comment on the verse because the translation has already been fitted to the interpretation the NIV supports.

In Galatians 1:8 and again in 1:9 (Passage 4), the Greek word *anathema* (ἀνάθεμα) is translated "eternally condemned." ("But even if we or an angel from heaven should preach a gospel other than the one we preached to you, let him be eternally condemned!... If anybody is preaching to you a gospel other than what you accepted, let him be eternally condemned!") Anyone reading this passage would think that eternal condemnation is an indisputable fact of the Bible. However, the sense of "eternally" is not inherent in the word; the Greek word has pretty much the same sense as the English cognate—cursed, banned, reviled, or denounced, not *eternally* damned.

In Colossians 1:19–20 (Passage 5), Paul says, "For God was pleased to have all his fullness dwell in him, and through him to reconcile to himself all things, whether things on earth or things in heaven, by making peace through his blood, shed on the cross." The note says of the phrase *reconcile to himself all things,* "Does not mean that Christ by his death has saved all people. Scripture speaks of an eternal hell and makes clear that only believers are saved." But the verse seems to say that the cross accomplishes the reconciliation of *all things* to God. In order to conclude that this verse "does not mean that Christ by his death has saved all people," you have to bring to it the presupposition that only some are saved. [For an extended exegesis of Col. 1:15–20, see "Reconciliation: The Heart of God's Grand Plan for Creation" (#7).]

Once I experienced the paradigm shift with respect to my assumption of eternal damnation, I started seeing how deeply (and how unknowingly) my presupposition had affected my understanding of the New Testament. For decades I had completely missed ideas that now seem plain. The well-ingrained belief in a traditional hell has had a tremendous impact on our interpretation of Scripture.

Here are a number of other NIV notes that interpret verses not according to their plain sense but according to a predetermined belief in eternal damnation. Try to look at each one with fresh eyes.

6) Verse: And all mankind will see God's salvation (Luke 3:6, quoted from Isaiah 40).

   NIV note: *all mankind.* God's salvation was to be made known to both Jews and Gentiles—a major theme of Luke's Gospel.

   My comment: The note waters down the force of the verse. The verse says that *all mankind* will see God's salvation, but the note says that God's salvation is *made known to both groups*—Jews and non-Jews—implying that only some from each group will really experience God's salvation.

7) Verse: But I, when I am lifted up from the earth, will draw all men to myself (John 12:32).

   NIV note: *all men.* Christ will draw people to himself without regard for nationality, ethnic affiliation or status.

   My comment: The note subtly changes the sense from *all men* to *all kinds of men*—that is, not all people from every group but some people from every group. See also John 6:33 ("For the bread of God is the bread that comes down from heaven and gives life *to the world.*")

8) Verse: For if the many died by the trespass of the one man, how much more did God's grace and the gift that came by the grace of the one man, Jesus Christ, overflow to the many! (Romans 5:15)

   NIV note: *the many.* The same as "all men" in v. 12 ["...sin entered the world through one man, and death through sin, and in this way death came to all men, because all sinned"]. *how much more.* A theme that runs through this section. God's grace is infinitely greater for good than is Adam's sin for evil.

21

My comment: The notes acknowledge that the phrases "the many" and "all men" refer to all of humanity when it comes to sin and death, but not when it comes to grace and life. Yet at the same time, the notes say, "God's grace is infinitely greater for good than is Adam's sin for evil." Is God's grace able to conquer sin completely and redeem as many people as sin has destroyed, or isn't it?

9) Verses: Consequently, just as the result of one trespass was condemnation for all men, so also the result of one act of righteousness was justification that brings life for all men. For just as through the disobedience of the one man the many were made sinners, so also through the obedience of the one man the many will be made righteous (Romans 5:18–19).

NIV note: *life for all men.* Does not mean that everyone eventually will be saved, but that salvation is available to all.

My comment: The verses have parallelism. One trespass brought condemnation for all men; one act of righteousness brought life for all men. The disobedience of the one man causes many to be sinners; the obedience of the one man causes many to be made righteous. The extent of the *all* or the *many* in the second half of each verse is the same as the extent of the *all* or the *many* in the first half of each verse. [For a fuller discussion of the parallelisms in Romans 5, see "By the Righteousness of One," #19.]

10) Verse: For God has bound all men over to disobedience so that he may have mercy on them all (Romans 11:32).

NIV note: *all men.* Both groups under discussion (Jews and Gentiles). There has been a period of disobedience for each in order that God may have mercy on them all. Paul is in no way teaching universal salvation.

My comment: Again the note assumes that Paul can't possibly be teaching universal salvation, so therefore the verse must not mean what it seems to say, i.e., that God will have mercy on all.

11) Verse: For as in Adam all die, so in Christ all will be made alive (1 Corinthians 15:22).

NIV note: *in Christ all will be made alive.* All who are "in Christ"—i.e., who are related to him by faith—will be made alive at the resurrection.

My comment: The *all die* is universal, but the *all will be made alive* is not?

12) Verses: For Christ's love compels us, because we are convinced that one died for all, and therefore all died. And he died for all, that those who live should no longer live for themselves but for him who died for them and was raised again (2 Corinthians 5:14–15).

NIV note: *for all.* For all mankind. *therefore all died.* Because Christ died for all, he involved all in his death. For some his death would confirm their own death, but for others (those who by faith would become united with him) his death was their death to sin and self, so that they now live in and with the resurrected Christ (v. 15). However, some hold that Paul is not speaking specifically here about the scope of Christ's atonement but about the effect of Christ's death on the Christian life. Thus "all" would refer not to mankind in general but only to the church.

My comment: The note suggests that Christ's death "for all" means "for all mankind," but for some of them "his death would confirm their own death" (i.e., they remain dead in their sins). Another possibility given is that "all" refers "not to mankind in general but only to the church" (i.e., He died only for the church, and the passage is talking "not about the scope of Christ's atonement but about the effect of Christ's death on the Christian life"). The more natural reading, which requires no fancy interpretation, is that Jesus did indeed die "for all" (i.e., all mankind), as stated in both verses, and that all died in Him. The passage goes on to say "that God was reconciling *the world* to himself in Christ, not counting men's sins against them" (v. 19). Our mission is to implore people on Christ's behalf to be reconciled to God (v. 20)—that is, to put their trust in Him.

13) Verses: Therefore God exalted him to the highest place and gave him the name that is above every name, that at the name of Jesus every knee should bow, in heaven and on earth and under the earth, and every tongue confess that Jesus Christ is Lord, to the glory of God the Father (Philippians 2:9–11).

NIV note: *bow...confess.* Cf. Isa 45:23. God's design is that all people everywhere should worship and serve Jesus as Lord. Ultimately all will acknowledge him as Lord (see Ro 14:9), *whether willingly or not.* [Emphasis added]

My comment: In 1 Corinthians, Paul declares that "no one can say, 'Jesus is Lord,' except by the Holy Spirit" (12:3), i.e., unless the Holy Spirit in him enables him to recognize Jesus as Lord. Compare to Romans 10:9—"If you confess with your mouth, 'Jesus is Lord,' and believe in your heart that God raised him from the dead, you will be saved." Here confessing Jesus as Lord is clearly genuine; it means agreeing to the truth that Jesus is Yahweh and that He is Lord of all. It is parallel and complementary to believing in your heart that God raised him from the dead. It is not simply a grudging assent or a forced submission. (If, as the note in Philippians claims, some are unwillingly acknowledging Him as Lord, then they are like the naughty little boy whose mother told him to sit in the corner, and he said, "I'm sitting down on the outside, but I'm standing up on the inside.") Did God send His Son to die on the cross just so He could coerce everybody into bending the knee and saying the words "Jesus is Lord"? No! His purpose is that all be in genuine worship and submission to Him. The phrase "every tongue confess that Jesus Christ is Lord" in Philippians 2:11 has the same structure and meaning as "confess with your mouth, 'Jesus is Lord'" in Romans 10:9; this confession is willing and heartfelt, and God's will is that ultimately *every tongue* will be doing it! As Revelation 5:13 says, "every creature in heaven and on earth and under the earth and on the sea, and all that is in them" will be praising the Lamb. [See "Is God Like Gargamel the Great?" (#23).]

14) Verses: He will punish those who do not know God and do not obey the gospel of our Lord Jesus. They will be punished with everlasting destruction and shut out from the presence of the Lord and from the majesty of his power (2 Thessalonians 1:8–9).

NIV note: *destruction*. Not annihilation (see note on 1 Th. 5:3). Paul uses the word in 1 Co. 5:5, possibly of the destruction of the "flesh" (see NIV text note there) for the purpose of salvation. Since, however, salvation implies resurrection of the body, annihilation cannot be in mind. The word means something like "complete ruin." Here it means being shut out from Christ's presence. This eternal separation is the penalty of sin and the essence of hell.

My comment: This whole paragraph is about the just judgment of God. The just penalty for those who do not know God and do not obey the gospel is "eternal destruction *apo* (Greek: ἀπὸ) the presence of the Lord." But does this destruction in the age to come mean that they will forever be excluded from the presence of God? As Thomas Talbott[2] points out, the idea of being "shut out" from the presence of God is not in the Greek text. It was inserted by the NIV translators, who give the preposition *apo* the meaning of "away from." Although *apo* sometimes does mean "away from," in other contexts it means "coming from," as in the familiar greeting "Grace to you and peace from (*apo*) God the Father and the Lord Jesus Christ." The American Standard Version translation of 2 Thessalonians 1:9 is preferable: "eternal destruction from the face of the Lord," meaning that God is the one who brings about the destruction of the wicked, just as He is *the source* of grace and peace. So the NIV note correctly states that this "destruction" is not annihilation in the sense that the person who is wicked goes out of existence, but it misses the point that God's glorious presence and the majesty of His power and the blazing fire serve to destroy the wickedness and purify the person. The verse referred to in the NIV note, 1 Corinthians 5:5 ("Hand this man [who sleeps with his father's wife] over to Satan, so that the sinful nature may be destroyed and his spirit saved on the day of the Lord"), actually supports the idea that the "destruction" is of that which is sinful, with the ultimate purpose of saving the spirit. The destruction of the wicked does not mean that the wicked cease to exist but that they cease to be wicked.

15) Verse: He is the atoning sacrifice for our sins, and not only for ours but also for the sins of the whole world (1 John 2:2).

NIV note: *for the sins of the whole world.* Forgiveness through Christ's atoning sacrifice is not limited to one particular group only; it has worldwide application (see Jn 1:29). It must, however, be received by faith (see Jn. 3:16). Thus this verse does not teach universalism (that all people ultimately will be saved), but that God is an impartial God.

My comment: The verse is interpreted not according to its plain sense ("Jesus' atoning sacrifice is for the sins of the whole world"), but according to the presupposition that universalism is not true ("...for the sins of people from every group in the world"). John 6:33 says that the one who comes down from heaven gives life *to the world*. Verse 37 says, "*All* that the Father gives me will come to me." And John 17:2 says, "For you [God the Father] granted him [God the Son] authority over *all* people that he might give eternal life to *all* those you have given him." Note the logic: Jesus will give eternal life to all those whom the Father has given Him. The Father has given Him authority over *all people*. Conclusion: Jesus will give eternal life to all people.

16) Verse: Who will not fear you, O Lord, and bring glory to your name? For you alone are holy. All nations will come and worship before you, for your righteous acts have been revealed (Revelation 15:4).

NIV note: Universal recognition of God is taught in both the OT (Ps 86:9; Isa 45:22–23; Mal 1:11) and the NT (Php 2:9–11).

My comment: This verse and the ones cited in the NIV note teach not merely universal "recognition" of God but universal *worship* of God. This verse says "all nations will come and *worship* before you." Psalm 86:9 says, "All the nations you have made will come and *worship* before you, O Lord; they will bring glory to your name." Malachi 1:11 says, "'My name will be great among the nations.... In every place incense and pure offerings will be brought to my name, because my name will be great among the nations,' says the Lord Almighty." These "pure offerings" are not coming from unregenerate people who are being forced to acknowledge God. Daniel 7:14 confirms that all peoples will enter into *true* worship of the Lord: "He [the one like a son of man whom Daniel saw in his vision] was given authority, glory and sovereign power; all peoples, nations and men of every language *worshiped* him." Both Isaiah and Philippians say that "every knee will bow" and every tongue will proclaim the name of the Lord. According to Isaiah, God has made a solemn promise in His own Name that He will bring all people to humbly acknowledge Him as Lord: "Turn to me and be saved, all you ends of the earth; for I am God, and there is no other. By myself I have sworn, my mouth has uttered in all integrity a word that will not be revoked: Before me every knee will bow; by me every tongue will swear" (Is. 45:22–23). As noted above in my comment on Philippians 2, this confession is not at gunpoint! It is willing and heartfelt, and one day every creature will join in the chorus of praise to our God!

17) Verse: Then I heard every creature in heaven and on earth and under the earth and on the sea, and all that is in them, singing: "To him who sits on the throne and to the Lamb be praise and honor and glory and power, for ever and ever!" (Revelation 5:13)

NIV notes: *heaven…earth…under the earth.* See note on v. 3. [Verse 3 note says about *in heaven or on earth or under the earth*, "'But no one in heaven or on earth or under the earth could open the scroll or even look inside it'—A conventional phrase used to express the universality of the proclamation—no creature was worthy."]

My comment: The notes acknowledge that the phrase "in heaven and on earth and under the earth" expresses universality, referring to every created being. The praise that is offered to God and to the Lamb by every creature in heaven and on earth and under the earth is not a grudging recognition of His power but heartfelt worship!

In another group of key passages that seem to teach the universal extent of God's love and salvation, the NIV study notes almost acknowledge it or simply fail to comment on it:

18) Verses: For God so loved the world that he gave his one and only Son, that whoever believes in him shall not perish but have eternal life. For God did not send his Son into the world to condemn the world, but to save the world through him (John 3:16–17).

NIV notes: *world.* All people on earth—or perhaps all creation (see note on 1:9). [The note about *world* in 1:9 says, "Another common word in John's writings, found 78 times in this Gospel and 24 times in his letters (only 47 times in all of Paul's writings). It can mean the universe, the earth, the people on earth, most people, people opposed to God, or the human system opposed to God's purposes."]

My comment: The note for John 3:16 says that in this case the word *world* means "all people on earth—or perhaps all creation." In other words, it acknowledges that God loves "all people on earth—or perhaps all creation," so much so that He gave His one and only Son for them. His purpose was that we could escape from perishing and have eternal life by believing in Him. The NIV study notes do not even mention the astounding fact stated in verse 17: that God sent His Son into the world *to save the world*—that is, all people on earth! Even more, He sent His Son to restore all creation!

19) Verse: …[W]e know that this man really is the Savior of the world (John 4:42).

NIV note: *the Savior of the world.* In the NT the expression occurs only here and in 1 Jn 4:14. It points to the facts that (1) Jesus not only teaches but also saves, and (2) his salvation extends to the world (see note on 3:16).

My comment: This note says that Jesus' salvation "extends to the world" and then sends us to John 3:16, where *world* is defined as "all people on earth—or perhaps all creation." The conclusion would be that Jesus' salvation extends to all people on earth.

20) Verse: And we have seen and testify that the Father has sent his Son to be the Savior of the world (1 John 4:14).

NIV note: None

My comment: Which of the definitions of *world* applies here? Compare to John 1:29, "the Lamb of God who *takes away the sin of the world*." The NIV note says, "Jesus would be the sacrifice that would atone for the sin of the world." Jesus will certainly *take away* the sin of the world—i.e., not just lock it up but eradicate it!

21) Verse: He must remain in heaven until the time comes for God to restore everything, as he promised long ago through his holy prophets (Acts 3:21).

NIV note: None

My comment: Will God restore everything *except* the majority of humanity? Bauer's Greek-English Lexicon (BDAG) says the "time of restoration of all things" (*chronōn apokatastaseōs pantōn*, χρόνων ἀποκαταστάσεως πάντων) is "the time for restoring everything to perfection." Thayer's Lexicon defines the restoration of all things as "the restoration not only of the true theocracy but also of that more perfect state of (even physical) things which existed before the fall." If these definitions are accurate, God will restore the universe to its pre-fall perfection, i.e., there will be no sin or rebellion or suffering, and all of creation will be in perfect harmony and fellowship with God.

22) Verse: [The ministry of reconciliation is the message] that God was reconciling the world to himself in Christ, not counting men's sins against them (2 Corinthians 5:9).

NIV note: None

My comment: "Reconcile" means to re-establish friendship or restore the favor of God, and this verse says that God reconciles the world to Himself in Christ, *not counting their sins against them*. If God shuts up people in hell forever, He is holding their sins against them perpetually.

23) Verse: And he made known to us the mystery of his will according to his good pleasure, which he purposed in Christ, to be put into effect when the times will have reached their fulfillment—to bring all things in heaven and on earth together under one head, even Christ (Ephesians 1:9–10).

NIV note: *to bring...under one head....* [I]n a world of confusion, where things do not "add up" or make sense, we look forward to the time when everything will be brought into meaningful relationship under the headship of Christ.

My comment: What kind of "meaningful relationship" under Christ do the damned have? How does it "make sense" that God's good pleasure is to bring all things in heaven and on earth together under Christ, if the majority of humanity is left out? Will the headship of Christ be like that of a prison warden, or will He be fully Savior, Lord, Shepherd, and Bridegroom?

Finally, some passages from the Apostle Peter. The NIV translation of 2 Peter 3:9 (Passage 24) says, "The Lord is not slow in keeping his promise, as some understand slowness. He is patient with you, not wanting anyone to perish, but everyone to come to repentance." The word translated "wanting" is *boulomenos* (βουλόμενός). Bauer's Lexicon says the root word *boulomai* (βούλομαι) can mean wish/desire or can refer to "decisions of the will after previous deliberation." The related noun *boulē* (βουλή) means purpose, counsel, resolution, decision, resolve. The NIV translation uses the weaker sense of the word *boulomenos* ("want" vs. "decree"), and the note skews the meaning of the verse: "God's seeming delay in bringing about the consummation of all things is a result not of indifference but of patience in waiting for *all who will come to repentance*" [emphasis added]. In other words, God does not *decree* that none shall perish—He just *wishes* they wouldn't—and His patience extends only to "all *who will come* to repentance" within a certain timeframe.

Another example of translating and interpreting a verse to suit a predetermined belief that the unsaved die and go straight to hell is 1 Peter 4:6 (Passage 25). Peter has been talking about the pagans who indulge in debauchery, lust, etc. Then he says, "But they will have to give account to him who is ready to judge the living and the dead. For this is the reason the gospel was preached even to those who are now dead, so that they might be judged according to men in regard to the body, but live according to God in regard to the spirit." The note explains the phrase *was preached even to those who are now dead* this way: "The word 'now' does not occur in the Greek, but it is necessary to make it clear that the preaching was done not after these people had died, but while they were still alive. (There will be no opportunity for people to be saved after death; see Heb 9:27.)"

When I first realized what that note was saying, I thought, "Wait, wait! Back up the truck! You can't just go and add words to the text to make it say what you want!" Adding the word *now* completely changes the sense of the verse. The Greek simply says *nekrois euangelisthē* (νεκροῖς εὐηγγελίσθη), "to the dead the gospel was preached" or "the dead were evangelized" or "the dead were addressed with good tidings." The verse seems to say that people who had already died were hearing the gospel, the "good news," which suggests that they were getting an opportunity to respond to it. (If it was a proclamation of judgment, it wouldn't be very good news for them.) But the NIV note says the verse can't possibly mean that the preaching was done after the people died, because "there will be no opportunity for people to be saved after death." Then it cites Hebrews 9:27 as proof that people cannot be saved after death: "Man is destined to die once, and after that to face judgment." But that verse simply says that you die and then face judgment; it never says there is no possibility of salvation after you die.

When Peter says the gospel was preached to the dead, perhaps he is referring in part to something he said a few verses earlier:

For Christ died for sins once for all, the righteous for the unrighteous, to bring you to God. He was put to death in the body but made alive by the Spirit, through whom also he went and preached to the spirits in prison who disobeyed long ago when God waited patiently in the days of Noah while the ark was being built (1 Pet. 3:18-20, Passage 26).

A different word is used for "preach"—*kēryssō* (κηρύσσω), which does not carry the idea of "good news" but simply to proclaim or announce. The NIV note gives three main interpretations: that Christ preached through Noah to the wicked generation of that time; that between His death and resurrection He preached to fallen angels; or that He went to the place of the dead and preached to Noah's wicked contemporaries. "What he proclaimed may have been the gospel, or it may have been a declaration of victory for Christ and doom for his hearers." The note then gives the problems with all three views.

There's another possibility that the note doesn't even mention. What about the idea that He was preaching the gospel to those who had died before He came to earth and were in Hades, including those who disobeyed during the time of Noah? The NIV note for Matthew 16:18 defines Hades as "the Greek name for the place of departed spirits, generally equivalent to the Hebrew *Sheol.*" The word *Sheol* is often translated as "grave," or it can mean the realm of the dead. What if these "spirits in prison" were those who had died without coming to faith and were stuck in the abode of the dead? Would Jesus offer up His life on the cross as a sacrifice for our sins—"Christ died for sins once for all, the righteous for the unrighteous, to bring you to God," as Peter puts it—and then immediately go to the place of the dead and proclaim judgment, rubbing it in that they were doomed forever? Why couldn't He be preaching the gospel, the good news, His victory over sin, release for the captives? He is the one who is anointed to preach good news to the poor, to bind up the brokenhearted, to proclaim freedom for the captives and release from darkness for the prisoners, and to turn their mourning into joy (Is. 61:1–3). Is Peter describing the time when Jesus "descended into the depths of the earth" and then "ascended higher than all the heavens, in order to fill the whole universe"? (Eph. 4:9–10). Are these the captives He led in His train when He ascended on high? (Eph. 4:8). Imagine Jesus dying on the cross, descending into hell, proclaiming the good news to the prisoners there, leading them out of darkness and captivity into freedom, and ascending higher than all the heavens in order to fill the whole universe!

## Conclusion

No single verse, no single passage, no single argument can seal the deal for either eternal condemnation or ultimate redemption. The goal is to take into account the whole counsel of Scripture and try to determine the understanding that is most in line with all that we know about God's character, His purposes, and the condition of humankind. This essay illustrates how we may inadvertently interpret the Bible to match our presuppositions, and it issues a challenge to reassess our assumptions before building interpretations on them.

Once we are aware of the fact that we filter all incoming information through our own grid, we can be very intentional about recognizing how our grid affects everything we perceive. If you have always viewed the Bible through a framework that includes eternal damnation as part of its given structure, I challenge you to try looking at Scripture through a lens of ultimate restoration. Try letting go of the assumption that eternal damnation is an indisputable fact of Scripture and an indispensable part of your faith. Be open to a paradigm shift that would allow you to see the fullness of the redemption theme throughout the Bible. And for those who already have the hope of ultimate redemption, come with me as we investigate many facets of this exquisite gem.

[1]Covey, Stephen R. *The Seven Habits of Highly Effective People.* 1988. pp. 30-31

[2]Talbott, Thomas. *The Inescapable Love of God.* 2014. pp. 88ff

[3]There are still other possible instances of reading one's presuppositions into the text. Taken together with the examples cited above, they show a pattern of basing interpretations on unquestioned assumptions.

27) Verses: And if your eye causes you to sin, pluck it out. It is better for you to enter the kingdom of God with one eye than to have two eyes and be thrown into hell (Gehenna, γέενναν), where "their worm does not die, and the fire is not quenched." Everyone will be salted with fire (Mark 9:47–49).

NIV note: Verse 48—Isa 66:24 [quoted in verse 48] speaks of the punishment for rebellion against God. As the final word of Isaiah's message, the passage became familiar as a picture of endless destruction. Verse 49—The saying may mean that everyone who enters hell will suffer its fire, or (if only loosely connected with the preceding) it may mean that every Christian in this life can expect to undergo the fire of suffering and purification.

My comment: The NIV note for verse 48 connects this passage with eternal destruction. The note for verse 49 acknowledges that "salted with fire" may refer to purification, but if so, it must be talking about what Christians experience "in this life." We should ask, why can't this "fire of suffering and purification" be in the afterlife? As Thomas Johnson says, "This description [Mark 9:48] was drawn from Isaiah 66:24, where it is applied to the dead bodies of those who have rebelled against the Lord. Is it a purifying fire, a destroying fire, or a fire of eternal conscious suffering? This passage does not give us the answer, though in context purification is suggested, since the next verse, Mark 9:49, says that 'everyone will be salted with fire,' a reference to salt's purifying function." H. Anderson notes, "We should not read into these sayings later speculations about the eternal punishment of the wicked in hell."

28) Verses: John answered them all, "I baptize you with water. But one more powerful than I will come, the thongs of whose sandals I am not worthy to untie. He will baptize you with the Holy Spirit and with fire. His winnowing fork is in his hand to clear his threshing floor and to gather the wheat into his barn, but he will burn up the chaff with unquenchable fire" (Luke 3:16–17).

NIV note: *and with fire.* Here fire is associated with judgment (v. 17). See also the fire of Pentecost (Ac 2:3) and the fire of testing (1 Co 3:13). *His winnowing fork.* See note on Ru 1:22. The chaff represents the unrepentant and the wheat the righteous. Many

Jews thought that only pagans would be judged and punished when the Messiah came, but John declared that judgment would come to all who did not repent—including Jews.

My comment: The notes on this passage and on Matthew 3:11-12 (parallel to Luke 3:16-17), Luke 12:49 ("I have come to bring fire on the earth"), Acts 2:3 ("tongues of fire"), and 1 Corinthians 3:13-15 ("[his work] will be revealed with fire, and the fire will test the quality of each man's work") recognize that the image of "fire" is applied figuratively in different ways in the New Testament. The notes indicate that fire is associated mainly with judgment, and sometimes with testing or with the divine presence. They do not even mention another important purpose of fire: purification. It is assumed that the burning up of the "chaff" in Luke 3:17 refers to the destruction of *people* ("The chaff represents the unrepentant"). The idea that the chaff could represent the worthless parts of a person's life, which are burned up in order to purify the person, is never even considered. Yet the context is about the baptism with the Holy Spirit and with fire, which suggests a sanctification process. And 1 Corinthians 3:13, cited in the NIV note, is about a judgment of purification: A man's work "will be shown for what it is…. It will be revealed with fire, and the fire will test the quality of each man's work. If what he has built survives, he will receive his reward. If it is burned up, he will suffer loss; *he himself will be saved,* but only as one escaping through the flames."

29) Verses: "Very truly I tell you, a time is coming and has now come when the dead will hear the voice of the Son of God and those who hear will live…. [A] time is coming when all who are in their graves will hear his voice and come out—those who have done what is good will rise to live, and those who have done what is evil will rise to be condemned" (John 5:25, 28–29).

NIV note: *is coming and has come.* Reference not only to the future resurrection but also to the fact that Christ gives life now. The spiritually dead who hear him receive life from him.

My comment: The NIV note identifies "the dead" who hear the voice of the Son of God as "the spiritually dead," in other words, people who are dead in their sins but still physically alive. This might be a reasonable interpretation except that "the dead" are identified three verses later as "all who are in their graves." The parallelism is strong: "the dead will hear the voice of the Son of God" / "all who are in their graves will hear his voice." Could all who are in their graves be hearing the Son of God preach the gospel, as 1 Peter 4:6 indicates ("the gospel was preached even to those who are dead")? If so, there is hope that the dead might hear the good news and rise to live!

# 6

# PICK TWO

A number of years ago I was trying to develop a budget for a project we were doing at the publishing company where I worked. My boss called me into her office to give me some guidelines and help me understand some of the obstacles to creating a high-quality product on time and on budget. She drew a triangle on a piece of paper and wrote one word at each vertex: Good, Fast, Cheap.

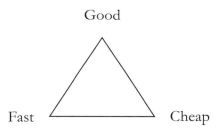

Good

Fast      Cheap

Then she said, "Pick two. If you want it to be fast and good, it won't be cheap. If you want good and cheap, it won't be fast. And if you want fast and cheap, don't expect it to be good." In the publishing world it's not an absolute impossibility to get high-quality work that is produced inexpensively and turned around quickly, but it's highly unlikely that all three conditions will be met simultaneously.

We might draw a comparison to the spiritual realm with the following three propositions, all of which can be defended from the Bible. In this case, not only is it improbable that all three will be true—it's impossible:

1) God will redeem
everyone Jesus died for.

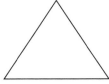

2) Jesus died for the                     3) Some people
sins of the whole world.              will never be redeemed.

One of the biggest divides in Christendom is over the whole question of God's sovereignty vs. man's free will. This conundrum is a major issue that sets Calvinists apart from Arminians. Although many Christians can't even give coherent explanations of Calvinism[1] and Arminianism,[2] they tend to fall in one camp or the other, or else believe a fuzzy mixture of the two. So how does this issue relate to the propositions in our triangle? Hang with me as we look at the logic.

Calvinists believe that by His sovereign decree, God will redeem everyone Jesus died for (proposition 1). They also believe that He died only for the elect, which means there are some people (the non-elect) who will never be redeemed (proposition 3). Arminians believe that Jesus died for the sins of the whole world, that is, all people (proposition 2), but there are some people who by their free will choose to reject Him so will not be redeemed (proposition 3).

At this point you might be thinking, "The Bible teaches all three of these truths: God is able to save all those for whom Jesus died *and* Jesus died for the sins of the whole world *and* some people reject Jesus' sacrifice for them and will be eternally separated from God. In His incomprehensible wisdom, which is far above our understanding, it can be so. I believe all three are true."

But the idea that all three could be true is not a paradox, it is not a mystery, it is not one of those inscrutable enigmas that we just have to accept by faith (like the fact that God is three and God is one, or that Jesus is fully God and fully man). It is simply a logical impossibility, an irrational contradiction. If God will redeem everyone Jesus died for and some people are never redeemed, then Jesus did not die for the whole world. If He did die for the whole world but some are not redeemed, it means that God does not redeem everyone Jesus died for. If propositions 1 and 2 are true as stated— God will redeem everyone Jesus died for, and Jesus died for the whole world—then by deductive logic, God will redeem the whole world, in which case proposition 3 is not true.

What are we to do? We want to be faithful to Scripture, and Scripture seems to teach all three of these truths, but they cannot all be true, as both Calvinists and Arminians fully understand. Both groups accept proposition 3, and they interpret Scripture in such a way as to defend their respective positions: Calvinists accept proposition 1 and add that Jesus died only for the elect, which means the rest are not saved; Arminians accept proposition 2 and say that because human beings have free will, some will reject Christ and therefore not be redeemed.

Aside from the possibility that only one proposition is true or that all three are false, which no Christians believe, the only other possibility is that proposition 3 is not true. In that case, it could be true that God will redeem everyone Jesus died for *and* that Jesus died for the sins of the whole world. The logical conclusion of those two truths is that God will redeem the whole world, which is another way of saying that He will save everyone. But if you even hint at that idea in a group of evangelical Christians, you are likely to be denounced by both Calvinists and Arminians!

Here's the irony: If I maintain that God will save everyone Jesus died for, I can find solid support for that belief from sound Calvinist theologians. If I believe that Jesus died for the sins of the whole world, I can get equally good support from Arminian scholars. But if I believe *both*—and the full implications of believing both—I may be considered a heretic by both camps!

Calvinists have a saying that Jesus' work on the cross is "sufficient for all, deficient for none, efficient only for those who believe." Makes for a nice little aphorism, but to say it is efficient only for those who believe is just a euphemism for saying it is *not* efficient for everyone else. Not efficient? Not effective? It doesn't work? For the majority of humanity? Do we really want to put such limitations on Jesus' sacrifice for us?

Arminians have their own problems: Can human free will[3] supersede God's will that all come to repentance? As Calvinists point out, if God can't manage to save everyone Jesus died for, what does that say about His sovereignty and power? Is Satan more effective in accomplishing his purposes than God is in accomplishing His?

To frame the dilemma another way, what is the relationship between God's goodness and His power? In a message about how to reach the world for Christ, one speaker identified the burning questions to which people are seeking YES answers. For example, they want to know "Is God both good and strong?"—a question that goes to the very core of the character of God. As the speaker explained,

> People often wonder, "Why does God let bad things
> happen?" Conventional wisdom says God can either
> be good and not quite able to keep control over things,
> or strong and tyrannical.

It's not just conventional wisdom that draws this conclusion; traditional theological systems say much the same. Calvinism says, in effect, God is VERY strong and pretty good. In contrast, Arminianism says God is VERY good and pretty strong. Taking the best of both, Christian Universalism says He is VERY good *and* VERY strong!

To use another analogy, Calvinism is like the *Titanic*: there were enough lifeboats for only a subset of all the passengers. Although hundreds were saved, it was still a colossal tragedy, even for those who themselves were rescued but had to watch others perish around them. Arminianism would be like the *Titanic* if there had been enough lifeboats for all the passengers but some chose not to avail themselves of the means of rescue offered to them. Universal salvation is like the Miracle on the Hudson: Captain Sully skillfully managed to land his damaged plane on the Hudson River, saving *all* 155 people aboard!

Obviously this chapter is a very simplified presentation of the viewpoints, but we cannot for that reason just dismiss the arguments or say that the problem is a lack of understanding of the intricacies and nuances of the issue. If we are going to be intellectually honest, we need to grapple with these questions and be able to give a reasonable confession of our faith. I suggest that we need to hang onto the truths that God will save everyone Jesus died for and that Jesus died for the sins of the whole world, and re-examine the assumption that some people are forever lost. God is *willing* to save, He is *able* to save, and *nothing*—not even our rebellion—can forever thwart His will.

---

[1]Here is a brief description of Calvinism, also known as Reformed Theology, from Matt Slick, the founder of the Christian Apologetics and Research Ministry: "The system of Calvinism adheres to a very high view of scripture and seeks to derive its theological formulations based solely on God's word. It focuses on God's sovereignty—stating that God is able and willing by virtue of his omniscience, omnipresence, and omnipotence to do whatever He desires with His creation. It also maintains that within the Bible are the following teachings: That God, by His sovereign grace, predestines people into salvation; that Jesus died only for those predestined; that God regenerates the individual to where he is then able to and wants to choose God; and that it is impossible for those who are redeemed to lose their salvation."

[2]Although he is a Calvinist himself, Matt Slick gives a fair and accurate description of Arminianism. He explains that there are five main tenets of Arminianism: "1) God elects or reproves on the basis of foreseen faith or unbelief, 2) Christ died for all men and for every man, although only believers are saved, 3) Man is so depraved that divine grace is necessary unto faith or any good deed, 4) This grace may be resisted, 5) Whether all who are truly regenerate will certainly persevere in the faith is a point which needs further investigation."

[3]God might be considered a "gentleman" by not forcing His will on us, but He would not be a good father; what good father stands back and allows his child to destroy himself?

# 7

# RECONCILIATION: THE HEART OF GOD'S GRAND PLAN FOR CREATION

He is the image of the invisible God, the firstborn over all creation. For by him all things were created: things in heaven and on earth, visible and invisible, whether thrones or powers or rulers or authorities; all things were created by him and for him. He is before all things, and in him all things hold together. And he is the head of the body, the church; he is the beginning and the firstborn from among the dead, so that in everything he might have the supremacy. For **God was pleased** to have all his fullness dwell in him, and through him **to reconcile to himself all things**, whether things on earth or things in heaven, by making peace through his blood, shed on the cross (Colossians 1:15–20).

This passage summarizes the whole sweeping scope of God's magnificent purposes for His creation, climaxing in the reconciliation of all things to Himself. What does Paul mean when he says that through Jesus, God will "reconcile to himself all things"? The context here, in conjunction with other passages, identifies the extent of the "all things" and defines the meaning of "to reconcile."

Verse 16 says, "For by him *all things (ta panta,* τὰ πάντα) were created." Paul goes to great lengths to show that "all things" means absolutely everything (with the exception, of course, of God Himself). In verse 15, he says that Christ is "the firstborn over *all creation*" (*pasēs ktiseōs,* πάσης κτίσεως), meaning that He came before all created things, which is also reiterated in verse 17. In verse 16 he elaborates on what he means by "all things": "things in heaven and on earth, visible and invisible, whether thrones or powers or rulers or authorities; *all* things were created by him and for him."

The phrase *things in heaven and on earth* is itself enough to show that he means everything without exception. (Cf. Jesus' use of the phrase in Matthew 28:18—"All authority *in heaven and on earth* has been given to me." Is there anything *not* under His authority?) Paul goes on to say "visible and invisible," which includes everything material and spiritual. He further specifies all kingdoms of every kind: "whether thrones or powers or rulers or authorities." To emphasize, he states the proposition again: "all things (*ta panta*, τὰ πάντα) were created by him and for him." Absolutely everything was brought into existence by and for Jesus Christ.

When Paul uses the phrase *all things* in the rest of the passage, he is referring to the same things. Verse 17 says, "He is *before all things* (*pro panton*, πρὸ πάντων), and *in him all things* (*ta panta*, τὰ πάντα) *hold together*." He was in existence before the created world came into being, and now He holds it all together. Furthermore, He is the head of the church, the beginning and the firstborn from among the dead, "so that in everything (*in all things, en pasin*, ἐν πᾶσιν) he might have the supremacy" (v. 18).

Verse 19 says that "God was pleased to have *all* his fullness (*pan to plērōma*, πᾶν τὸ πλήρωμα) dwell in him." And verse 20 is the climax of this passage: God was pleased "through him to reconcile to himself *all things* (*ta panta*, τὰ πάντα), whether things on earth or things in heaven, by making peace through his blood, shed on the cross." Paul identifies the "all things" in verse 20 using a phrase very similar to the one in verse 16:

16: by him **all things** were created: *things in heaven and on earth*

20: to reconcile to himself **all things**, whether *things on earth or things in heaven*

It stands to reason that "all things" in verse 16 is parallel to "all things" in verse 20, so the extent in each case must be the same. By Jesus, all things were created; through Jesus, all things will be reconciled.

So this passage seems to say that all created things will be reconciled to God. Since human beings are created things, it suggests that all human beings will be reconciled to God. But what does it mean to be reconciled? Again, the context of this passage, along with information from other passages about reconciliation, will give the meaning. The dictionary definition and the etymology of the word will also shed light on the meaning.

Verse 20 itself suggests the meaning of the word by the phrase that is set in apposition to it:

...[20]and through him to **reconcile** to himself all things, whether things on earth or things in heaven, by *making peace* through his blood, shed on the cross.

The phrase *making peace* indicates that the reconciliation involves peace between the two parties, in this case, God and all things.

The next verse contains two phrases that describe the *opposite* of reconciliation—the state we were in before we were reconciled:

[21]Once you were *alienated from God* and were *enemies in your minds* because of your *evil behavior.*

We were "enemies" of God. Our sin ("evil behavior") caused us to be "alienated" from God—estranged from Him, hostile toward Him, on unfriendly terms with Him. So being reconciled to God would change us from enemies of God to friends of God.

The next verse amplifies the meaning of reconciliation:

[22]But now he has **reconciled** you by Christ's physical body through death to present you *holy in his sight, without blemish and free from accusation.*

Jesus' death on the cross enables Him to present us "holy in his sight, without blemish and free from accusation." Because Jesus has paid for our sin, we can be in the presence of God without guilt or stain. So being reconciled also involves getting rid of the sin that stands between us and God; then we can have a free and open friendship with Him.

The word *reconcile* (*apokatallassō*, ἀποκαταλλάσσω) is also found in Ephesians 2, which adds to the understanding of what the word means and what its opposite is:

> [R]emember that at that time you were separate from Christ, excluded from citizenship in Israel and foreigners to the covenants of the promise, without hope and without God in the world. But now in Christ Jesus you who once were far away have been brought near through the blood of Christ. For he himself is our peace, who has made the two one and has destroyed the barrier, the dividing wall of hostility, by abolishing in his flesh the law with its commandments and regulations. His purpose was to create in himself one new man out of the two, thus making peace, and in this one body to **reconcile** both of them to God through the cross, by which he put to death their hostility. He came and preached peace to you who were far away and peace to those who were near. For through him we both have access to the Father by one Spirit." [19]Consequently, you are no longer foreigners and aliens, but fellow citizens with God's people and members of God's household (Eph. 2:12–19).

This passage teaches that in Christ, God is not only reconciling people to Himself, but also reconciling people to one another (in this case, Jews and Gentiles—who constitute all of mankind). He is bringing near those who were once far away, drawing them into the covenants of the promise and making them members of God's household. The following phrases in the passage describe being reconciled and not being reconciled:

**Not Reconciled**
separate from Christ
excluded from citizenship in Israel
foreigners to the covenants of the promise
without hope and without God in the world
far away, hostile
separated by a barrier, the dividing wall of hostility

**Reconciled**
brought near through the blood of Christ
he himself is our peace
has made the two one
has destroyed the barrier, the dividing wall of hostility
to create in himself one new man out of the two
making peace
*in this one body to reconcile both of them to God through the cross*
put to death their hostility
preached peace to you who were far away and peace to those
    who were near
we both have access to the Father by one Spirit
no longer foreigners and aliens
fellow citizens with God's people
members of God's household

A prominent theme here is "peace": Jesus is our peace, He makes peace, He preaches peace—to those near and far. When we are reconciled, the hostility is gone and there is peace between God and mankind and peace among people.

Similar words for reconcile (*katallassō,* καταλλάσσω) and reconciliation (*katallagē,* καταλλαγή) are found in Romans 5:

> For if, when we were God's enemies, we were **reconciled** to him through the death of his Son, how much more, having been **reconciled**, shall we be saved through his life! Not only is this so, but we also rejoice in God through our Lord Jesus Christ, through whom we have now received **reconciliation** (Rom. 5:10–11).

This passage shows that we are reconciled through the death of God's Son and saved through the life of His Son. When we are reconciled to God, we are no longer His enemies, so we can rejoice in Him.

The words *katallassō* and *katallagē* are used five times in 2 Corinthians 5. This passage sheds further light on what it means to be reconciled.

> Therefore, if anyone is in Christ, he is a new creation; the old has gone, the new has come! All this is from God, who **reconciled** us to himself through Christ and gave us the ministry of **reconciliation**: that God was **reconciling** the world to himself in Christ, not counting men's sins against them. And he has committed to us the message of **reconciliation**. We are therefore Christ's ambassadors, as though God were making his appeal through us. We implore you on Christ's behalf: Be **reconciled** to God. God made him who had no sin to be sin for us, so that in him we might become the righteousness of God (2 Cor. 5:17–21).

This passage says that God "reconciled us to himself through Christ" and that "God was reconciling the world to himself in Christ." What does that mean? Again, phrases in the passage give the clues:

> new creation
> not counting men's sins against them
> in him we might become the righteousness of God

As with the other passages, "reconciliation" here means a complete cessation of hostility and restoration of our relationship with God, as we "become the righteousness of God."

The dictionary definition of the word *reconcile* confirms this meaning of the word. Its definition is "to re-establish friendship between" (American Heritage Dictionary); "to win over to friendliness; cause to become amicable" (Random House Dictionary). Thayer's Greek-English Lexicon says that the New Testament uses the word *katallagē* to refer to the restoration of the favor of God. Similarly, *katallassō* means to reconcile those who are at variance or to be restored to the favor of God. The word *apokatallassō* means "to reconcile completely," "bring back to a former state of harmony."

Returning to Colossians 1, we see the entire scope of the history of the universe and God's grand plan for it:

In the beginning, Jesus created all things (v. 16).
In the present, all things hold together in Him (v. 17).
In the end, He will reconcile to Himself all things (v. 20).

The passage even says that Christ existed before the created world came into being: "He is before all things" (v. 17).

So Jesus existed before all things, He created all things, He holds together all things, and He will reconcile all things. And what does it mean for God to "reconcile to himself all things"? It is clear that the word *reconcile* means much more than just squashing opposition. It means a full restoration of peace and harmony for anyone and anything that has been out of harmony. It is friendship where there was once enmity, peace where there was once hostility, wholeness where there was once brokenness.

It is true that the word *all* in Scripture does not always mean "absolutely all," but in this lofty declaration of the supremacy of Christ, I believe that the word *pas* (πᾶς) in its different forms (πάσης/πάντα/πάντων/πᾶσιν/πᾶν) does mean "all without exception" in each of the eight instances where it is used in this passage:

15—He is the firstborn over **all** creation
16—by Him **all** things were created
16—**all** things were created by Him
17—He is before **all** things
17—in Him **all** things hold together
18—He has supremacy in **everything**
19—**all** God's fullness dwells in Him
20—through Him God reconciles **all** things

The "all things" of verse 20 is as extensive as the "all things" of verse 16. So just as God created everything and everybody through Christ, so He will reconcile everything and everybody through Christ (not everything *except* most of humanity!) The universe will be completely restored to its original perfection and peace. No one will be at enmity with God or with one another. He will completely fulfill "the mystery of his will according to his good pleasure"—"to bring all things in heaven and on earth together under one head, even Christ" (Eph. 1:10). Going from the depths of mankind's depravity to the total reconciliation of everyone to God and to each other will be more glorious than if we had never fallen in the first place. The restoration of every single relationship to perfect harmony through the work of reconciliation on the cross will be the most spectacular demonstration imaginable of the grace and justice and wisdom and power and love of God.

# 8

# TERROR AT THE MARATHON

On the morning of April 15, 2013—Patriots' Day—I stood near the finish line of the Boston Marathon and snapped a picture to send to my daughter Michelle. It showed the place the 27,000 marathon runners set their sights on, the goal of their years of training and discipline. In the background was another special place, the hotel where Michelle's upcoming wedding reception was to take place.

Unlike the year before, when it was brutally hot, it was a perfect day for a marathon—sunny and brisk. The whole city was festive, anticipating a great day of competition and camaraderie with runners from around the world and half a million spectators coming to the world's oldest annual marathon. Spirits on our volunteer team were high; we had what we felt was the very best volunteer job—placing well-deserved medals around the necks of the finishers.

Not long after the picture was taken, the runners started arriving, at first just a few of the elite runners, but then the trickle swelled to a flood as thousands of exhausted but happy runners streamed across the finish line to the sound of enthusiastic cheers and whistles and applause. They bowed their heads to receive their medal and a smile and words of congratulations and sometimes a hug, and then they gathered with family and friends to celebrate.

The tide of runners continued for two hours, and then came the moment when everything changed. At about 2:50 p.m. a blast rocked the area around the finish line, followed quickly by another one nearby. As the runners who had already crossed the finish line reached the medals area, they looked first confused, and then shocked, and then terrified and frantic. Then there were no more incoming runners, and as the gravity of the situation set in, we were told to run in the opposite direction. My friend and I reached Boston Common, where we tried to get information, which became increasingly gruesome.

Through the rest of that day and night and into the next day, the horrible news continued as the toll increased: 2 dead...several injured...shrapnel flying...limbs severed...23 wounded...3 dead, including an eight-year-old boy...40+ wounded, many critical... 50+...70+...100+...140+...170+. Each new report of injuries felt like another blow.

It defies all reason that any human being could think it's justified or even noble to murder innocent people, even children, who are simply enjoying a community event with their family and friends. And yet, I find that such tragic events reinforce my conviction that God will one day make all things right. We human beings have made an irreparable mess of our world. Good people try, with some success, to make things right. The courage and compassion of the good people on Marathon Monday far outweighed the cowardice and cruelty of the evil ones. And yet, we can never bring about complete justice or restore all that has been lost. We cannot make amputees grow new limbs or heal a person's shattered sense of well-being or bring the dead back to life. **But God can and will!** Clearly this full restoration is not accomplished in this life, but God is not limited to this life to fulfill His purposes. I am confident that He will continue His work in the ages to come until everything is restored under Jesus Christ.

As Peter proclaimed in his sermon in Acts, God has *promised* to restore everything:

> Heaven must receive him [Christ] until the time comes for God to *restore everything,* as he promised long ago through his holy prophets (Acts 3:21).

Paul also declared God's wise purpose to bring unity to *all*:

> With all wisdom and understanding, he made known to us the mystery of his will according to his good pleasure, which he purposed in Christ, to be put into effect when the times reach their fulfillment—to *bring unity to all things* in heaven and on earth under Christ (Eph. 1:8–10).

For those who want evil people like the Marathon bombers to pay dearly for their crimes, rest assured that God "will by no means leave the guilty unpunished" (Ex. 34:7; Nah. 1:3). Proverbs also declares, "Assuredly, the evil man will not go unpunished" (11:21). We don't know exactly what the punishment will look like for each person, but because of God's holy and just character, we can be certain that it will be both severe and fair. I believe that at least part of the judgment that evil people will face will be to experience personally the pain they have inflicted on others—that somehow they will become fully aware, in an excruciatingly personal sense, of the suffering they have caused to others. Though now their conscience may be seared to such an extent that they cannot feel the pain of others, I believe that one day God will open their eyes so that they know fully what it is like to be the victim of senseless suffering or to lose their own children to violence. Perhaps it will be similar to what happens to us when He brings us under conviction for sin. The wicked will see God in all His holiness, and they will see themselves for who they really are. Imagine if you can the horror of such a judgment.

And yet, I don't believe this judgment will be endless or purposeless. God's will is that none should perish but all should come to repentance (2 Pet. 3:9), and He will do whatever it takes to achieve that purpose. By His kindness *and* His severity He deals with us to bring us to repentance, though for some it will take a great deal of severity. He wants all men to be saved and come to a knowledge of the truth (1 Tim. 2:4), and He will reveal truth to them. Jesus gave Himself as

the ransom for *all* men (1 Tim. 2:6). He is the atoning
sacrifice for the sins of the *whole world* (1 Jn. 2:2). He promised
that through His death and resurrection, He would draw all
people to Himself (Jn. 12:32), and He will not fail.

So how can we make any sense of unfathomable evil and
suffering juxtaposed with promises of complete restoration
and joy? I am not a person who gets visions from the Lord,
but years ago He gave me a picture that sustained me then
and has come to mind frequently since then. I applied it to
myself at the time, but more recently I have seen that it really
has a broader application. In this vision, I saw myself in a
deep, dark pit, with steep, slimy sides. It was impossible to
climb out; if you tried, you only slipped back down into the
mud. But then the Lord reached down and lifted me out of
the pit and set me beside it. I felt like the Psalmist who said,
"He brought me up out of the pit of destruction, out of the
miry clay, and He set my feet upon a rock making my foot-
steps firm" (40:2). And then God filled in the pit, leaving no
trace of the ugly, inescapable prison.

But it was what He did next that really gripped my heart.
On the spot where the pit had been, He built a mountain that
was as high as the pit had been deep. I thought of Psalm 103,
which says that God not only redeems my life from the pit,
but also crowns me with lovingkindness and compassion (v.
4). This image spoke to me of the fact that God will not only
take away the pain and even the memory of our trials, but He
will redeem our trials to the extent that the coming glory will
be as great as and even far greater than the past hardship and
anguish. It brought to life verse 18 of Romans 8: "For I consider that the sufferings of this present time are not worthy to
be compared with the glory that is to be revealed to us."

And this image applies not just to me and other people,
but to the whole creation. As Romans 8 says, we ourselves
groan now (v. 23), and indeed the whole creation is groaning
now (v. 22). But we look forward to a cosmic redemption.
We have hope that "the creation itself will be set free from its
bondage to corruption" (v. 21) in order to experience free-

dom and joy. As we walk through this broken world, by faith we need to live into the reality of the coming restoration— not only to believe that it will happen, but to actively work toward it by striving in our own small way, in our own little corner of the world, to bring about the restoration and reconciliation that one day God will fully bring to pass. As Peter puts it, "in keeping with his promise we are looking forward to a new heaven and a new earth, where righteousness dwells" (2 Pet. 3:13). Therefore, "You ought to live holy and godly lives as you look forward to the day of God and *speed its coming*" (2 Pet. 3:11–12).

At a prayer service for the victims of the bombing the following night, it was noted that events like the Marathon point to a universal desire for goodwill and harmony. There is a longing inside us to be part of a community of love and kindness. God made us with that longing, and He will not allow it to go forever unfulfilled. The spirit of unity and goodwill at the Marathon gives us a small foretaste of the perfect harmony that God will create when He "brings unity to all things in heaven and on earth under Christ" (Eph. 1:10).

The Bible makes it very clear that evil is an ever-present reality in this fallen world. *But evil will not have the last word.* As the resurrection chapter, 1 Corinthians 15, shows, God will have the final victory, and He will become all in all (v. 28). Life will overcome death: "As in Adam all die, so also in Christ shall all be made alive" (v. 22). He will "put all his enemies under his feet" (v. 25). "The last enemy to be destroyed is death" (v. 26). Thanks be to God, "Death is swallowed up in victory!" (v. 54).

This theme is also echoed in many hymns that speak of God's final victory:

**I Heard the Bells on Christmas Day**
And in despair I bowed my head
"There is no peace on earth," I said,
"For hate is strong and mocks the song
Of peace on earth, good will to men."

Then pealed the bells more loud and deep:
"God is not dead, nor doth He sleep;
The wrong shall fail, the right prevail
With peace on earth, good will to men."
                    —Henry W. Longfellow, 1864

### This Is My Father's World

This is my Father's world. O let me ne'er forget
That though the wrong seems oft so strong, God is
     the ruler yet.
This is my Father's world: the battle is not done:
Jesus Who died shall be satisfied,
And earth and Heav'n be one.
                    —Maltbie D. Babcock, 1901

As the writer of Proverbs said of the wicked, "their feet
run to evil, and they make haste to shed blood" (1:16). But in
the words of a nineteenth-century writer,

We do not think man's evil can, in the long run of the
ages, finally outspeed God's ever-pursuing mercy.

# 9

# COME WHAT MAY

*"Terror at the Marathon" (#8), is an account of that awful April day in 2013 when the joy and camaraderie of the Boston Marathon were shattered by terrorist bombs. In my first book I wrote about the aftermath of the 2013 Boston Marathon and told stories of runners in the 2014, 2015, and 2016 Marathons. Here are some more inspiring Marathon stories. Let every story of goodness in this broken world be a glimpse of the Kingdom of God and a foretaste of its fullness.*

"Come what may, *I will run.*" I picture every runner of the Boston Marathon echoing these words of Ahimaaz, the messenger who was determined to run to King David to deliver the news of victory in battle (2 Sam. 18:23). Each one has his or her own reasons and faces unique challenges and hardships, but all are absolutely determined to run the race, despite the obstacles.

In 1966, Roberta "Bobbi" Gibb applied to run the Marathon but was denied entry. "Women aren't allowed, and furthermore are not physiologically able," wrote the race director. At that time, AAU rules did not allow women to run more than a mile and a half competitively, but Gibb had been training for Boston every day for two years, sometimes running as much as 40 miles in a day. Fired up, she took a four-day trip on a Greyhound bus from her home in San Diego, arriving in Boston the day before the race. On race day, she slipped into the pack with the men and ran the entire route, becoming the first woman to complete the Boston Marathon.

A year later, Kathrine Switzer registered for the race under the name "K. V. Switzer." She received bib number 261 and took her place with the men at the start line. Partway into her run, an angry race official tried to grab her and pull her off the course bellowing, "Get the hell out of my race, and give me those numbers!" Her boyfriend, an ex-All-American football player, tackled the official out of the way, and Switzer finished the Marathon. In 2017, on the fiftieth anniversary of her historic run, Switzer ran again with bib number 261, at age 70. Her foundation, 261 Fearless, was created to "provide networking, healthy running support and education, and a sisterhood to women all over the world. It is the mission of 261 Fearless to bring active women together through a global supportive social running community—allowing fearless women to pass strength gained from running onto women who are facing challenges." The Boston Athletic Association (BAA) has retired Switzer's number in her honor.

Running the Marathon to raise money for worthy causes has a long history. In 1946, Styliano "Stelios" Kyriakides sold his furniture to buy a ticket to come to Boston from his war-torn village in Greece. Although he had not competed for six years and was physically depleted from the famine conditions in his country—some doctors in Boston advised him not to run at all for fear he would die in the streets—somehow he summoned up the strength to give it his all for his homeland, shouting "For Greece!" as he crossed the finish line as the winner. He appealed to America to help his country, and he returned to Greece with cash and 25,000 tons of supplies for his people.

Today, thousands of athletes run for charitable causes and to honor loved ones. My friend Paul Reardon ran for Spaulding Hospital's Race for Rehab team for the third time in 2017, again raising thousands of dollars for those "living with or recovering from illness, injury, and disability."

Brian Alexander, a US Army Captain, ran for the Rodman for Kids organization, to raise money to serve at-risk children in Massachusetts. "The youth they serve are homeless, seriously ill, academically at-risk, economically disadvantaged, living in foster care, have developmental disabilities, are abused or neglected or malnourished." Their mission is "to have every kid in our community live as we would want our own kids to live."

On the Saturday before the Marathon, hundreds of military members and civilian supporters do a 26.2-mile marathon route through Concord, Massachusetts. Participants in the "Tough Ruck" carry full packs, along with the names of fallen service members. In addition to honoring the fallen, they raise funds to support military families. Finishers become the first to receive the Boston Marathon medal for that year. My daughter Christine has now earned a third medal for her participation in the Tough Ruck.

Each athlete has very personal reasons for making the sacrifices necessary to run Boston. Belinda Stoll witnessed firsthand the 2013 bombings and wanted to run for her grandchildren. When she arrived at the finish line, she was looking for another grandma to bestow her medal. I was honored to place her medal around her neck. Another woman crossed the finish line with her five children, each one wearing a T-shirt with one letter: G-O-M-O-M.

These dedicated folks received the Six Star Finisher medal for completing six major marathons—in New York City, Tokyo, Berlin, London, Chicago, and now Boston.

Mark Sullivan had run thirty consecutive Boston Marathons and was determined not to let knee surgery forty days before the 2017 race stop him. He did complete his thirty-first Boston—174 marathons in total!

In 2016 Tyson Park finished his fourth consecutive Boston Marathon *barefoot*. In 2017 he made it five in a row, at age 75!

In my 2016 Marathon report I featured Earl Granville, a US Army veteran who lost his leg in Afghanistan and completed the Marathon on a handcycle, and Andi Marie Piscopo, who did the 24-hour GoRuck Heavy two days before running Boston. In 2017

they ran together—Earl on his prosthesis and Andi as his partner and guide. In a memorable Marathon moment, Earl picked Andi up and carried her across the finish line, as she carried the American flag. Their emotional finish was captured on TV and spread all over social media, inspiring thousands.

We will never know all the hardships faced by the athletes just to get into the Boston Marathon and then to run it and finish, but I hope that getting a glimpse into some of their stories will inspire you to run your own life race with courage and perseverance and to look forward to the day of final victory when God will make all things new.

# 10

# A WORD TO THE "ELECT"

This poem is by Anne Brontë, the youngest of the famous Brontë sisters. It was first published in 1846 in *Poems by Currer, Ellis, and Acton Bell*, a collection of poems by Charlotte, Emily, and Anne Brontë, using pseudonyms because of the prejudice against female writers at the time. Anne's life was cut short by tuberculosis in 1849 at age 29, within ten months of the death of her brother Branwell at age 31 and her sister Emily at age 30. The work expresses poetically Anne's response to the idea that God chooses a "favoured few" to be with Him in heaven, while the rest are "excluded from that happiness." If she were alive today, would you reprove her as a friend did to me: "This doctrine [that all will be saved] is damnable and I urge you—and anyone else who has either influenced you or whom you have influenced in this regard—to repent and do so as publicly as you have proclaimed error"? Or would you agree that all sinners will one day "live by Him that died"?

### A Word to the "Elect"
### by Anne Brontë

You may rejoice to think yourselves secure;
You may be grateful for the gift divine—
That grace unsought, which made your black hearts pure,
And fits your earth-born souls in Heaven to shine.

But, is it sweet to look around, and view
Thousands excluded from that happiness
Which they deserved, at least, as much as you,—
Their faults not greater, nor their virtues less?

And, wherefore should you love your God the more,
Because to you alone his smiles are given;
Because he chose to pass the many o'er,
And only bring the favoured few to Heaven?

And, wherefore should your hearts more grateful prove,
Because for ALL the Saviour did not die?
Is yours the God of justice and of love?
And are your bosoms warm with charity?

Say, does your heart expand to all mankind?
And, would you ever to your neighbor do—
The weak, the strong, the enlightened, and the blind—
As you would have your neighbor do to you?

And, when you, looking on your fellow-men,
Behold them doomed to endless misery,
How can you talk of joy and rapture then? —
May God withhold such cruel joy from me!

That none deserve eternal bliss I know;
Unmerited the grace in mercy given:
But, none shall sink to everlasting woe,
That have not well deserved the wrath of Heaven.

And, oh! there lives within my heart
A hope, long nursed by me;
(And, should its cheering ray depart,
How dark my soul would be!)

That as in Adam all have died,
In Christ shall all men live;[1]
And ever round his throne abide,
Eternal praise to give.

That even the wicked shall at last
Be fitted for the skies;
And, when their dreadful doom is past,
To life and light arise.

I ask not, how remote the day,
Nor what the sinners' woe,
Before their dross is purged away;
Enough for me, to know

That when the cup of wrath is drained,
The metal purified,
They'll cling to what they once disdained,
And live by Him that died.

Do you have within your heart "a hope, long nursed...
That as in Adam all have died, / In Christ shall all men live; /
And ever round his throne abide, / Eternal praise to give. /
That even the wicked shall at last / Be fitted for the skies; /
And, when their dreadful doom is past, / To life and light
arise"? If you want to have that hope but it eludes you, please
read on. God's Word contains the assurance for those who
want it.

---

[1]From 1 Corinthians 15:22

# 11

# THE INESTIMABLE WORTH
# OF EVERY PERSON

In a sermon series about the "DNA points" of our church—the key truths that animate our life as the Body of Christ—our pastor spoke of "the inestimable worth of every person." Because each and every human being is created in the image of God, we all have infinite value in His eyes. As David so eloquently put it:

> For you formed my inward parts;
>     you knitted me together in my mother's womb.
> I praise you, for I am fearfully and wonderfully made.
> Wonderful are your works;
>     my soul knows it very well.
> My frame was not hidden from you,
> when I was being made in secret,
>     intricately woven in the depths of the earth.
> Your eyes saw my unformed substance;
> in your book were written, every one of them,
>     the days that were formed for me,
>     when as yet there was none of them.
> (Ps. 139:13–16)[1]

In my first book I laid out some of the far-reaching ramifications of this truth—both in terms of how God views and treats people and in terms of how we ourselves view and treat other people. If God imprints His own image on a person, He will love and value that person as a treasured daughter or son.[2] Since His capacity to love is limitless, *every* individual can be the recipient of His boundless love. *No one*—from the tiniest baby lost in the womb to the most powerful kings of the earth—is insignificant to Him. Nobody is a nobody. Not a single human being will be forgotten or neglected by Him.

In the middle of the book of Lamentations, Jeremiah calls to mind God's great love:

> Because of the Lord's great love, we are not consumed,
>    for his compassions never fail.
> They are new every morning;
>    great is your faithfulness (Lam. 3:22–23).

The hymn "Great is Thy Faithfulness" has made those words well known, but for a long time I never noticed what Jeremiah says a few verses later. He assures us that because of God's unfailing love, He does not reject anyone forever!

> For no one is cast off
>    by the Lord forever.
> Though he brings grief, he will show compassion,
>    so great is his unfailing love (Lam 3:31–32).

As far as the way we ourselves treat other people, should we not see them all through God's eyes and love them with His love? Obviously, our love, unlike God's, is severely limited, so it will be focused on those closest to us. But we can still have a caring attitude toward everyone who crosses our path, and even toward those we will never meet. The next time you are out in public—at the mall, in an airport or bus station, at a stadium or concert, or just on the street—take a closer look at the faces passing by. Do you think most of those people are hurtling toward hell with no one to rescue them? No! Each one has immeasurable value and is loved by God just as you are. Not a single soul is expendable to Him![3]

---

[1]Here's a challenge question for those who want to go deeper. To whom do David's declarations in Psalm 139 apply? David was confident about his *own* worth in God's eyes:

O Lord, you have searched *me* and known *me*!
You know when *I* sit down and when *I* rise up.
You are acquainted with all *my* ways.
You hem *me* in, behind and before.
You lay your hand upon *me*.
Your hand shall lead *me*.
You knitted *me* together.
*I* am fearfully and wonderfully made.
Your eyes saw *my* unformed substance.
In your book were written the days that were formed for *me*.

But right after his beautiful declaration of his own value in God's sight, David says, "Oh, that you would slay the wicked!... Do I not hate those who hate you, O Lord?... I hate them with complete hatred" (Ps. 139:19–22). David seems to think that not everyone is as precious to God as he is. Is David expressing the heart of God in his hatred of the wicked, or only his own feelings? Is it OK for us to have the same attitude toward our enemies as David had toward his? Should we hate those who hate the Lord? Should we desire that God slay those who are evil?

[2]There is a special sense in which only those who are in Christ are children of God (Jn. 1:12–13, Rom. 8:14, 1 Jn. 3:1–2, 10, etc.). But there is also a general sense in which God is the Father of all those whom He has created in His image. Malachi asks, "Do we not all have one Father? Did not one God create us?" (Mal. 2:10), thus linking His fatherhood with the fact that He created us. Paul told the Athenians that "we are God's offspring," so we understand that the divine being is not made in our image "by human design or skill," but rather that we are made in His image (Acts 17:29). He also spoke of "one God and Father of all, who is over all and through all and in all" (Eph. 4:6).

[3]In "Glimpses of English Poverty" (1863), Nathaniel Hawthorne speaks of the misery of London's poor and the fact that if even one is lost, truly we all are lost:

> How difficult to believe that anything so precious as a germ of immortal growth can have been plunged into this cesspool of vice! Oh, what a mystery! Slowly, slowly, as after groping at the bottom of a deep, noisome pool, my hope struggles upward to the surface, bearing the half-drowned body of a child and bearing it aloft for its own life, and my own life, and all our lives. Unless these slime-clogged nostrils can be made capable of inhaling celestial air, I know not how the purest and most intellectual of us can reasonably expect ever to taste a breath of it. The whole question of eternity is staked there. If a single one of those helpless little ones be lost, the world is lost.

# 12

# IN WHAT WAY ARE GOD'S WAYS HIGHER THAN OUR WAYS?

Whenever someone is struggling with the concept of billions of people being eternally separated from God in hell, sooner or later somebody will offer the concepts in Isaiah 55:8–9:

> "For my thoughts are not your thoughts, neither are your ways my ways," declares the Lord. "As the heavens are higher than the earth, so are my ways higher than your ways and my thoughts than your thoughts."

The idea of invoking this passage is to say that God must have wonderful, glorious purposes in allowing most of His creatures to suffer in hell forever, but we can't comprehend them because our minds are so tiny compared to His.

However, a closer look at Isaiah 55 shows that the passage is saying nothing of the sort—in fact, virtually the opposite. The Israelites wanted their enemies to be punished and non-Jews to be excluded from God's people, but God, contrary to their expectations, offers abundant mercy to all. What the Israelites can't fathom is how vast and inclusive His *mercy* is.

The theme of Isaiah 55 is in verse 1: "Come, all you who are thirsty," and in verse 3: "Give ear and come to me; hear me that your soul may live." The verse immediately preceding the often-quoted ones says, "Let the wicked forsake his way and the evil man his thoughts. Let him turn to the Lord, and he will have mercy on him, and to our God, for he will freely pardon." What we cannot comprehend is *how freely He pardons*.

The theme of God's desire to abundantly pardon and bless is present in chapter 54 (coming right on the heels of the Suffering Servant passage in chapter 53) and continues through chapter 55 and into chapter 56. In chapter 54, God acknowledges that He has been angry with His people, but His anger is completely overshadowed by His compassion:

> For a brief moment I deserted you,
>> but with great compassion I will gather you.
> In overflowing anger for a moment
>> I hid my face from you,
> but with everlasting love I will have compassion on you.
>> says the Lord, your Redeemer (Is. 54:7–8).

The verses immediately following the "my ways are higher than your ways" passage reinforce the idea that God has a merciful purpose for His creation. Verses 10 and 11 of chapter 55 say that, like the rain and snow that water the earth so it yields bread, so God's Word "shall accomplish that which I purpose, and shall succeed in the thing for which I sent it." His purpose is identified in Isaiah 45 and 49 (and confirmed in Acts 13:47)—to bring salvation to the ends of the earth:

> "Turn to me and be saved,
>> all you ends of the earth;
>> for I am God, and there is no other.
> By myself I have sworn;
>> my mouth has uttered in all integrity
>> a word that will not be revoked:
> Before me every knee will bow,
>> by me every tongue will swear" (Is. 45:22–23).

> "I will make you a light for the Gentiles,
>> that my salvation may reach to the ends of the
>> earth" (Is. 49:6).

Verses 12 and 13 of Isaiah 55 talk about joy, peace, and song, and the fact that pine trees and myrrh will grow instead of thorns and briers. "*This* will be for the Lord's renown," not billions of people suffering eternal punishment!

Chapter 56 invites *foreigners* to partake of God's goodness: "Let no foreigner who has bound himself to the Lord say, 'The Lord will surely exclude me from his people'" (v. 3). God promises to give to faithful foreigners "a memorial and …an everlasting name that will not be cut off" (5). He will bring these foreigners to His holy mountain and give them joy in His house of prayer, which will be *"for all nations"* (7).

So this passage is really talking about how *inclusive* God's mercy is (which the Israelites couldn't comprehend), not that He excludes vast numbers of people from His kingdom and that we just have to accept it. He wants to keep on gathering people to Himself:

> The Sovereign Lord declares—he who gathers the exiles of Israel: I will gather still others to them besides those already gathered" (56:8).

The wicked can't come in while they remain in their wickedness, but God urges them to turn to Him so He can have mercy on them and freely pardon them.

The theme of judgment is strong throughout Isaiah, but God's boundless mercy is seen to triumph over judgment. In chapters 13 through 24, the prophet pronounces a series of oracles against the nations, including Babylon, Assyria, Egypt, Philistia, Moab, and even God's own people, culminating in the judgment of the whole earth in chapter 24. Yet promises of restoration of the nations are interwoven with judgment:

> In that day there will be an altar to the Lord in the midst of the land of Egypt…. When they cry to the Lord because of oppressors, he will send them a savior and defender, and deliver them. And the Lord will make himself known to the Egyptians, and the Egyptians will know the Lord in that day and worship with sacrifice and offering, and they will make vows to the Lord and perform them. And the Lord will strike Egypt, striking and healing, and they will return to the Lord, and he will listen to their pleas for mercy and heal them.

In that day there will be a highway from Egypt to Assyria, and Assyria will come into Egypt, and Egypt into Assyria, and the Egyptians will worship with the Assyrians. In that day Israel will be the third with Egypt and Assyria, a blessing in the midst of the earth, whom the Lord of hosts has blessed, saying, "Blessed be Egypt my people, and Assyria the work of my hands, and Israel my inheritance." (Is. 19:19–25).

Israel's archenemies—Egypt and Assyria—will be in a covenant with her and will be blessed along with her! And not just Egypt and Assyria; these two enemies of Israel—one to the south and one to the north—are representative of all the nations of the earth. *Striking and healing*. God strikes in order to heal. He is not only Judge, but also Savior, Defender, and Deliverer—for the Gentile nations as well as for Israel.[1] The judgment on the whole earth in chapter 24 is followed by blessings on the whole earth in chapter 25:

> On this mountain the Lord of hosts will make for *all*
>     *peoples*
>   a feast of rich food, a feast of well-aged wine....
> And he will swallow up on this mountain
>     the covering that is cast over *all peoples*,
>     the veil that is spread over *all nations*.
> He will swallow up death forever;
>     the Lord God will wipe away tears from *all faces*,
>     and the reproach of his people he will take away
>       from *all the earth*,
>   for the Lord has spoken" (Is. 25:6–8).

In Romans 9, Paul makes a point similar to Isaiah's when, in answer to the question "Is there injustice on God's part?" he quotes the Lord's words to Moses, who was interceding on behalf of Israel: "I will have mercy on whom I have mercy, and I will have compassion on whom I have compassion" (Rom. 9:15; from Ex. 33:19). The point is not that God arbitrarily singles out certain individuals to receive His mercy and casts off the rest, but rather that He freely extends His mercy to all.

As in Isaiah 55, this extravagant mercy is contrary to the desire and expectation of the Jews, who think they alone—not the Gentiles—should be the recipients of God's grace. Paul confirms that the extent of God's mercy is not just to all Israel but to all people when he says, "For God has consigned all to disobedience, *that he may have mercy on all*" (Rom. 11:32).

Psalm 145 also expresses the unfathomable greatness of God and the boundless extent of His mercy: "Great is the Lord and most worthy of praise; *his greatness no one can fathom*" (v. 3). The chapter talks about His mighty acts and glorious splendor and majesty and dominion (4–6, 10–13), and especially about His "abundant goodness" (7–9, 13ff). He is "gracious and compassionate, slow to anger and rich in love" (8). He is "good to all" and "has compassion on all he has made" (9). He is "loving toward all he has made" (13, 17). He "upholds all those who fall and lifts up all who are bowed down" (14).

As Isaiah and Paul and the Psalmist all try to convey, it is God's wonderful love, which is so much higher than our ways, that humans cannot fathom!

> "The mountains may depart and the hills be removed, but my steadfast love shall not depart from you, and my covenant of peace shall not be removed," says the Lord, who has compassion on you (Is. 54:10).

---

[1]The New Living translation of Psalm 87 says that Egypt, Babylon and other Gentile nations will become citizens of Jerusalem and enjoy its blessings:

I will count Egypt and Babylon among those who know me—
    also Philistia and Tyre, and even distant Ethiopia.
    They have all become citizens of Jerusalem!
Regarding Jerusalem it will be said,
    "Everyone enjoys the rights of citizenship there."
    And the Most High will personally bless this city.
When the Lord registers the nations, he will say,
    "They have all become citizens of Jerusalem" (Ps. 87:4–6).
Psalm 22 begins with the Suffering Servant and ends with the Victorious King ministering to all the afflicted and being worshiped by all nations:
    *The whole earth* will acknowledge the Lord and return to him.
    *All the families of the nations* will bow down before him.

# 13

# PARADISE REGAINED

Some friends went on a fabulous trip to his birthplace—
Hawaii—to celebrate his seventieth birthday. All seven-
teen members of their family were able to go—Mom,
Dad, five kids, three spouses, and seven grandkids.

As I looked at their pictures and heard about their adventures, I have to admit that I felt some twinges of envy—not
just for the spectacular place where they gathered, but even
more so for the fact that their *whole* family was together.
Everyone was there, down to their newest little grand-
daughter, who was only six weeks old. And even better than
the fact that they were all together—they all got along! As the
mom reported, "Family members still on speaking terms after
all this togetherness!"

Relatively few people will ever experience a reunion with
the entire family in such an exotic location. It has been
several years since our whole family has been together, and
with everyone's life circumstances, I don't know when it might

happen again. Some haven't even met our newest grandchild. As a mother and grandmother, I long for such a reunion, yet even when or if it does happen, I know it won't be perfect; conflict and friction will never be completely absent.

Who wouldn't be thrilled to have a vacation in a beautiful place like Hawaii surrounded by people who love you and get along with you? For most, it is an impossible dream, made unattainable by a multitude of factors. I especially feel for those who can't even *hope* for such a reunion—even if money were no object—because they have lost family members due to death or estrangement.

So will this universal longing go unfulfilled for the vast majority of people on earth? Yes. Even the rich can't pull it off if their family members are at odds with one another.

But wait. Did God put such longings inside us only to have them go forever unfulfilled? No! He created us with a desire for fellowship, love, and beauty, and He can and will fulfill that desire, beyond our wildest expectations.

Clearly such a complete fulfillment will not happen in this life. But God is not limited to this life to accomplish His purposes and bless His people. He promised long ago that the day will come when He will restore *everything* (Acts 3:21). He has made known to us the mystery of His will—to bring *all* together in unity under the headship of Christ (Eph. 1:9–10).

Some might be thinking, "Gag me—I couldn't stand to be with my family for more than five minutes." But don't worry—they will not be the same as they are now, and neither will you! We will all go through the refining fire of God's judgment, until we are fit to live in His kingdom (Rom. 14:10–12). And the earth itself, which now is in bondage to decay, will be transformed into a paradise that will make Hawaii pale in comparison (Rom. 8:21). And all suffering will end and there will be no more tears or fears or strife or pain or mourning or death (Rev. 21:4).

Does your heart feel a thrill of hope to imagine that such a paradise might exist—a place of exquisite beauty and perfect harmony? This hope can be realized only through Jesus Christ.

He is the one who brings good news and sets free those who are oppressed (Luke 4:18–19). He died and was raised to life, and in Him we will be resurrected to new life (1 Cor. 15:20–22). Come to Him, allow Him to transform the ashes of your life to beauty, and embrace the hope of the resurrection.

Or do you already have assurance that you yourself will experience bliss, but feel fear for your loved ones who don't know Christ? Remember who it is you have put your faith in. He loves your family members more than you do. He loves *you* more than you can imagine. You will not arrive at the reunion only to find that those you love have been cast off. Their presence will not be *automatic*—they have to come to Christ, acknowledge Him as their Savior, and submit to His transforming work in their lives—but it is *assured* because He loved them enough to give His life for them, and He will surely see to it that His sacrifice for them was not in vain.

So when you see people experiencing joy and beauty and harmony that may seem elusive to you, don't let it become a cause of envy. (I'm speaking to myself here!) Rather, let it be a cause for hope. As you catch a glimpse of what true joy and peace can be, let it serve as a small foretaste of the spectacular future that God has in store for us—to restore His entire creation to a state that will be even more wonderful than it was before we messed it up.

When my dad passed away, I reminded my mom that their separation is only for a time. Someday there will be a stupendous family reunion where not only will they be together, but the entire family will be present and at perfect peace with one another. Praise God that His ways are infinitely beyond all we could ask or even imagine!

> What no eye has seen,
> what no ear has heard,
> and what no human mind has conceived—
> the things God has prepared for those who love him—
> these are the things God has revealed to us by his Spirit.
> 1 Corinthians 2:9–10

Now to him who is able to do
immeasurably more than all we ask or imagine,
according to his power that is at work within us,
to him be glory in the church and in Christ Jesus
throughout all generations, for ever and ever! Amen.
Ephesians 3:20–21

# 14

# THE UNMENTIONABLE SUBJECT

I used to be afraid to share the gospel, for fear that the conversation would come around to the subject of hell. I was afraid someone would ask, What about those who have never heard? or How can a good God allow billions of people to be tormented forever? or What's the point of bringing people into existence only to suffer in this life, die, and then suffer forever? I had no good answers. I knew all the standard answers, but they didn't satisfy me any more than they would satisfy those who asked the questions.

As Grady Brown writes in his foreword to Gerry Beauchemin's book *Hope Beyond Hell,*[1]

> The doctrine of "endless punishment" has for centuries been the "crazy uncle" that the Church, with justifiable embarrassment, has kept locked in the back bedroom. Unfortunately, from time to time, he escapes his confinement, usually when there are guests in the parlor, and usually just at the time when we are telling them about a loving God who gave His Son to die for their sins. It's no wonder that the guests run away never to return. But instead of shunting the "crazy uncle" back to his asylum, and trying to cover our embarrassment (by ever more loudly shouting "God is Love!"), we need to get our "crazy uncle" healed.

Now I see that there *is* a way for the crazy uncle to be healed: by going back to Scripture and rediscovering the true purpose, nature, and duration of hell. The purpose of hell is redemptive—it is God's will to restore the whole creation, including all of humanity, to a state even more glorious than its original perfection. His desire is *to eradicate sin* from the universe by transforming sinners into saints. Christ appeared "once for all at the culmination of the ages *to do away with sin* by the sacrifice of himself" (Heb. 9:26). As Thomas Allin puts it, the end is "*the extinction of sin* and the restoration of the sinner; for no other end is worthy of God." Yes, that process can be described as a fiery ordeal; rooting out sin is always painful and wrenching. And it may take a long time; people can be *very* resistant to God. But ultimately, He will have complete victory; by His kindness and His severity, every soul will be brought to repentance. Then *every* knee will willingly bow and *every* tongue will joyfully confess that Jesus Christ is Lord.

Now I'm free to share the gospel without worrying about getting trapped by good questions that have no good answers. I can confidently proclaim that God is Love, that He is *not* a monster who allows people to spend eternity in perpetual suffering apart from Him. At the same time, I can confidently proclaim that He is holy and righteous, He is a consuming fire, and He will not let anyone get away with anything. We will all have to stand before the judgment seat of Christ and give an account of our lives. He will do whatever it takes to make sinners holy, fit for spending eternity in His presence, and the more rebellious we are, the more difficult that process will be. We are called to cooperate in that process here and now, and to encourage others to do the same.

Jesus died not just for an elect few but for the whole world. As in Adam all die, so in Christ all are made alive. His work on the cross will be effective for everyone He created. The process of counteracting all the evil we have caused will be long and painful, but ultimately God will have complete victory. And we can share the gospel as the **Good News** it was meant to be—that God was in Christ reconciling the *whole* sinful, messed-up world to Himself (2 Cor. 5:11–21)!

---

[1]Beauchemin, Gerry. *Hope Beyond Hell: The Righteous Purpose of God's Judgments.*

[2]Allin, Thomas. *Christ Triumphant.*

# 15

# DOES GOD LOVE EVERYBODY?

I became a Christian through Campus Crusade for Christ (now Cru), with the use of "The Four Spiritual Laws." Law #1 stated:

God loves you and has a wonderful plan for your life.[1]

**GOD LOVES YOU!** *
*Some restrictions apply

This message is appealing, and I'm sure it has helped to draw many (like me) to faith in Christ. *But is it true?* Is it biblically accurate to tell unbelievers "God loves you"?

There are some who flat-out say that God does *not* love the whole world—that God's love is reserved for the elect, that only the saints are the recipients of His love. For example, Arthur W. Pink (1886–1952) states:

> One of the most popular beliefs of the day is that God loves everybody, and the very fact that it is so popular with all classes ought to be enough to arouse the suspicions of those who are subject to the Word of Truth. God's love towards all His creatures is the fundamental and favorite tenet of Universalists, Unitarians, Theosophists, Christian Scientists, Russell-ites, etc.... So widely has this dogma been pro-claimed, and so comforting is it to the heart which is at enmity with God, we have little hope of convincing many of their error....
>
> To tell the Christ-rejector that God loves him is to cauterize his conscience as well as to afford him a sense of security in his sins. The fact is, the love of

God is a truth for the saints only, and to present it to the enemies of God is to take the children's bread and to cast it to the dogs.

A contemporary preacher who holds a similar belief is Mark Driscoll. He told his congregation,

Some of you, God hates you. Some of you, God is sick of you. God is frustrated with you. God is wearied by you. God has suffered long enough with you…. He doesn't think your excuse is merited. He doesn't care if you compare yourself to someone worse than you; He hates them too.

God hates right now, personally, objectively, hates some of you.

Those who believe that God loves and calls only the elect cannot even have confidence that He loves and calls their own beloved children. Some time ago I read some words by John Piper that grieved me greatly. Writing in 1983, when his three sons were small, he spoke of his deep love for them and his high hopes that they would grow into powerful men of God. Then he added, *"But I am not ignorant that God may not have chosen my sons for his sons."*[2] He said that he himself would give his life for their salvation, but he could not be sure that Jesus had died for them! Do you parents resonate with what Piper says? Or do you find it overwhelmingly sad that he thinks God could pass over his dear sons?

In my experience, it seems that those who already believe that God loves only the elect are as unlikely to change their opinion as they think those who believe God loves everybody are to change theirs. ("So widely has this dogma been proclaimed, and so comforting is it to the heart which is at enmity with God, we have little hope of convincing many of their error.") Therefore, a dialog between these two camps would probably make little headway in either direction.

For that reason, here I would like to address those who say, "Yes, God loves all people, *but…*" There are many who affirm the biblical truth that God loves the world, but they often add a caveat or condition or restriction:

> ...*but* He is also holy.
> ...*but* His love is not like human love.
> ...*but* love is not His primary attribute.
> ...*but* He is also just.
> ...*but* He has to punish sin.
> ...*but* He doesn't force anyone to believe.

For example, in a correspondence with a friend, he said regarding the relationship between God's love and holiness,

> You seem to want to place God's love as the controlling factor in his planning and decisions. To me the central attribute around which all the others revolve is His holiness. He is called the Holy One of Israel 31 times (e.g. 2 Kings 19:22; Psalm 71:22, 41:14; Isa 55:5; 60:9, etc.). His name is holy (Isa 57:15). I do not see His love as the central issue or motivation in God.

I replied,

> I think a case could be made that God's love is at least as central as His holiness (God IS love—you don't get any more essential than that), but I don't think it's necessary or wise to do so, because God's love is not in conflict with His holiness (or with any of His other attributes). It's not that some of His actions are driven by His holiness and some by His love; everything He does is driven by the totality of who He is. So we should never say, "God is holy, *but* He's also loving" nor "God is loving, *but* He's also holy"; both are part of His essential nature and are in no way at odds with each other.

In other words, I believe it's a mistake to say "God is loving, *but* anything." He's loving *and* He's holy *and* He's just *and* He's infinitely more than we can ever know. His love is at the core of His being, just as all His other attributes are at the core of His being. But the question remains, Does He love *everybody*? Or does He hate some, as Pink and Driscoll say? Does He love everybody in a vague, fuzzy kind of way? Does He love in a way that we find difficult to recognize as love? Does He love everybody at first but stop loving them depending on what they do? Or stop loving them when they die?

*God IS love.* His loving holiness and holy love are inseparable; in fact, it could be said that they are one and the same. He always operates in love, He loved us while we were sinners, and He will always love us. And by "us" I mean the whole human race. And by "love" I mean the quality that in God is infinitely higher and purer than the best human love but *not* radically different from it.[3] And by "always" I mean that He will *never stop loving* us—not when we sin, not when we rebel against Him, not when we die.

Let's look first at the Old Testament. One might read certain parts of the Old Testament and conclude that God does not love everyone, but let's see how we might better understand passages that suggest that God loves only certain people or even that He hates and destroys the rest.

Certainly God's steadfast love is evident throughout the Old Testament, but some say it is directed only to His chosen ones, the people of Israel. It's true that the children of Israel are the apple of His eye—He set His affection on them and chose them above all others and made a covenant of love with them. But are they alone the objects of His love? And it's not hard to find passages that indicate that God will destroy His enemies. Do these passages represent His heart in the matter? In what way might He destroy His enemies?

It could also be said that His love is conditional: He keeps His covenant of love with His people *if* they continue wholeheartedly in His way and are careful to follow His laws. He shows love to those who love Him and keep His commands. He loves the just, and His unfailing love surrounds those who trust in Him. His love is great for those who fear Him, but He hates evildoers. The psalmist says, "The wicked of the earth you discard like dross" (119:119). He detests the way of the wicked, but He loves those who pursue righteousness.

So shall we conclude that God's love is only for a select segment of humanity? No! The people of Israel were specially chosen by God, but not to be the *exclusive* recipients of His love. Rather they were to be the instrument for declaring His name to the world and making known His holiness and His love so that others might be drawn into His family. They didn't do a very good job of it, but God's desire was that they be a light to all the nations rather than keeping the light for themselves. Psalm 107 repeatedly says to give thanks to the Lord for His unfailing love and His wonderful deeds for *mankind* (or *the children of men*). David's song of praise in Psalm 145 extols the Lord for His graciousness toward all:

> The LORD is gracious and merciful, slow to anger and abounding in steadfast love. The LORD is good to all, and his mercy is over all that he has made.... The LORD is righteous in all his ways and kind in all his works.... Let all flesh bless His holy name forever and ever (Ps. 145:8–9, 17, 21).

In what sense does God "destroy" the wicked? Does He put them out of existence? Or lock them in hell to be punished forever and ever? Consider another way that He might destroy His enemies: in the sense that Abraham Lincoln spoke of when he said, "Do I not destroy my enemies when I make them my friends?" God is more than able to get rid of all enemies by transforming them into friends, just as He did to you and me who were once dead in our trespasses and now have been made alive together with Christ.

Is God's love is reserved for those who are faithful to Him? In one sense, perhaps; those who follow Him are the recipients of His love, while those who are in rebellion against Him do not experience His love. Yet on another level, God's love is spoken of as an essential part of who He is, which is not dependent on how we respond to it. He can no more stop being loving than He can stop being holy. Over and over the Bible declares that He is a forgiving God, gracious and compassionate, slow to anger and abounding in love. His love is steadfast and unfailing, it reaches to the heavens, it stands firm forever. Psalm 136 declares 26 times that His love endures forever. His love does not depend on our obedience, any more than His faithfulness does; as Paul says, "If we are faithless, *he remains faithful*" (2 Pet. 2:13).

So if you want to limit God's love in any way, you can find verses to support your position. But I would encourage you to do the opposite; rather than limiting His love—or any of His attributes—think *bigger*. With all of God's attributes, however great you think they are—they're greater. (Ps. 145:3—"His greatness no one can fathom.") However holy you think He is—He's holier. However just you think He is—His justice is more complex and perfect. However powerful you think He is—His power exceeds what you can imagine. However vast you think the love of God is—it's more so. His "love divine, all loves excelling" extends to all of space and time and beyond space and time, because God is beyond space and time and God is love.

And what do we see in the New Testament? Again there are those who say God's love is only for His people.[4] It has been pointed out that, other than John 3:16, God's love is hardly mentioned in the gospels; it's not until the epistles, which are addressed to the people of God, that the love of God is revealed in its fullness. Should we therefore understand that God's love is restricted to the elect? Does He love the elect before they come to faith (knowing that they will)? Does He love little children? All little children, or only those who will one day come to Him in repentance and faith? If He loves them all, does He stop loving some if they fail to trust Him personally?

Or does God love everybody in this life but stop loving unbelievers if they die without coming to faith? One person stated that God "turns off" His love when unbelievers die:

God makes the choice to turn His love off once a lost person enters into eternity.... For God to turn His love off means you can no longer experience that

82

love. Once a lost person enters into eternity God no longer expresses His love towards them. Instead all the lost person knows is the judgment of God.

So she believes that God's love for the lost stops at their death and turns into judgment. Others believe that God's love is an immutable part of His nature, so it does not stop when a person dies, but they say that allowing people to go to hell is somehow an expression of His love. I can only wonder by what strange logic it can be considered "love" to consign people to never-ending suffering with no hope of relief. God has given us a sense of right and wrong, and we know in our hearts that cruel and unusual punishment is wrong, even for the worst of criminals. If "love" means allowing people to suffer endlessly, then the word "love" has completely lost its meaning and become indistinguishable from hate.

Of course God deals with people differently depending on their response to Him, and of course their perception of Him depends greatly on their own moral condition and their relationship to Him. The consuming fire of His presence is experienced as intense love by those who love Him but intense conviction by those who do not. But it seems to me that you get trapped in a logical quagmire if you say that God's love or lack thereof is somehow dependent on the worth or character or faith or actions or standing of the recipients.

Yes, you can find verses that suggest that God's love for a person is determined by the person's value or actions (He loves His own beloved children; He hates the wicked, etc.), but I think those verses should be understood in light of the character of God and the constancy of His love. Otherwise you get tangled up in all kinds of quandaries and contradictions: "God loves the righteous but hates evildoers"; in other words, He loves you if you're good, and He hates you if you're bad. So does He hate believers when they do evil? Does He love unbelievers when they do good? Why do some merit His love while others do not? Or if no one merits it, why does He single out some to get it and leave others with no hope of ever getting it? If He is the one who grants (or withholds) salvation, how does He choose who will get it and who won't? Does He automatically love people who are unable to choose between good and evil (infants and mentally handicapped)? Does He stop loving them when and if they become able to choose? Does He love beforehand those whom He knows will eventually come to faith, or does He hate them until they do? Does He love people in this life and keep calling them to Himself up to their deathbed, and then set His face against them with implacable wrath the moment they take their last breath?

I don't think we need to go through any philosophical or theological contortions to try to explain God's love. It's not complicated: God is love, He loves you and me and everyone else, and His love never ceases. He loved us when we were dead in sin, and He continues to love us if we fall into sin again. Just like any good father, He never gives up loving us. The goal of His holy love/loving holiness is to make us holy, to eradicate sin, and to restore His creation to a state of sinless perfection even greater than it would have been if we had never sinned. He pursues us tirelessly—throughout our lives on earth and beyond, through kindness and severity—to draw us to Himself in a relationship of love. As George MacDonald has said, "Every soul that is ultimately lost is a defeat of the love of God." Conversely, the salvation of every soul is the full triumph of His love.[5]

God's love and holiness in no way clash with one another; in fact, they are even more than complementary. As Stephen Ford put it,

> God's judgments (because of His Holiness) are, in reality, simply manifestations of His Love. (For God would not be loving if he never judged sin and simply allowed it to go unchecked and bring about ever more evil.) And His Love—which has been manifested to the world (all of humanity) through the cross—is an expression (and "satisfaction") of His Holiness.... In

the final analysis, I am convinced that to say "God is Holy" or "God is Love" is to say the same thing.

As I tried to explain to a Calvinist:

> I was once a child of wrath. But I think God loved me even then: "But God, who is rich in mercy, for his great love wherewith he loved us, even when we were dead in sins, hath quickened us together with Christ, (by grace ye are saved)." And I think that He loves others who are still dead in sins, so much so that He sent His Son to die for them: "But God commendeth his love toward us, in that, while we were yet sinners, Christ died for us" (Rom. 5:8).

The justification that Jesus brings through the cross is as extensive as the condemnation that Adam brought upon us in the garden: "Therefore as by the offence of one, judgment came upon all men to condemnation; even so by the righteousness of one the free gift came upon all men unto justification of life. For as by one man's disobedience many were made sinners, so by the obedience of one shall many be made righteous" (Rom. 5:17–18). How could Adam's sin be greater than Christ's righteousness? The power of the cross is that Jesus by His righteousness can completely undo the destruction caused by man's sinfulness.

So yes, all little children can sing "Jesus Loves Me" with confidence that it is true—not that there are some He does not love, or that He may stop loving some when they get older. His love is not limited to a fraction of humanity; it is big enough to go around. And though we can and do rebel against Him and walk according to the prince of the power of the air and become children of disobedience, yet HE IS SOVEREIGN and will not allow any of us to thwart His good purposes forever. He is not limited in power, He is not limited by our "free will," and He is

85

not limited to this one age to accomplish His eternal purposes. He will draw all by His irresistible grace and reconcile all to Himself through the blood of the cross.

A. W. Pink says, "To tell the Christ-rejector that God loves him is to cauterize his conscience as well as to afford him a sense of security in his sins." Others say that if unbelievers think God will rescue all in the end, they will see no point in coming to Christ now. On the contrary, what keeps many away is a twisted picture of God that shows Him treating unbelievers in a way that is unrecognizable as love. For example, one commenter's response to the question "What Would Jesus Say to Justin Bieber?" was "I love you Justin. Repent and live for me or I will thrust you out of my presence on judgment day and declare to you that I never knew you." Is God really that schizophrenic? Consider this scenario, which occurred to me when I read the commenter's "gospel" message:

> Suppose your daughter met a man who professed undying love for her. He asked her to marry him and promised a wonderful life together. He vowed that if she became his wife, he would love her unconditionally and protect her with tender care. But if she turned down his offer, she would be miserable. If she doubted or rejected his love, she would receive his fury. Not only would she miss out on all he promised to do for her, but he would see to it that she met a terrible fate. What would you advise your daughter to do? Avoid that kind of guy, or hurry up and marry him in order to receive the blessings and avoid the misery?

Does our witnessing for Jesus ever look like the latter? "Ask Jesus into your heart now so you get the blessings and go to heaven and avoid hell." Do we not cheapen the gospel of grace when we hold out the carrot of heaven and/or the stick of hell? Salvation is *so* much more than getting into heaven, and when we present it as a get-out-of-hell-free card, we horribly misrepresent the Lord and His message.

Unlike many Calvinists, I think God loves everyone and Jesus died for everyone (not just the elect). However, I do agree with one statement made by a Calvinist. He said, "To die for the world (everyone) and fail to redeem all is an epic failure." I replied, "I think you're absolutely right about one thing: 'To die for the world (everyone) and fail to redeem all is an epic failure.' I believe He died for the world and will *succeed* in redeeming all. **Epic success**."

---

[1]If my memory serves me, back in the 70s the first law stated, "God loves you and *has* a wonderful plan for your life." It now reads, "God loves you and *offers* a wonderful plan for your life." I don't know whether the change is incidental, whether it reflects a change in theology, or whether it is just me not remembering what it actually said.

[2]"I have three sons. Every night after they are asleep I turn on the hall light, open their bedroom door, and walk from bed to bed, laying my hands on them and praying. Often I am moved to tears of joy and longing. I pray that Karsten Luke become a great physician of the soul, that Benjamin John become the beloved son of my right hand in the gospel, and that Abraham Christian give glory to God as he grows strong in his faith.

"But I am not ignorant that God may not have chosen my sons for his sons. And, though I think I would give my life for their salvation, if they should be lost to me, I would not rail against the Almighty. He is God. I am but a man. The potter has absolute rights over the clay. Mine is to bow before his unimpeachable character and believe that the Judge of all the earth has ever and always will do right." (John Piper, 1983. desiringgod.org)

[3]C. S. Lewis echoes this idea in *The Problem of Pain*: "If God's moral judgement differs from ours so that our 'black' may be his 'white', we can mean nothing by calling him good, for to say 'God is good', while asserting that his goodness is wholly other than ours, is really only to say 'God is we know not what'."

[4]Many Jews wanted God's favor to be restricted to "the chosen people" (the Jews) and not extended to the Gentiles (everyone else). Paul faced this mindset: "And now I am standing trial for the hope of the promise made by God to our fathers.... And for this hope, O King, I am being accused by Jews. Why is it considered incredible among you people if God does raise the dead?" (Acts 26:6-8). We might ask, "Why is it considered incredible among you people if Jesus does save the world?"

[5]We often speak of omnipotence, omniscience, and omnipresence as the key qualities of God's character. I believe we should add omnibenevolence.

# 16

# SHOULD WE LOVE EVERYBODY?
## PART 1

The question "Does God love everybody?" (#15) prompts the question "Should we love everybody?" which leads to the bigger question "How should (or how does) the way we live reflect what we believe about the character of God?" My short answers to the first two questions are "Yes" and "Yes." My short answer to the third question is that, for good or for ill, our lives do tend to reflect what we believe about God.

If it's true that God loves everybody, then it follows that we His children should try to love everybody as He does. And even if you don't believe that God loves everybody, if you're a Christian you probably agree, at least in theory, that we should love our neighbors. Jesus Himself considered the command to love our neighbors of utmost importance, second only to loving God with our whole heart, soul, mind, and strength (Lk.10:27).

In order to see the connection between God's love for people and our love for people, let's explore the third question—the relationship between our view of how God acts and our view of how we should act, particularly how our love for other people is an expression of how we believe He loves people.

In a discussion of this question, I commented that "our theology (how we view God) has a direct and profound effect on our behavior (how we live)." Another person was thinking along the same lines as I was but saw the dynamics working in the opposite direction:

You suggest that "our theology (how we view God) has a direct and profound effect on our behavior (how we live)." I have lately been thinking much the same. But while I agree with your thought to a certain extent, I think it might more accurately be viewed from almost 180 degrees the other way: our outlook (which is reflected in our behavior) has a direct and profound effect on how we view God.

He went on to give examples of how different people's experiences had affected their perception of God. I suspect that it works both ways: the experiences we go through shape our view of God, and our view of God informs the way we behave. For example, it is well documented that our relationship with our earthly father has an early and lasting effect on how we perceive our heavenly Father. A recent book by John Bishop, *God Distorted: How Your Earthly Father Affects Your Perception of God and Why It Matters* (2013), explains that "Regardless of the type of father you grew up with—or without—it is likely that your view of God is influenced by the relationship you had with your father." Your view of God, in turn, influences the way you parent; the tendency is to model your parenting after the fatherhood of God, as you perceive it.

Consider the child who grows up with an abusive, violent father. Chances are that he will picture God as harsh, critical, and unreasonable. And with such an image of God, it will be difficult for him not to repeat that pattern in his own parenting. Conversely, a child whose father is kind and fair is more likely to believe that God is loving and just and will be more likely to reflect those characteristics when he becomes a father himself.

I could give many illustrations of how people's words, attitudes, and actions mirror their understanding of what God is like. For example, consider three people who were involved in the dialog on this topic. One of them is adamant that the damned will suffer eternal conscious torment in hell. She believes that God turns His back on unbelievers when they die and remembers them no more. Her attitude toward those who have died without Christ, as expressed at another time, is similar to what she thinks God's attitude is:

> Once they die it is all over with. I barely even remember them if at all. Do I care they died in their sins and that they are suffering because of it? No, I don't because that is not a reality to me.

> God isn't going to burden my heart for them or bring them to mind for prayer when He doesn't remember them anymore nor does He work with them to ease their pain by showing them mercy and bringing them to salvation.

Another person, a staunch Calvinist, believes that God loves the elect but hates the non-elect. His treatment of other people is similar to the way he thinks God treats them. He claimed of himself, "I'm gracious to all of God's Elect," and I did not disagree. I said to him, "I've seen you speak very graciously to others who line up with your beliefs. But I've seen very *un*gracious comments to and about those outside your group of hard-core Calvinists."

He is not an isolated case. I encountered very similar attitudes among some Calvinists in another forum—"Bless you, brother" and "Amen, sister" to fellow Calvinists, but downright nasty toward those they did not consider to be elect. It's tragic when Christians treat each other that way, but I must say there is a certain consistency about it, given the Calvinist understanding of God's own attitude toward the lost.[1]

In contrast, another person who participated in that dialog was genuinely gracious to all. His comments were thoughtful and kind, and he was a peacemaker, a voice of reason in the midst of a lot of hostility. Although I do not know him personally, he seems like a person I would like to get to know. Significantly, he believes that God loves everyone and keeps on pursuing all His lost sheep, meaning not just the "elect" but all of humanity. Like the others, his attitudes are consistent with his theology, in this case, resulting in good fruit.

You may have seen humorous pictures of dogs who look like their masters. Similarly, we come to look more and more like our Master, however we perceive Him to be. So please make sure your perception of God is true to who He really is; it's not simply a matter of getting your theology right—it will have a profound impact on how you live your life and how you treat other people.[2]

*Here in Part 1 I have observed that our attitudes and actions toward others tend to be a reflection of how we think God treats people. In Part 2 we will take a closer look at why it matters.*

---

[1]Dr. Thomas Talbott points out the parallels between racist ideology and exclusivist theology: "Consider more closely, then, the racist who sincerely believes that, because the African races are less than fully human, we may therefore treat them as an inferior species. If our racist is a Southern gentleman, he may be very gracious, very loving towards his family and friends, and a person with many good qualities; his demeanor may be utterly different from that of skinheads and members of the American Nazi Party. But his racist ideology will interfere with his capacity for love nonetheless, and the theological name for any belief that interferes with that capacity is sin. Our racist cannot *both* hold his racist beliefs *and* properly love all of his neighbors. And what is true of a racist ideology is no less true of an exclusivist theology. One cannot believe that God has divided humanity into the elect, whom he loves, and the non-elect, whom he despises *and* believe that God is nonetheless worthy of worship *and*, at the same time, love one's neighbor as oneself" (*The Inescapable Love of God,* pg. 131).

[2]The way we treat others, especially the poor and needy, is an indication of whether or not we know God. Speaking to Shallum, the son of the good King Josiah, God says, "Did not your father eat and drink and do justice and righteousness? Then it was well with him. He judged the cause of the poor and needy; then it was well. *Is not this to know me?* declares the Lord" (Jer. 22:15–16).

# 17

# SHOULD WE LOVE EVERYBODY?
# PART 2

In Part 1 of this series (#16) I started exploring the relationship between our view of God and our behavior, and I concluded that there is a direct connection

> **"Belief in a cruel God makes a cruel man."**
> **—Thomas Paine**

between the two. What is the dynamic that is going on here? Psalm 115 gives us a clue; it indicates that we tend to become like whatever we worship. The psalmist speaks of idols made by human hands and says, "Those who make them will be like them, and so will all who trust in them" (v. 8). In his book *We Become What We Worship,*[1] Greg Beale exegetes Isaiah 6 to show that we take on the characteristics of whatever we worship— whether idols of wood and stone, the modern idols that we run after, or the true God.

And why does it matter? If it's true that we become like the God we worship, then it is critically important to know what He is really like so that our lives accurately reflect and represent the true God. As one of the reviewers of Beale's book writes,

> Beale argues that humans are "imagining" beings, necessarily reflecting one image or another, and so it becomes crucial to determine who or what we are reflecting and to whom or what we are becoming conformed.[2]

Consider all the ways the Bible exhorts us to be like the Lord:

Be holy, *for I am holy* (Lev. 1:44–45, 19:2, 20:7,26, 1 Pe. 1:16).

Love your enemies *so that you may be sons of your Father* who is in heaven (Mt. 5:44).

Be perfect, *as your heavenly Father is perfect* (Mt. 5:48).

*Be imitators of God*, as beloved children (Eph. 5:1).

And walk in love, *as Christ loved us* and gave himself up for us (Eph. 5:2).

Put on the new self, which is being renewed in knowledge *in the image of its Creator* (Col. 3:10).

Forgive each other, *as the Lord has forgiven you* (Col 3:13).

We are being *conformed to the image of Christ* (Rom. 8:29).

In particular, we are to love as God loves. Certainly we are to love the *brothers* (1 Jn. 3:14), but our love is not to be limited to other believers. The second of the two great commandments is to love our *neighbors* (Mt. 22:39), who may or may not be Christians. And if we truly want to be like God and love as He loves, we must go one step further and love even our *enemies*; then we will truly be children of our heavenly Father (Mt. 5:44):

> But love your enemies, and do good, and lend, expecting nothing in return, and your reward will be great, and *you will be sons of the Most High*, for he is kind to the ungrateful and the evil (Lk. 6:35).

Our pastor did a sermon series on the book of 1 John, with its great themes of "God is light" (1:5) and "God is love" (4:8, 4:16). The word *love* appears more than 40 times in this short book, and the connection between God's love for us and our love for others is inescapable. Love originates in God, and His true children act like Him because He perfects His love in them. Read these representative verses and consider how our love is to reflect His love.

Whoever keeps his word, in him truly the love of God is perfected. By this we may know that we are in him: whoever says he abides in him ought to *walk in the same way* in which he walked (2:5-6).

*See what kind of love the Father has given to us*, that we should be called children of God; and so we are (3:1).

*By this we know love*, that he laid down his life for us, and we ought to lay down our lives for the brothers (3:16).

Beloved, let us love one another, for *love is from God*, and whoever loves has been born of God and knows God. Anyone who does not love does not know God, because God is love (4:7-8).

Beloved, *if God so loved us, we also ought to love one another.* No one has ever seen God; if we love one another, God abides in us and his love is perfected in us (4:11-12).

We love *because he first loved us* (4:19).

The rest of Scripture also teaches us to know God as He really is and to reflect His character qualities in our own lives, especially His love.

This is my commandment, that you love one another *as I have loved you* (Jn. 15:12).

*God's love has been poured into our hearts* through the Holy Spirit who has been given to us (Rom. 5:5).

Your attitude should be *the same as that of Christ Jesus,* who...made himself nothing, taking the very nature of a servant, being made in human likeness (Phil. 2:5–6).

Put on the new self, which is being renewed in knowledge *after the image of its creator....* Put on then, as God's chosen ones, holy and beloved, compassionate hearts, kindness, humility, meekness, and patience, bearing with one another and, if one has a complaint against another, forgiving each other; as the Lord has forgiven you, so you also must forgive. And above all these put on love, which binds everything together in perfect harmony (Col. 3:10-14).

Does not the Bible make it abundantly clear that God is love, He loves us, and we as His children ought to love one another with the same love? And what could be more important than understanding the true character of God so that we might worship Him properly and reflect His character accurately in our own lives? As Greg Beale says in his book *We Become What We Worship,* "What people revere, they resemble, either for ruin or restoration." In the words of Thomas Thayer,

If, then, we would make mankind what they should be, we must begin with the object of their worship; we must first make their religion what it should be. We must cast out from the holy place all the dark and ferocious superstitions of the past and the present, whether Pagan or Christian, and in the place of these set up, in all its divine beauty and simplicity, the merciful and loving religion of Jesus Christ.[3]

How would setting up "in all its divine beauty and simplicity, the merciful and loving religion of Jesus Christ" impact our world? Jesus said it would cause people to recognize Christians as His disciples:

A new commandment I give to you, that you love one another: just as I have loved you, you also are to love one another. By this all people will know that you are my disciples, if you have love for one another (Jn. 13:34-35).

If Christians are known for their love, people will be drawn to their fellowship, and even more importantly, drawn to the God who transformed them and created the love and unity among them. Our lives can be a powerful testimony to the truth of the words of the gospel, *if* we present the true God who is light and love and *if* our lives match our words. Sadly, the converse is also true; people can be driven away from God by the behavior of His children, who presumably reveal what He is like.[4] When our picture of the Father is distorted, our reflection of Him becomes even more distorted than it is already by our sin nature.[5]

We are called to be conformed to the image of God's Son, to become like Him—not, of course, in the qualities that God alone possesses, like omniscience and omnipotence, but in His character qualities like love, justice, kindness, righteousness, and patience. According to 1 Corinthians 13, we can have faith, knowledge, prophetic powers, the ability to speak in tongues, and the courage to be a martyr, but without love we are nothing. If we lack the fruit of the Spirit, the first of which is love, the world will not see God in us. But if we love as He loves, God's love will be perfected in us—and the world will take note.

My prayer for all of us is Paul's prayer from Ephesians 3:14–19:

> For this reason I kneel before the Father, from whom every family in heaven and on earth derives its name. I pray that out of his glorious riches he may strengthen you with power through his Spirit in your inner being, so that Christ may dwell in your hearts through faith. And I pray that you, being rooted and established in love, may have power, together with all the Lord's holy people, to grasp how wide and long and high and deep is the love of Christ, and to know this love that surpasses knowledge—that you may be filled to the measure of all the fullness of God.

---

[1]Beale, Gregory. *We Become What We Worship: A Biblical Theology of Idolatry.* 2008

[2]On Journeying with those in Exile, poserorprohet.wordpress.com, January 1, 2009

[3]Thayer, Thomas. "Religious Cruelty," from *The Origin and History of the Doctrine of Endless Punishment,* 1855. For historical evidence of the truth of Thomas Paine's statement "Belief in a cruel God makes a cruel man," see excerpts from Thayer's "Religious Cruelty" (#52). Here is a representative statement: "If [a Christian] believe the God of the Bible hates any portion of mankind, or regards them with any dislike or displeasure, he also will come to hate them, and to entertain towards them the same feelings which he supposes reside in the bosom of God." Obviously this statement is not true of all people who believe that God hates unbelievers or subjects them to eternal conscious torment. And clearly our laws and our sensibilities prevent us from acting on these feelings to the extreme detailed in Thayer's essay. But the logic is sound.

[4]As I said to one person who treats non-Calvinists with contempt, "If I were an unbeliever and thought you were representative of Christians in general, I would want no part of you and your friends and your religion. And I would figure that your god is like you, so I would want no part of him either."

[5]Two other books that deal with the connection between our view of God and our attitudes and actions are *Cruel God, Kind God: How Images of God Shape Belief, Attitude, and Outlook,* by Zenon Lotufo, Jr. and *The God-Shaped Brain: How Changing Your View of God Transforms Your Life,* by Timothy R. Jennings, M.D.

# 18

# A CHILD'S TESTIMONY

*S*everal years ago a woman who is now in her thirties wrote this story about her childhood and sent it to me. It brought tears to my eyes. As you read it, think about how to share the gospel with children without instilling terror in them.

The following is an example of an understatement: I am not a proponent for the teaching of brimstone and hellfire. My childhood was riddled with anxiety over my fears of hell. I had been told that if Jesus saves you, you are safe for all of eternity. This never quite quelled my fears. I was always terrified that Satan had been lurking in the shadows of my subconscious when I asked this Jesus into my heart, rendering my acceptance of him useless and blocking him from saving me. For this reason, I accepted Jesus into my heart frequently, praying that he would save me and praying that this time it would work, even if on none of the previous times I had been sincere. I watched older kids who had once been like me, devout little Christian children falling away from this Lord and the church and imagined they had suffered the fate I was so scared of: Satan had blocked Jesus from getting into their hearts when they had asked. Due to this I was afraid of growing older, afraid that I, too was headed for this same fate.

I watched the movie Top Gun in 1989. My nine year old little self fell hopelessly in love with Tom Cruise. This unrequited love would last many years to come (until he went crazy that is—I hadn't taken a for sicker or poorer vow!) but I would never love him more than I did when I was 9. It immediately became my mission to find out if Tom Cruise was a Christian. I scoured the magazines whenever I went to

CVS and one day I came across the dreaded words: according to People Magazine, Tom Cruise was a Scientologist. My little heart was crushed, so deeply saddened by the notion that while most likely I would go to heaven, my one true love would spend all of eternity dying a slow, excruciating death a million times over. I prayed for Tom Cruise like someone prays for a terminal relative. And I kept searching the magazines for evidence that my prayers had been answered. I obviously never found it.

Sadly, Tom Cruise was not the only person whose fate I feared. The anxiety I felt over the notion that most of my little friends would spend the afterlife in such great suffering bordered on depression sometimes. I prayed constantly but it did little to soothe my terror. I tried to convert some of them but this never worked and they only thought I was strange. How could I possibly explain to them that I wasn't doing this because I was weird, but because I was afraid for their eternal souls?

Looking back, I think the thing that scared me the most was how alone I so often felt with this knowledge. Children need to feel protected and the main ones they turn to are their parents. How should a child be expected to feel that parental protection when they're told, from such a young age, that even their parents can't save them from a fate worse than death?

The bigger question is why a child should be so heavily burdened like this. In fact, why should any of us live our lives in fear of the afterlife? It doesn't seem a God with a good heart would even create such a place, let alone send people there. There is a happy ending to my story, luckily. I grew up and grew out of that particular anxiety. I left (most) of those fears behind several years after I had reached an age where I could reason. And the good news is also that my child will never be exposed to "hell," "brimstone," "fiery grave," and other fear-evoking concepts. If my child grows up exposed to a church, it certainly won't be one that preaches these words. And if one day my child comes home from Sunday School talking about hell, it will be the last time she or he attends.

*This is the story of just one little girl, but I wonder if other children have had similar experiences. I am doing a survey to collect information about what people learned about hell as children and how it has affected their beliefs as adults. If you would like to participate in the survey, please see Appendix D.*

# 19

# BY THE RIGHTEOUSNESS OF ONE

The epistle reading in church on the first Sunday of Lent was Romans 5:12–19. It made me take a closer look at the whole chapter to see what Paul is trying to communicate in this pivotal passage. I wanted to gain a deeper understanding of what it means to "have peace with God" and to "rejoice in hope of the glory of God" (5:1–2), and what it is we are proclaiming when we celebrate the Resurrection.

> **Just as one trespass resulted in condemnation for all people, so also one righteous act resulted in justification and life for all people.**
>
> **Romans 5:18 (NIV)**

Romans 5[1] declares that God loves sinners and that Jesus died for them:

> [6]For **when we were yet without strength**, in due time **Christ died for the ungodly**. [7]For scarcely for a righteous man will one die: yet peradventure for a good man some would even dare to die. [8]But God commendeth his love toward us, in that, **while we were yet sinners, Christ died for us**. [9]Much more then, being now justified by his blood, we shall be saved from wrath through him. [10]For if, **when we were enemies, we were reconciled to God** by the death of his Son, much more, being reconciled, we shall be saved by his life (Rom. 5:6–10).

Christ died for His enemies, the sinners, the ungodly—that's us! God's love for us is shown in the fact that Jesus died for us *while we were yet sinners*—when we were yet without strength, when we were mired in ungodliness. And now that Jesus has laid down His life for His enemies, will He ever cast them off irretrievably? By no means!

> **Much more** then, being now justified by his blood, we shall be saved from wrath through him. For if, when we were enemies, we were reconciled to God by the death of his Son, **much more**, being reconciled, we shall be saved by his life (Rom. 5:9–10).

Some will say that these verses apply only to believers—to those who choose to come to Christ before they die, or those whom God has chosen out of all the people on earth. But in multiple parallelisms throughout the chapter, Paul shows the full extent of Christ's saving work. For example,

> [18]Therefore as by the offence of one, judgment came upon all men to condemnation; even so by the righteousness of one the free gift came upon all men unto justification of life. [19]For as by one man's disobedience many were made sinners, so by the obedience of one shall many be made righteous.

Let's break down the passage into its parts:

> 18a—Therefore as by the offence of one, judgment came upon all men to condemnation,
> 18b—even so by the righteousness of one the free gift came upon all men unto justification of life.
> 19a—For as by one man's disobedience many were made sinners,
> 19b—so by the obedience of one shall many be made righteous.

Notice the strong parallels within and between the verses: 18a is parallel to 18b (18a ‖ 18b), 19a is parallel to 19b (19a ‖ 19b), and 18a–b is parallel to 19a–b (18a–b ‖ 19a–b):

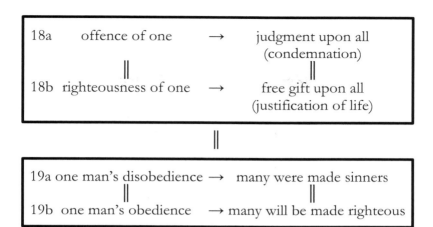

So verse 18 says that judgment and condemnation came upon all because of the offence of one, and justification and life came upon all because of the righteousness of one. In other words, Adam's sin resulted in condemnation for all people, and Jesus' righteous act resulted in the free gift of life for all people. Verse 19 is a restatement of verse 18, to emphasize the fact that the extent of the justification is just as great as the extent of the condemnation. "Many" certainly means all in the first half of the verse; the second half is parallel so the extent of "many" is the same!

There are similar parallels in the preceding verses in Romans 5:

[15]But not as the offence, so also is the free gift. For if through the offence of one many be dead, much more the grace of God, and the gift by grace, which is by one man, Jesus Christ, hath abounded unto many. [16]And not as it was by one that sinned, so is the gift: for the judgment was by one to condemnation, but the free gift is of many offences unto justification. [17]For if by one man's offence death reigned by one; much more they which receive abundance of grace and of the gift of righteousness shall reign in life by one, Jesus Christ (Rom. 5:15–17).

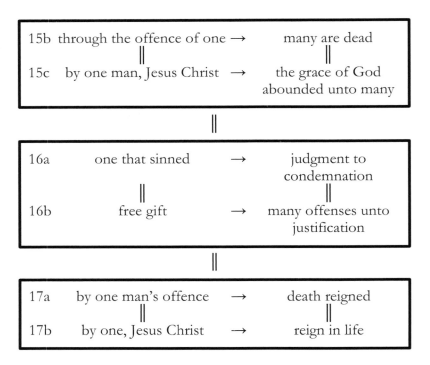

1 Corinthians 15:21–22 is similarly parallel:

[21]For as by a man came death, by a man has come also the resurrection of the dead. [22]For as in Adam all die, so also in Christ shall all be made alive (1 Cor. 15:21-22).

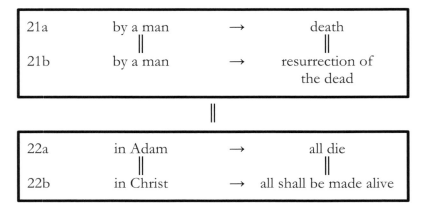

Romans 3:23 is often quoted as part of the "Romans Road" path to salvation, but do we forget verse 24?

<sup>23</sup>All have sinned and fall short of the glory of God, <sup>24</sup>and all are justified freely by his grace through the redemption that came by Christ Jesus (NIV).

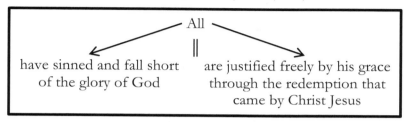

*All* have sinned and fall short of the glory of God. The same *all* are being justified freely by his grace. One might point out that the passage goes on to say that this propitiation is "through faith in his blood" and that God is the justifier "of him which believeth in Jesus." But these statements do not *limit* the number of those who are being justified by His grace; rather they explain *how* people are justified. *All* are justified freely by his grace through faith in his blood.

Over and over Paul states unequivocally that all are under the condemnation of sin and all will be justified by God's grace, that Adam brought death to all and Jesus brings life to all. And in the verses that use the term "many," we all agree that "many" means everybody (except Jesus Himself) when it comes to sin and death; the strong parallelism suggests that "many" also means everybody when it comes to grace, justification, and life. In fact, when Paul says, "But not as the offence, so also is the free gift" and "not as it was by one that sinned, so is the gift," he means that the gift is far *greater* than the offense! Throughout the chapter, when Paul uses the terms "much more," "abound," "abundance," he's talking about the fact that grace far surpasses sin.

**Much more** then, being now justified by his blood, we shall be saved from wrath through him (v. 9).

For if, when we were enemies, we were reconciled to God by the death of his Son, **much more**, being reconciled, we shall be saved by his life (v. 10).

But not as the offence, so also is the free gift. For if through the offence of one many be dead, **much more** the grace of God, and the gift by grace, which is by one man, Jesus Christ, hath **abounded unto many** (v. 15)

For if by one man's offence death reigned by one; **much more** they which receive **abundance of grace** and of the gift of righteousness shall reign in life by one, Jesus Christ (v. 17).

Where sin abounded, grace did **much more abound!**" (v. 20).

Friends, please read Romans 5 again. Read it in different translations. Meditate on it. Let the full weight of the words sink in. Ask yourself what you celebrate at Easter. That you along with a fraction of humanity have been rescued from hell? Or that Jesus Christ will have complete victory over sin and death? That He will bring about the full reconciliation of all humanity to Himself and to one another? That He will truly wipe away every tear? Does grace really reign (v. 21)? Can you fully rejoice in the hope of the glory of God (v. 2)?

---

[1] I have chosen to look at this passage in the King James Version, but you can choose any translation you like; the parallels are unmistakable.

# 20

# WHY AREN'T WE ALLOWED TO BELIEVE WHAT WE SING, SAY, AND PRAY? PART 1

In an article entitled "Let's Stop Singing These Ten Worship Songs," Corrie Mitchell maintains that some of the most popular Christian songs aren't worth singing. Mitchell says, "Some of the songs on this list are theologically questionable, others are merely uncomfortable—and some sound like thinly disguised teenage crush songs." I completely concur that we should be more careful about the words we use when we worship God.

I also have another problem with some of the songs we sing in church—that we sing them without really believing what we're saying, and in some cases we're not allowed to believe what we sing. I'm talking about songs and hymns that speak of the full breadth of Jesus' saving work—that He died for the sins of the whole world and will actually save the world. This idea finds its way into our Christian music, as well as our prayers and statements about our faith, but most of the Christian church rejects the idea that Jesus will save all.

Look closely at the selected words to the sampling of hymns below. They hint at or declare openly the hope that God will draw all to Himself, give life to all, and be adored and worshiped by all.

### Lift High the Cross
George W. Kitchin 1887

Lift high the cross, the love of Christ proclaim,
Till all the world adore His sacred Name.

O Lord, once lifted on the glorious tree,
As Thou hast promised, draw the world to Thee.

## God Is Love
Timothy Rees (1874–1939)

God is Love; and love enfolds us,
all the world in one embrace:
with unfailing grasp God holds us,
every child of every race.

Sin and death and hell shall never
o'er us final triumph gain;
God is Love, so Love forever
o'er the universe must reign!

## The Love of God
Frederick M. Lehman 1917

Oh, love of God, how rich and pure!
How measureless and strong!
It shall forevermore endure—
The saints' and angels' song.

When hoary time shall pass away,
And earthly thrones and kingdoms fall,
When men who here refuse to pray,
On rocks and hills and mountains call,
God's love so sure, shall still endure,
All measureless and strong;
Redeeming grace to Adam's race—
The saints' and angels' song.

## Jesus Loves the Little Children
Clare Herbert Woolston (1856–1927)

Jesus loves the little children
All the children of the world.
Red, brown, yellow, black and white
They are precious in His sight.
Jesus loves the little children of the world.

## Hark the Herald Angels Sing
Charles Wesley 1739

Hail the heav'n-born Prince of Peace!
　　Hail the Sun of righteousness!
Light and life to all He brings,
　　Ris'n with healing in His wings:
Mild He lays His glory by,
　　Born that man no more may die;
Born to raise the sons of earth;
　　Born to give them second birth.

## The Great Creator of the Worlds
Bland F. Tucker 1939

He came as Savior to his own,
　　the way of love he trod;
he came to win us by good will,
　　for force is not of God.

Not to oppress, but summon all
　　their truest life to find,
in love God sent his Son to save,
　　to ransom all mankind.

## Come, Now Is the Time to Worship
Brian Doerksen 2002

One day ev'ry tongue will confess You are God
One day ev'ry knee will bow
Still the greatest treasure remains for those
Who gladly choose you now.

## All Praise to Thee
Bland F. Tucker 1938

Wherefore, by God's eternal purpose, thou
art high exalted o'er all creatures now,
and given the name to which all knees shall bow:
Hallelujah; hallelujah!

Let every tongue confess with one accord
in heaven and earth that Jesus Christ is Lord;
and God eternal be by all adored:
Hallelujah; hallelujah!

## All Hail the Power of Jesus' Name
Edward Perronet 1780

Let every kindred, every tribe
on this terrestrial ball,
to him all majesty ascribe,
and crown him Lord of all.
To him all majesty ascribe,
and crown him Lord of all.

## O Day of Peace that Dimly Shines
Carl P. Daw, Jr. 1982

O day of peace that dimly shines
through all our hopes and prayers and dreams…

Then enemies shall learn to love,
all creatures find their true accord;
the hope of peace shall be fulfilled,
for all the earth shall know the Lord.

## O Zion, Haste
Mary Ann Thomson (1868)

O Zion, haste, thy mission high fulfilling,
to tell to all the world that God is Light;
that He who made all nations is not willing
one soul should perish, lost in shades of night.

Publish glad tidings, tidings of peace,
tidings of Jesus, redemption, and release.

Proclaim to every people, tongue, and nation
that God, in whom they live and move, is Love;
tell how He stooped to save His lost creation,
and died on earth that we might live above.

**I Cannot Tell**
William Y. Fullerton 1929

I cannot tell how all the lands shall worship,
When, at His bidding, every storm is stilled,
Or who can say how great the jubilation
When all the hearts of men with love are filled.
But this I know, the skies will thrill with rapture,
And myriad, myriad human voices sing,
And earth to Heaven, and Heaven to earth, will answer:
At last the Savior, Savior of the world is King!

**He Comes to Us as One Unknown**
Timothy Dudley-Smith 1982

He comes in love as once he came
   by flesh and blood and birth,
to bear within our mortal frame
a life, a death, a saving name,
   for every child of earth
   for every child of earth.

There are also countless hymns that speak of the greatness of God's grace, the wideness of His mercy, and the vastness of His love. Do you sing these songs and others like them with full conviction that what you are singing about is true? Or do the words go right over your head without a thought about their meaning? Or do you fudge them in your mind or water them down to mean something less than the complete restoration of all creation?

Or perhaps you take another approach. The leaders of some churches actually *do* listen to what they are singing—and change the words to fit their theology. A Reformed church I used to attend made slight revisions to some old hymns to correspond to their belief in limited atonement, resulting in a weakened gospel. Here is their version of the first verse of "To God Be the Glory":

To God be the glory, great things He hath done;
So loved He the world that He gave us His Son,

111

Who yielded His life, an atonement for sin,
And opened the lifegate, that we may go in.

Did you catch the difference? "And opened the lifegate,
that *we* may go in" (i.e., the "elect") instead of "that *all* may go
in," as Fanny Crosby originally wrote. Why must we remove
any suggestion that *everybody* might go in? Or how about their
version of "And Can It Be":

He left his Father's throne above
(so free, so infinite his grace!),
humbled himself (so great his love!)
and bled for all his chosen race!
'Tis mercy all, immense and free,
for, O my God, it found out me!

The real one by Charles Wesley says:

He left His Father's throne above
So free, so infinite His grace—
Emptied Himself of all but love
And bled for Adam's helpless race:
'Tis mercy all, immense and free,
For O my God, it found out me!

Even before I had any idea that there was such a thing as universal restoration, I refused to sing the adulterated versions. I
just knew something wasn't right about the idea that only "we
the chosen" could go in.

Some friends have alerted me to other instances of lyric-
tampering to tone down a Universalist thrust. Two stanzas of
John Wesley's translation of "Jesus, Thy Blood and Righteousness" read:

Lord, I believe were sinners more
Than sands upon the ocean shore,
Thou hast for all a ransom paid,
For all a full atonement made.

Jesus, be endless praise to Thee,
Whose boundless mercy hath for me,

> For me, and all Thy hands have made,
> An everlasting ransom paid.

The first of these stanzas does not appear in the Trinity Hymnal at all, and the second reads:

> Jesus, be endless praise to thee,
> Whose boundless mercy hath for me—
> For me a full atonement made,
> An everlasting ransom paid.

Ironically, the verse speaks of Jesus' "boundless mercy," but the "full atonement" is just "for *me*," not "for me, and all Thy hands have made"! In another irony, the verse at the top of the page in the hymnal is Romans 3:24: "Justified freely by his grace through the redemption that came by Christ Jesus." This verse follows and complements 3:23, which speaks of the universal fall. The NIV makes the connection clear:

> For all have sinned and fall short of the glory of God, and all are justified freely by his grace through the redemption that came by Christ Jesus (Rom. 3:23–24).

Sadly, not even children's songs are safe from tampering. In some churches, "Jesus loves the little children, all the children of the world" becomes "Jesus loves His little children, all His children of the world." How tragic that someone would feel compelled to make sure that little children don't believe that Jesus loves *all* of them.

What's going on here, that we find a conflict between what we sing with the heart and what we believe with the head? A comment by Snitzelhoff explains this tension:

> A lot of our worship music, from old hymns to contemporary choruses, from the deepest, most contemplative to the fluffiest, carries undertones of Universalism. I find it absolutely fascinating, since most of the artists and composers would deny being Universalists, as would most of those that joyfully sing the songs in worship. The conflict between the heart that

longs for God to save the world and the mind that pessimistically declares that He cannot or will not do it is never clearer than in a church that expresses belief in a hopeless, eternal Hell in its statement of faith and then turns right around and sings that the love of God "reaches to the lowest Hell." They sing about "streams of mercy, never ceasing," while warning in their sermons that mercy will one day be cut off. Children's songs about the God who's "got the whole world in His hands" belie doctrine that insists that most of the world will be ripped out of His hands.

Deep in the heart of Christians is the hope of the ultimate victory of God, and while bad theology obscures that hope, music has a way of bringing it out.

Next time you sing a hymn or worship song, really think about the words. If you have simply been uttering the words, or if you cannot whole-heartedly affirm what you are singing, then maybe it's time to take stock of what you really believe.

*In Part 2 I will take a look at some of the prayers used in our church that express Universalist themes. Do we pray these prayers as wishful thinking, knowing that what we pray for won't really happen? Or are we actually laying hold of God's promises by faith?*

---

For more examples of songs with Universalist overtones, see "Songs that reflect God's unfailing love," compiled on the website godslovewins.com. A new one to me was included in our worship on 2/4/2018, "Through All the World," by Bryan Jeffery Leech. It is a prayer that God be King and Christ be Lord in all the world. The first verse anticipates that Christ will reign where He is now rejected:

Through all the world let every nation sing to God the King:
as Lord may Christ preside where now he is defied,
and sovereign place his throne in lands not yet his own.
Through all the world let every nation sing to God the King.

The second verse articulates the longing that *all* "express true righteousness," be conformed to Christ, and be cured from sin. The third verse confirms that "then *all* the world in every part shall hear, and God revere."

# 21

# WHY AREN'T WE ALLOWED TO BELIEVE WHAT WE SING, SAY, AND PRAY? PART 2

In Part 1 of this series (#20), I talked about the fact that there are hymns and songs in all Christian traditions that speak of a hope that Jesus will save the world and draw all people into His kingdom. Here in Part 2 we will look at prayers that express the same idea. Most of these prayers come from the Anglican *Book of Common Prayer*,[1] but similar ones can be found in many other denominations.

I first started noticing this theme in our prayers when a friend drew my attention to the Collect for Christ the King Sunday:

> Almighty and everlasting God, whose will it is to restore all things in thy well-beloved Son, the King of kings and Lord of lords: Mercifully grant that the peoples of the earth, divided and enslaved by sin, may be freed and brought together under his most gracious rule; who liveth and reigneth with thee and the Holy Spirit, one God, now and for ever. Amen.

Two statements jumped out at me: "whose will it is to restore all things in thy well-beloved Son" and "Mercifully grant that the peoples of the earth…may be freed and brought together under his most gracious rule." God's will is to restore all things in Christ; will He accomplish His will? Are we asking that He bring all people together, knowing that in reality it will only be some? Or are we fully laying hold of His promise to reconcile *all* to Himself through the cross?

115

Many of our Prayers of Consecration include the idea that God in His mercy sent His Son, whose sacrifice is completely sufficient to atone for the sins of the whole world:

All praise and glory is yours, God our heavenly Father, because of *your tender mercy*, you gave your only Son Jesus Christ to suffer death upon the cross for our redemption; who made there, by his one oblation of himself once offered, *a full, perfect, and sufficient sacrifice, oblation, and satisfaction, for the sins of the whole world*; and instituted, and in his Holy Gospel commanded us to continue a perpetual memory of his precious death and sacrifice, until his coming again.

Holy and gracious Father: In *your infinite love* you made us for yourself; and, when we had fallen into sin and become subject to evil and death, you, in *your mercy*, sent Jesus Christ, your only and eternal Son, to share our human nature, to live and die as one of us, *to reconcile us to you, the God and Father of all*. He stretched out his arms upon the cross, and *offered himself in obedience to your will, a perfect sacrifice for the whole world*.

Almighty God, our heavenly Father, in *your tender mercy*, you gave your only Son Jesus Christ to suffer death upon the cross for our redemption. He offered himself and *made, once for all time, a perfect and sufficient sacrifice for the sins of the whole world*.

The Prayer of Consecration from *Our Modern Services* of the Anglican Church of Kenya expresses the same belief that Jesus made "full atonement for the sins of the whole world":

Therefore, heavenly Father, hear us as we celebrate this covenant with joy, and await the coming of our Brother, Jesus Christ. He died in our place, making a *full atonement for the sins of the whole world, the perfect sacrifice, once and for all*. You accepted his offering by raising him from death, and granting him great honor at your right hand on high.

If His sacrifice is perfect and if He made full atonement for the sins of the whole world, why would we ever think that His sacrifice won't work to atone for the sins of all?

The 1662 Book of Common Prayer includes this prayer for those who are outside the faith:

> O Merciful God, who has made all men, and hatest nothing that thou hast made, nor desireth the death of a sinner, but rather than he should be converted and live: Have mercy upon all Jews, Turks, infidels, and Hereticks, and take from them all ignorance, hardness of heart, and contempt of thy word; and so fetch them home, blessed Lord, to the flock, that they may be saved among the remnant of the true Israelites, and be made one fold under one shepherd, Jesus Christ our Lord; who liveth and reigneth with thee and the Holy Spirit, one God, world without end.

The power of the cross to draw all people to Christ is a theme that is particularly prominent at Easter time.[2] This Preface of Holy Week says that God gave His Son to redeem mankind; does He redeem only a fraction of mankind?

> Because you gave your only Son, our Savior Jesus Christ, *to redeem mankind from the power of darkness*; who, having finished the work you gave him to do, *was lifted high upon the cross that he might draw the whole world to himself*, and...might become the author of eternal salvation to all who obey him.

This Preface of Easter includes John's declaration that Jesus *takes away* the sin of the world. And if by His death He has *destroyed* death, how can anyone be subject to eternal death?

> But chiefly are we bound to praise you for the glorious resurrection of your Son Jesus Christ our Lord; for he is the true Paschal Lamb, who was sacrificed for us, and *has taken away the sin of the world; by his death he has destroyed death*, and by his rising to life again he has won for us everlasting life.

This Collect for the Triduum (the three-day period from Maundy Thursday to Resurrection Sunday) expresses the hope that all nations will one day be saved and all people will be numbered among the children of Abraham. As we pray that all the people of the earth may become children of Abraham, do we believe that it will actually come to pass?

> O God, whose wonderful deeds of old shine forth even to our own day, you once delivered by the power of your mighty arm your chosen people from slavery under Pharaoh, to be *a sign for us of the salvation of all nations* by the water of Baptism: *Grant that all the people of the earth may be numbered among the offspring of Abraham*, and rejoice in the inheritance of Israel, through Jesus Christ our Lord. Amen.

Not only at Easter but throughout the year we declare our belief in Jesus' power to redeem the world, and we pray that He would do it. This Prayer for the Persecuted Church asks that God would deliver us from hatred and enable us all to stand reconciled before Him. Would not "the Father of all, whose Son commanded us to love our enemies," also love His own enemies and make sure that in the end they too experience His saving mercy?

> O God, *the Father of all*, whose Son commanded us to love our enemies: Lead them and us from prejudice to truth: deliver them and us from hatred, cruelty, and revenge; and in your good time *enable us all to stand reconciled before you*.

When we confess, we are assured with "The Comfortable Words" from 1 John 2:1–2. Do they not tell us that Jesus Christ is the advocate and atoner for the whole world?

> If anyone sins, we have an advocate with the Father, Jesus Christ the righteous. He is the propitiation for our sins, and not for ours only but also *for the sins of the whole world*.

In the *Agnus Dei*, we call upon the Lamb of God who "takes away the sin of the world." In our Prayers of the People we ask that "the whole created order" would worship at Jesus' feet. Will God bring His entire creation—*except* the majority of humanity—to bow in true worship to the Savior?

> Jesus Christ, keep the Church in the unity of the Spirit and in the bond of peace, and *bring the whole created order to worship at your feet*; for you are alive and reign with the Father and the Holy Spirit, one God, now and for ever.

When you pray prayers like these, are you thinking that they express a nice sentiment, but you know it won't really turn out that way? When you proclaim that God's mercy endures forever, does your theology tell you that He cuts off His mercy when an unbeliever takes his last breath? Or can you lay hold of the certainty that Jesus will truly take away the sin of the world, redeem mankind from the power of darkness, and draw the whole world to Himself?

---

[1]The *Book of Common Prayer* also contains the Thirty-Nine Articles, which define the doctrines and practices of the Anglican Church. Dating from the sixteenth century, the Thirty-Nine Articles were based on the Forty-Two Articles, which were never ratified. Article 42 was one of the items that were dropped. It read, "*All men shall not bee saved at the length.*. Thei also are worthie of condemnacion who indevoure at this time to restore the daungerouse opinion; that al menne, be thei never so ungodlie, shall at length bee saved, when thei have suffered paines for their sinnes a certaine time appoincted by Goddes justice." The Thirty-Nine Articles do not have a similar statement, do not speak of everlasting damnation, and do not condemn Universalism.

[2]*Certain Sermons or Homilies Appointed to be Read in Churches in the Time of Queen Elizabeth of Famous Memory* is a sixteenth-century collection of "wholesome and godly exhortations" to be read on Sundays and holy days in all Anglican churches. The purpose is stated in the Preface: "the word of God, which is the only food of the soul, and that most excellent light that we must walk by, in this our most dangerous pilgrimage, should at all convenient times be preached unto the people." The homily for Easter Day includes this statement: "He destroyed the devil and all his tyranny; and openly triumphed over him, and *took away from him all his captives*; and hath raised and set them with himself among the heavenly citizens above."

# 22

# IS THERE GRACE BEYOND THE GRAVE?

If coming to Jesus Christ in repentance and trust is necessary for salvation—and I believe that it is—then the doctrine of universal redemption hinges on whether there can be repentance and salvation after physical death. Many people go to their graves without ever acknowledging Jesus as their Savior—some without ever hearing His name. If it is true that they will ultimately be redeemed, then there must be a way for them to attain salvation after they die.

The Bible never says, "People can be saved after they die." Neither does it say, "People cannot be saved after they die." The answer to the question of whether they can be saved after they die must come by examining what the Bible *does* say about God and His work and purposes.[1]

Although our physical death, like our physical birth, marks a dramatic change in our lives, I believe that God sees our whole life as a continuum, and He is continuously working in us throughout. Those of us who have trusted Him as Lord and Savior understand that He knew us before we were conceived, He knitted us together in our mother's womb, He calls us to Himself and sanctifies us in this life, He completes the good work He began in us, and He continues to draw us into deeper knowledge of Him throughout eternity. Thankfully we are not locked in to the condition we are in when we die; the transformation that started in this life needs to be completed in the next.

Neither are unbelievers locked in to their condition when they die. Experiencing God's judgment and seeing Jesus face to face will not leave them unchanged. Some people say that if a person resists God until the end of his life, he will continue to do so after he dies. Perhaps for a time, but can a person remain forever defiant before our magnificently holy and loving God? At the very end of his life, Muammar Gadhafi changed from an arrogant, ruthless tyrant to a terrified, whimpering child, just in the face of the wrath and judgment of men. What will he do before God Almighty?

To insist that no unbeliever would ever turn to Christ after death, even if he were given the chance, is a tacit admission that something is not right: If we say that there is no chance to repent, then we find ourselves compelled to say that no one would take it anyway, because we recognize that if some would indeed ask for forgiveness, then it is unfair not to offer it. So the standard position is to maintain that no one who has rejected God in this life would ever receive Him in the next, even if he had the opportunity.

Yet that assertion flies in the face of common sense. For one thing, there will be no atheists after death. All the philosophical questions about the existence of God will go out the window when a person stands before the living God. And any illusions a person may have about his own goodness will be dispelled when he stands before the holy God. Those who rejected Him in this life thinking He was cruel will see that He is truly a loving God. The girl who hated God, believing He was like her abusive father, may say, "Now I see who you really are; I know I can trust you, and I want to come to you." The aborigine who sought for Him in nature will discover the Creator of the sun and moon and trees and flowers. The lost souls who have stumbled through this life in "quiet desperation" may catch a glimpse of the joy that belongs to the redeemed and long to have it. Will God say to each of these, "Sorry, pal, you're too late"? Does it make any sense that 100 percent of those who die without Christ will forever remain in rebellion against Him?

So it is unlikely that all people who have rejected Christ in this life will continue to do so forever in the next. It is even more unlikely that God will instantly change His attitude toward all unbelievers the moment they die. Virtually all Christians agree that there can be genuine death-bed conversions; God continues to call people to Himself as long as they live, and some do come to Him in their last moments. So does God woo people with His love up until the end of their lives and then turn into the God of wrath the instant they draw their last breath? Does He cut off His mercy when one dies OR does His mercy endure forever? Does His nature change radically just because an individual transitions from one state to the next? No. We may experience different facets of God's nature at different times, but His immutable qualities are always completely present and at work in Him.

These reflections are based on what we know from Scripture about the character of God, but they are philosophical and logical, not exegetical. However, I have also presented some passages in 1 Peter that suggest that people in the place of the dead (the "spirits in prison") have a chance to hear the preaching of the gospel. (See "Presuppositions and Interpretations, #5.") Peter explicitly says, "the gospel was preached to the dead." What was this "good news" that the dead were hearing? That Jesus had accomplished atonement on the cross and risen from the dead, but it was too late for them and they were hopelessly doomed? Or were they being given a chance to respond to the gospel "that they might live according to God in regard to the Spirit"? (1 Pet. 4:6)

Before closing I want to mention Hebrews 9:27, as it is often quoted as "proof" that there is no opportunity for salvation after death. But the verse says nothing of the sort; it simply says, "man is destined to die once, and after that to face judgment"; in other words, "you die, and then you get judged." The fact that a person will be judged after death in no way rules out the possibility that sometime in the eternal ages to come, the person might yet come to Christ in repentance and trust.[2]

So although Scripture does not state explicitly whether salvation is possible after death, there are sound reasons to believe that God will not withdraw His offer of salvation the moment a person takes his last breath. It is entirely consistent with His nature and purposes that He will continue to reach out in mercy until every lost sheep is found, until the cross accomplishes its complete work of redemption of every human being.

---

[1]P. T. Barnum was most famous for founding the Barnum & Bailey Circus, which ran from 1871 to 2017. He was also a committed Christian Universalist. On the question of whether there can be grace beyond the grave, he gives this illustration:

> Suppose a certain number of men should agree that no man has moral opportunity after 1890. I deny their belief. They say, "Show a text which says a man can repent after 1890." I reply, "the burden of proof rests on you who have set up the external, mechanical, arbitrary and artificial date." The fact is that Scripture and reason declare that "now is the accepted time." Now is the time to live, to do, to be. No wise man defers it. It is as wise and as safe to defer it a day after death as it is a day after any other date. It is neither wise nor safe to defer it at all. There is nothing in the event of death that fixes character and ends a soul's moral possibilities more than there is in the date 1890 or any other arbitrary date. Those who set dates, such as death, after which moral beings cease to be moral beings, must show their proofs.

He goes on to affirm the principle that God's character and purposes do not change when we die: "The principles of God's government are not suddenly changed at death or any other date. He is 'Our Father,' and 'the same yesterday, to-day and forever.'"

The tract in which Barnum articulates his belief in Christian Universalism is worth reading in its entirety. Google "PT Barnum" and "Why I Am a Universalist."

[2]The verses immediately preceding and following Hebrews 9:27 speak of the fact that Jesus' ultimate purpose is to *take away sin*, not to punish it perpetually:
"But he has appeared once for all at the culmination of the ages *to do away with sin* by the sacrifice of himself" (Heb. 9:26b)
"So Christ was sacrificed once *to take away the sins of many*" (Heb. 9:28a).

# 23

# IS GOD LIKE GARGAMEL THE GREAT?

While visiting my granddaughters I read to them the book *Gargamel the Great*, about the evil wizard who is the archenemy of the Smurfs. The vain and wicked Gargamel has a magic show and uses trickery to try to get his audience to admire him. In one scene, he forces the crowd to bow to him:

> Gargamel looks at the crowd.
> "Get on your knees and bow," he says.
> The crowd laughs.
> "I said BOW!" Gargamel shouts.
> Gargamel waves his wand at his fans.
> He puts them under a spell.
> They all fall to their knees and bow.
> "That's better," Gargamel says.[1]

As I read those words I thought, This is not so different from what many Christians believe God will do to His enemies: He will force them to bow the knee and say Jesus is Lord *against their will*. For example, the NIV Study Bible says of Philippians 2:9–11, "Ultimately all will acknowledge him as Lord, *whether willingly or not*. The Philippians passage declares:

> God exalted him to the highest place and gave him the name that is above every name, that at the name of Jesus every knee should bow, in heaven and on earth and under the earth, and every tongue confess that Jesus Christ is Lord, to the glory of God the Father.

The NIV study notes state, "God's design is that all people everywhere should *worship and serve Jesus as Lord.*" How is it worship if people are *forced* to bow to Him? To *confess* something is to *agree* with it. How is it true confession if people say the words against their will? In 1 Corinthians, Paul declares that "no one can say, 'Jesus is Lord,' except by the Holy Spirit" (12:3). How can one acknowledge the Lordship of Jesus unless the Holy Spirit in him enables him to recognize Jesus as Lord? Philippians 2 says that bowing to Jesus and confessing Him as Lord is "to the glory of God the Father." How does it glorify God if people are coerced into paying homage to Him? In Philippians 1:10–11 Paul tells how God will be truly glorified: when we are "pure and blameless" and "filled with the fruit of righteousness that comes through Jesus Christ," it will truly be "to the glory and praise of God."

Romans 10:9 says, "If you confess with your mouth, 'Jesus is Lord,' and believe in your heart that God raised him from the dead, you will be saved." Compare it to Philippians 2:11:

Romans: "confess with your mouth 'Jesus is Lord'"
Philippians: "every tongue confess that Jesus Christ is Lord"

In Romans, confessing Jesus as Lord is clearly genuine; it is not simply a grudging assent or a forced submission. It is parallel and complementary to believing in your heart that God raised him from the dead, and it is the ground of true regeneration. The construction in Philippians is nearly identical, so the logical conclusion is that it too refers to sincere confession and true salvation. Rather than forcing people to bow and cry uncle against their will (which anyone with enough brute strength can do), God exercises *His* mighty power to transform the human heart, which is far more glorifying to Him!

The Old Testament also declares that every knee will bow to the Lord. God Himself calls all people to turn to Him and be saved, and He affirms that it absolutely will happen:

Turn to me and be saved,
    all you ends of the earth;
    for I am God, and there is no other.
By myself I have sworn,
    my mouth has uttered in all integrity
    a word that will not be revoked:
Before me every knee will bow;
    by me every tongue will swear (Is. 45:22–23).

So is God like Gargamel the Great? Does He want to coerce everybody into bending the knee and saying the words "Jesus is Lord"? No! His purpose is that all be in genuine worship and submission to Him, that the words on their lips would match the love in their hearts for Him. The confession of Jesus as Lord is willing and heartfelt, and God's will is that ultimately *every tongue* will be doing it! Psalm 145 affirms that "*All flesh* will bless his holy name forever and ever" (Ps. 145:21). And as Revelation 5:13 says, "*every creature* in heaven and on earth and under the earth and on the sea, and all that is in them" will be honoring and worshiping the Lamb with joyful praise—all to the glory of God.

---

[1]*Gargamel the Great*, Adapted by Tina Gallo, Simon Spotlight, 2013

# 24

# TOWARD A UNIFIED FIELD THEORY OF THE SPIRITUAL UNIVERSE PART 1

For decades scientists have been searching for a "unified field theory"—an explanation of all the fundamental forces in the universe within a single theoretical framework. Albert Einstein coined the term and spent much of his life trying to formulate such a theory, but neither he nor anyone else has been successful so far. With respect to spiritual truths, I believe that the doctrine of ultimate restoration is as close as we have come to a unified field theory of the spiritual universe. It harmonizes many apparently contradictory or competing truths and resolves many dilemmas that have confounded theologians and lay people alike (and caused division and enmity and even war). Each part of this series examines how different truths can be integrated within this framework.

In Ephesians 1, Paul reveals God's ultimate purpose for the universe: "He made known to us the mystery of his will according to his good pleasure, which he purposed in Christ— to bring all things in heaven and on earth together under one head, even Christ" (vv. 9–10). In Colossians 1, Paul presents the framework for God's work from eternity past to eternity future (See "Reconciliation: The Heart of God's Grand Plan for the Universe," #7):

> From eternity past, Christ is before all things (v. 17).
> At the beginning of time, Christ created all things (v. 16).
> In the present, Christ holds all things together (v. 17).
> In the future, God in Christ will reconcile all things to
> Himself (v. 20).

The idea of ultimate restoration, or ultimate reconciliation—that God will reconcile all to Himself in full harmony—constitutes what I believe is the most unified understanding of God's overall purposes and work. It would be rather presumptuous for me to think that I have come up with such a grand theory, but I have not come up with it at all; it comes straight out of the Bible. Scripture presents a glorious overarching picture of God's universe and His purposes for it. We are called not to fashion our own understanding of how the world ought to be, but to believe God's revealed truths. Our God-given reason is not to be used to come up with our own theories but to enable us to grasp the magnificence of God's plan. This series will explore the beauty and harmony of God's purposes for His creation and attempt to show that His revealed plan makes sense of the world and is extremely coherent and satisfying.

One conflict that vanishes immediately is the one between Calvinists and Arminians, or between God's sovereignty and man's free will. In the ultimate restoration framework, the Arminian belief is right in that God loves all people and wants *all* to come to repentance and knowledge of the truth. Calvinists are right in that God is fully able to accomplish all His holy will and to save all those He has chosen to save without being thwarted by man's choice. The harmonization is that God *wills* the salvation of all, and He *accomplishes* the salvation of all. (See "Pick Two," #6.)

The relationship between God's sovereignty and man's free will remains a complex one, but not absolutely contradictory. God gives us a great deal of autonomy and free will, but ultimately our will cannot prevail against His will. Yet God does not force His will upon us or coerce us to love Him. Rather, He draws us so powerfully—by both blessings and discipline—that ultimately every human being will bow the knee willingly and choose to love Him freely.

One of the most incongruous ideas in Calvinism is the concept of "limited atonement." How can anyone speak of the work of Christ on the cross and say "limited" in the same breath? How could the Son of God, the Savior of the world (John 4:42), lay down His life for the sake of His creatures, and yet somehow His sacrifice is not enough for all of His creatures? Is God's master plan of salvation only for a fraction of His creation? Does He want "to reconcile to Himself all things, whether things on earth or things in heaven" (Colossians 1:20) but find Himself unable to pull it off? No! He desires full reconciliation and He will make it happen.

Sooner or later, most people who hear the traditional gospel will ask, "How can a loving God allow any of the people He created (never mind *most* of them) to suffer torment endlessly with no hope of relief?" Christians have devised many responses to this question ("God's ways are higher than our ways," "If people don't repent they will be separated from God forever," "God is God and can do as He pleases," "We deserve it because of our sin," "If it weren't for His grace, *nobody* would be saved," "People who oppose God in this life will continue to defy Him in the next," "They would not want to be in His presence anyway," etc.), but none are very satisfying.

The restoration answer to this question is that God does *not* act in a way that would be considered monstrous if it were done by a man. He is like any good father; He does not allow His children to get away with anything and He makes sure they face the consequences of their sin, but He does not allow them to suffer permanent, irreparable harm. His goal is not to get back at us for what we do wrong; His purposes are *redemptive*, not just retributive. We will face judgment for our sin, but we will not be utterly cast out into excruciating torment with absolutely no hope of relief. Our fallible human system of justice forbids cruel and unusual punishment; would God's allow it?

True justice is not served by ordinary, bungling sinners spending eternity in torment, nor by evil monsters guilty of heinous acts getting off scot-free just by asking Jesus into their heart at the last minute. Nor is it right that Christians should go straight to heaven for having correct doctrine while

129

being guilty of broken relationships, dishonest dealings, or just being downright nasty people. We can't begin to comprehend God's perfect justice, but He created us in His image and we have an innate sense of right and wrong. We know what's fair and unfair—we understand that the punishment should fit the crime, and good human justice systems attempt to mete out justice fairly. Isn't it reasonable that God Himself would exercise justice in a way far superior to—but *consistent with*—the sense of justice He gave us? That He would judge with perfect knowledge and absolute fairness?

Another objection often raised by unbelievers (and believers too) is the exclusivity of Christianity. In the traditional view, unless a person acknowledges/accepts/trusts/receives/believes in Christ (however that action or process is defined) in this life, he cannot be a Christian and cannot go to heaven. Even though we have attempted to soften this doctrine ("God knows a person's heart and will find a way to reach him," "No one will stand before God and say He is unfair," etc.), it still strikes us as unfair and exclusive.

Christian Universalism holds firmly to the belief that Jesus is the Way, the Truth, and the Life and that no one comes to the Father except through Him. The *only* means of salvation is through the cross. The only difference is that God will continue to extend His grace after death. Those who have never heard of Jesus or know only a distorted caricature of Him will have opportunity to see the real Jesus face to face and to hear the real gospel, undistorted by flawed human vessels.

Predestination (and even more so, double predestination) is an enormous problem in the traditional view. People have built an entire theology around the concept of the sovereignty of God with the idea that God predestines some to go to heaven (and in some systems, that He also predestines the rest to go to hell). For example, the Westminster Confession of Faith says, "By the decree of God, for the manifestation of his glory, some men and angels are predestinated unto everlasting life, and others foreordained to everlasting death."[1] These systems maintain that God somehow sovereignly ordains our eternal destiny and yet we are responsible for our sin and He is not unfair. They do mental and exegetical gymnastics to try to justify the idea that it's OK for God to decree, either directly or by default, that people end up in torment forever.

Yet the term *predestined* (from προορίζω) occurs in only four passages[2] in the English Bible, and none says anything about heaven and hell. Ephesians 1 says we were predestined to be adopted as God's children: "In love He predestined us to be adopted as his sons through Jesus Christ, in accordance with his pleasure and will" (v. 5). "In him we were also chosen, having been predestined according to the plan of him who works out everything in conformity with the purpose of his will" (v. 11). Romans 8 says we were predestined to become like Jesus: "For those God foreknew he also predestined to be conformed to the likeness of his Son" (v. 29).

Why do we assume that predestination is about going to heaven or hell, when the Bible never talks about it in that context? There is a simpler and more sensible explanation of predestination that does not require us to go through logical contortions: When the Bible talks about being "predestined," "elected," "called," or "chosen," it is referring to the fact that some have been called by God to be the firstfruits—to know God now, to become more like Jesus in this life, and to have the privilege of serving Him by spreading the gospel to others. We are the firstfruits, but we are not the last! As Peter says, the purpose of being chosen is in order to proclaim the greatness of God that others might also glorify Him:[3]

> You are a chosen people...that you may declare the praises of him who called you out of darkness into his wonderful light. Once you were not a people, but now you are the people of God; once you had not received mercy, but now you have received mercy.... Live such good lives among the pagans that...they may see your good deeds and glorify God on the day he visits us (1 Peter 2:9–12).

*Part 2 will examine several other issues that are very problematic in the traditional paradigm but are neatly resolved when seen through the lens of ultimate restoration.*

---

[1]Chapter III, Article III. Articles VI and VII go on to say, "They who are elected…are kept by His power through faith, unto salvation. Neither are any other redeemed by Christ, effectually called, justified, adopted, sanctified, and saved, but the elect only. The rest of mankind God was pleased, according to the unsearchable counsel of His own will, whereby He extendeth or withholdeth mercy, as He pleaseth, for the glory of His Sovereign power over His creatures, to pass by; and to ordain them to dishonour and wrath for their sin, to the praise of His glorious justice."

[2]In addition to Ephesians 1 and Romans 8, the other passages are Acts 4:28 (Herod, Pontius Pilate, the Gentiles, and the people of Israel gathered against Jesus "to do whatever your hand and your purpose predestined to occur") and 1 Corinthians 2:7 ("we speak God's wisdom in a mystery, the hidden wisdom which God predestined before the ages to our glory").

[3]Like many other Christians, I always assumed that "election" and "predestination" were about being chosen to go to heaven. One explanation was that there is a banner over the door to heaven saying, "Whosoever will may come." Once you enter, you look back and see these words over the door: "Predestined before the foundation of the world." In other words, it *seems* as if you are making a free choice to enter heaven, but in reality your election is *God's* sovereign choice. Now I see that election isn't even about being chosen to go to heaven or not; it is about being chosen as a vessel to participate in God's grand purpose of redeeming His entire creation. It started with the choosing of Abraham. God promised to bless him and make his name great and make him into a great nation, but these blessings were *not* just for Abraham and his family. God told him, "you will *be* a blessing…and *all peoples on earth will be blessed through you*" (Gen. 12:2–3; see also Gen. 22:18). The choosing of Abraham was to be a blessing to "all peoples on earth"! God's electing work continued with the choosing of Jacob (rather than Esau) to be the father of the nation of Israel, which was to be "a light for the Gentiles, that my salvation may reach to the ends of the earth" (Isa. 49:6). Paul and Barnabas took this statement as a command for themselves: "For this is what the Lord has commanded us: 'I have made you a light for the Gentiles, that you may bring salvation to the ends of the earth'" (Acts 13:47). And we today are chosen in order to declare the praises of Him who called us into His wonderful light (1 Pet. 2:9).

# 25

# TOWARD A UNIFIED FIELD THEORY OF THE SPIRITUAL UNIVERSE PART 2

*Part 1 of this series suggested that the doctrine of ultimate reconciliation—the idea that God will fully accomplish His purpose of reconciling the whole world to Himself—can serve as a kind of "unified field theory" of the spiritual universe, one that makes sense of many truths about God, ourselves, and the meaning of life. In Part 2 we look at more problems raised by the doctrine of eternal damnation and show how they can be resolved by a paradigm shift to ultimate restoration.*

Another dilemma that cannot be resolved in the traditional understanding is the question of how we can be completely joyful in heaven knowing that billions of people, including many we love, are simultaneously suffering unbearable pain. We believe that God will wipe away every tear and give us boundless joy, that He will remove all the sources of sorrow and create the conditions that provide untainted joy. Yet what is the cause of our deepest sorrow and our greatest delight? Is it not people—the pain of broken relationships, of seeing others suffer, of watching loved ones reject Christ; and the joy of restored relationships, of relief from suffering, and of watching loved ones come to Christ? When you imagine heaven, what are the primary images that come to mind—golden streets, magnificent mansions, lavish banquets, creature comforts? Those realities are far overshadowed by looking forward to being reunited with loved ones, having all brokenness healed, and experiencing perfect fellowship. Will the source of pain still exist and the joy be limited? The thought of others still suffering is particularly difficult for parents; any good parent understands that it is more painful to see your child suffer than to experience suffering yourself.[1]

Again, the typical answers are unsatisfying ("We'll be so holy that we'll share God's righteous hatred of sin," "Those who seem like nice people will be revealed as the incorrigible evildoers they really are," "They stand as a testament to God's grace—their fate would be that of all mankind were it not for God's kindness," "We won't remember those who set their faces against God," "We'll be so blissful that any concern for the lost will fade from our consciousness," "We don't understand how it can be that we will experience perfect joy while others are suffering unspeakable pain, but God can make it so"). Unbelievers have no qualms about saying those answers don't make sense. If they are honest, most Christians admit that the rationale is hard to swallow, but they feel they have to accept it by faith.

Believing in ultimate restoration removes this problem entirely. God will *not* erase our loved ones from our memory. He will not leave us with no hope of ever seeing them again. We will not have to set our faces against them in righteous anger over their sin. We will be able to fully enjoy the blessings of heaven, knowing that all the people we care about will be welcomed with open arms to participate in those blessings when they come with repentant hearts and bowed knees. All the relationships that were broken on earth will be healed in heaven. God will *truly* wipe away *every* tear. The greatest rejoicing of all will come as the worst sinners humble themselves, repent, and come into the kingdom. (See "True Joy, #47)

In fact, the whole question of why God ever allowed sin and suffering in the first place finds its answer in the doctrine of ultimate redemption. In the traditional view, people are born into the world, suffer in this life, and then, if they have not trusted Christ, pass into never-ending suffering in the next life. For all the talk about the value of suffering—to identify us with Christ, refine our character, make us more like Jesus, cause us to long for heaven, give us more compassion for others, etc., etc.—in many cases it does not have these effects at all. People are born, they suffer here, they die, they suffer forever—without ever coming to Christ or becoming more like Him. Suffering can and does produce the positive results the Bible talks about, but often it drives people away from God. And if they end up in everlasting torment, their suffering is strictly punitive, with no hope of having any redemptive value for them. So what's the point of it all?

In the ultimate redemption view, there is a wonderful point, stated by Paul in Romans 11: "For God has bound all men over to disobedience [and the consequent suffering] **so that he may have mercy on them all**" (v. 32). In other words, God gave us genuine free will. He allows us to exercise our free will, and we have made a mess of the world. But He exercises His mercy toward us! The suffering we experience in this life *and* the next is designed not just to punish us but to humble us and correct us and draw us into a relationship of love and gratitude toward Him. God longs to have mercy on us *all*. The glory of our redemption from the depths of sin will be greater than the glory there would have been had we never sinned in the first place. We were once objects of God's wrath (Eph. 2:3), but He makes us objects of His mercy. As Paul says in Romans 9, God put up with our sin when we were objects of His wrath in order to make known the riches of His glory as we become objects of His mercy:

> What if God, choosing to show his wrath and make his power known, bore with great patience the objects of his wrath—prepared for destruction? What if he did this **to make the riches of his glory known to the objects of his mercy, whom he prepared in advance for glory**? (Rom. 9:22–23)

Another insuperable problem for the traditional view is how to explain God's treatment of the Canaanites. Even people with little knowledge of the Bible are aware that God performed or allowed some pretty cruel-sounding actions in the Old Testament, including the annihilation of men, women, and children. We have enough trouble just explaining why it's OK for Him to allow wholesale slaughter, and if those people go straight to unending torture that is far worse than anything they experienced on earth, then we have no reasonable defense for the goodness of God.

Some of the events of the Bible, like the genocide in the Old Testament, will never be easy to explain, but there is a far more reasonable explanation than the traditional view can offer. If the killing of masses of unbelieving people is the tragic end of their story—or worse yet, only the beginning of a never-ending tragedy—then we are hard-pressed to prove that God is loving. But what if their physical death is only the entrance to another phase of their lives? A phase in which there may be further judgment, but which also offers the hope of knowing God and experiencing eternal life? Such a possibility would put God's actions in an entirely different light: His allowing their physical death would be the means to lead to greater good, not just in some vague sense "for God's glory," but eternal good for the individuals themselves.[2]

On another front, with an understanding of ultimate restoration, the question of whether a believer can lose his salvation becomes a non-issue. In the traditional view, a person receives salvation and then either possesses it forever ("eternal security") or else can run the risk of losing it ("falling away"). In the restoration model, "salvation" is not like a ticket to heaven that you either have or don't have, that you obtain at a point in time and maybe keep forever (despite what you do or don't do) or maybe lose somewhere along the line. Rather, God has foreordained each person to eternal life, and He takes absolutely everything into account and judges with unlimited knowledge and perfect justice to create a tailor-made destiny for every individual.

The criteria on which salvation is based are very ill-defined in the traditional view. (See "What Does It Take to Get into Heaven?" #44.) When you have only two possible destinies—heaven or hell—which are diametrically opposed to each other, it is imperative to be able to identify with clarity the way to get into the one and stay out of the other. I have never heard a totally coherent explanation of what constitutes the minimum requirements for getting into heaven and staying out of hell. As soon as you start trying to define the conditions, you run into unanswerable questions. It is impossible to state the conditions clearly without raising a thousand ifs, ands, and buts.

One biblical answer is to say you have to "Believe in the Lord Jesus Christ and you will be saved." A very honest question is "What about the person who has never heard of Jesus Christ?" Or "If you confess with your mouth 'Jesus is Lord' and believe in your heart that God raised him from the dead, you will be saved." Another biblical answer, but what if you just believe it in your heart and never confess it with your mouth? And what about babies and children? And the mentally handicapped? And people who think they believe in Jesus but have been taught wrong doctrine, for example, that Jesus is not fully God? What about people who have received a totally distorted picture of God, as from an abusive father? They may well reject the god they know without rejecting the true God.

Another way to look at this problem of defining the criteria is that if there are two and only two distinct possibilities for our eternal destiny, then there must be a dividing line somewhere between them. Where is the dividing line? How can you be sure that someone at least squeaks over onto the right side? What makes the difference between the lowest person in heaven and the top person in hell? (If you have good answers for these questions, please let me know.)

In contrast, the restoration view eliminates these quandaries and absurdities. In this understanding, there is no problem trying to identify the dividing line—there is no final dividing line. We don't have to panic about the people who never heard the gospel or didn't quite get it or even resisted or rejected it. We don't have to be in torment wondering whether or not our loved ones got their ticket to heaven before they died. Though many will undergo the painful fire of purification as God deals with them in a very personal way, they will not be forever shut out from the blessings of heaven.

*Part 3 will conclude this series with a look at still more problems with the traditional position that can be resolved by viewing the world through the lens of ultimate restoration.*

---

[1]Paul experienced deep pain as he thought about his unbelieving people. He spoke of his "great sorrow and unceasing anguish" over his kinsmen who did not know Christ. He loved them so intensely that he would be willing to trade his own salvation for theirs: "I could wish that I myself were accursed and cut off from Christ for the sake of my brothers, my kinsmen according to the flesh" (Rom. 9:2–3). His anguish was not the hopeless despair of believing they were cut off forever, but it shows the intensity of his affection for them. It is unimaginable that he would cease to care about them or turn against them after he himself entered into glory.

[2]Thomas Allin points out that some of the Church Fathers "seem to regard death (not of the righteous merely), but death in itself, as a provision designed in mercy for healing sin." For example, Clement writes of Sodom, "The just vengeance on the Sodomites became an image of the *salvation* which is well calculated for men."

**26**

# TOWARD A UNIFIED FIELD THEORY OF THE SPIRITUAL UNIVERSE PART 3

*This series of essays proposes that the doctrine of ultimate reconciliation can serve as a kind of "unified field theory" of the spiritual universe, one that makes sense of many truths about God, ourselves, and the meaning of life. Part 3 is the conclusion of the series but not the end of the story— I believe that as our understanding grows, we will see more ways that God's truths are in complete harmony with one another.*

The whole question of faith vs. works is a huge issue that cannot be adequately resolved with the traditional view. Luther's re-discovery of the doctrine that "The just shall live by faith" ignited the Reformation, but may also have caused us to lose sight of the tremendous emphasis that the Bible puts on works. The Bible does require us to have faith, but it also has a great deal to say about the importance of works. For example, when people use Matthew 25:46 as a proof text for eternal damnation, they miss the main point of the passage—that we are to feed the hungry, give drink to the thirsty, welcome the strangers, clothe the naked, and visit the sick and prisoners.[1] In the restoration view, there is no conflict between faith and works; God calls on us to exercise faith and to practice good works, and He will figure out all the complexities of how they work together and how our lives are to be evaluated. There is no need for some elusive dividing line between saved and unsaved with ambiguous criteria regarding faith and works, because God has a glorious final destination for every human being.

Something else that doesn't make sense about the traditional view is the idea that this short wisp of life on earth should determine our entire eternal destiny, that our stumbling around and bad choices and rebellion in this life consign us to an eternity of suffering in the next. How can any system of justice require infinite punishment for finite sin, even if it is against an infinite Being? We're told that anyone who rejects God in this life will continue to harden his heart and reject God for all eternity. But is that really true, or is it just an attempt to make us swallow the idea that it's fair to allow such a person to go to hell?

We all agree that deathbed conversions are possible—like that of the thief on the cross. So does God woo us and keep calling us to Himself until the moment we take our last breath, and then set His face against us with implacable wrath? Does it make sense that the moment of physical death marks the last opportunity we will ever have to come to Christ? What if a person died and met the real Jesus and wanted to enter into a relationship of love with Him? Would God say no? The doctrine of ultimate restoration recognizes that life is a continuum and that God's mercy endures forever—not just until we die—and that He will continue to reach out to us in love and grace until He has not just ninety-nine sheep but the whole flock.

There are yet other inconsistencies in the doctrine of eternal damnation. Carried to its logical conclusions, it can produce horrendous results. If there is a likelihood, or even a small chance, that a child might grow up to reject Christ and suffer everlasting punishment, then it would be better for the child to die in infancy before having a chance to bring condemnation on himself. If the traditional view is true, then for a mother to kill her babies would be a logical and loving thing to do. After drowning her five small children, Andrea Yates said she took their lives in order to prevent them from going to eternal hell. Believing that such a fate was possible for them led to an unspeakable crime. Although she was mentally ill, the doctrine of eternal damnation contributed to the crime.

Another problem with the traditional view is the concept of "the age of accountability." This idea has been introduced to try to explain at what point a child becomes responsible for his own sin, but it is not a biblical concept. Every evil person started out as a baby; at what point was he transformed from a confused little child (perhaps a victim of abuse himself) into an evil adult, fully responsible for his own actions? The traditional view has no good definition for the so-called "age of accountability," whether a chronological age or some kind of "moral" age at which the individual understands sin enough to be guilty of it. In the restoration view, there is no need for an age of accountability, beyond which an individual is responsible for his own sin and has to suffer eternally if he fails to consciously turn to Christ for salvation. Each human being is treated by God with absolute fairness, infinite wisdom, and infinite love.

Another serious problem[2] with the traditional view of hell is what to do with the hundreds of promises of restoration in the Old Testament. Each passage needs to be considered individually, but there are some general questions that must be asked. What should the original hearers believe regarding promises that are not fulfilled in their lifetimes? Should they believe that they themselves will somehow experience the fulfillment of the promise (by being raised back to life in the future), or that it refers to some general fulfillment for the people of God as a community, not particular individuals?

If the latter, then the promises are essentially meaningless for the original hearers themselves. It might be comforting to think that your great-great-...grandchildren or your nation as a body will experience restoration, but it has little personal relevance. If, on the other hand, the fulfillment of the promises is to be experienced by the original hearers, will it be *all* of the hearers or only some of them? Promises of redemption and hope were often given when the people of God were in a state of rebellion; if the promises applied only to those who were faithful at the time, then those who could expect to see redemption would be few indeed.

The last twenty-seven chapters of Isaiah, for example, are filled with promises of the restoration of Israel. Yet the biblical record shows that the history of Israel is filled with sin and rebellion. The faithful ones are the few, the remnant. Do the promises of restoration apply only to the faithful few? Do many, if not most, of the chosen race (not to mention the rest of humanity) go by the wayside because they rebelled against God in this life? Or does God plan to yet restore even those who died without honoring Him? It seems to me that God is giving hope not just to those who manage to stand strong for Him, but even to those who stumble through this life in sin and wandering.

Finally, if everyone's eternal destiny depends upon accepting Christ in this life, then we have no business doing anything but sharing the gospel day and night for our whole lives. Everything else is frivolous. How can we allow ourselves a moment of rest or fun when people are rushing into hell and will be there forever and ever? Imagine what life would be like if we actually lived as if we believed that every person who is without Christ is in a train rushing toward a cliff that plunges into an abyss of never-ending horror. Between the pressure and the guilt, life would be unbearable—for us and for our evangelistic targets.

If the doctrine of eternal damnation doesn't make sense, perhaps the reason is because it is nonsense. Maybe we should stop trying so hard to convince ourselves to believe it and start examining our presuppositions to see if they are true. While we can never comprehend God fully, I think He can help us to know Him accurately. Our knowledge is necessarily incomplete, but it doesn't have to be faulty. There are many paradoxes in the Christian faith that Gods wants us to just accept and hold in tension, but I don't think He asks us to believe something that violates every shred of reason and compassion and justice in us. If we can get beyond the "proof texts" that supposedly prove eternal damnation and look at the whole scope of Scripture, I believe we will find the true heart of God, and our hearts will be able to rest in that truth.

My own experience of encountering the beauty of ultimate restoration was more gradual than that of Thomas Talbott but very similar in outcome:

> Almost from the moment I began to examine the doctrine of universal reconciliation with an open mind, something akin to a paradigm shift in science, as Thomas Kuhn has called it, or a Copernican Revolution in philosophy, as Immanuel Kant called it, took place in my theological outlook. Suddenly, everything seemed to fall into place. Paul's theological essay in Romans 9–11 finally began to make sense to me, as did the warnings against apostasy in Hebrews 10 and Jesus' remarks about the unpardonable sin. Whole areas of tension between faith and reason, between the supposed teachings of the Bible and my philosophical reflections, between theology and ordinary common sense, simply dissolved and evaporated. But above all, I finally understood why the gospel really is good news, indeed the best possible news for those in our present condition, and why it should not be confused with the twisted message of fear that we humans sometimes make it out to be.[3]

As Owen Gingerich (former professor of astronomy and of the history of science at Harvard) has said of science, and of theories of origins in particular, it's not about *proof* but about *coherence*. We cannot *prove* what happened at the beginning of time; we did not witness it, we cannot reproduce it. We can, however, try to come up with explanations that are *coherent*— that best fit the facts and make them hang together. Similarly, we cannot prove what will happen at the end of time and in the afterlife; we haven't experienced it and we can't simulate it. But we can take what we observe and what has been revealed in Scripture and use our reason to try to come to an understanding that is coherent—that best unifies what we know about God, the world, and ourselves. All in all, the doctrine of ultimate restoration is a far more unified system than the traditional gospel with eternal damnation or annihilation. It offers a framework that ties together many paradoxes and seeming contradictions. It is true to Scripture and thoroughly satisfying to our sense of reason, justice, and compassion. It's elegant. It's biblical. It's beautiful. Is it not true?

---

[1]For an excellent treatment of the judgment in Matthew 25, google the sermon by Rev. Dr. Jeffrey A. Hanson at the Church of the Advent on Sunday, November 26, 2017, the Feast of Christ the King.

[2]The passage that brought this problem to my attention is Luke 13:34–35: "O Jerusalem, Jerusalem, you who kill the prophets and stone those sent to you, how often I have longed to gather your children together, as a hen gathers her chicks under her wings, but you were not willing! Look, your house is left to you desolate. I tell you, you will not see me again until you say, 'Blessed is he who comes in the name of the Lord.'"

The words *you* or *your* are used nine times in these two verses. I started wondering, Whom is Jesus addressing? Who is *you*? First Jesus speaks to "you who kill the prophets and stone those sent to you," which would seem to mean those who are opposed to God and His messengers. They are not willing to be gathered by Jesus, and their house is left desolate. But then in the same breath, He says, "You will not see me again *until* you say, 'Blessed is he who comes in the name of the Lord.'" Now who is *you*? Jesus seems to be saying that those who have rejected Him will one day receive and bless Him.

I have not solved the problem of who Jesus is talking to or about in this passage, but thinking about it raised a whole category of questions regarding the promises in the Bible, particularly in the Old Testament. Do the promises of restoration apply to the original hearers (if only some, which ones?) and/or to their descendants or to the nation of Israel as an entity? If the latter, then the promises are quite meaningless to the individuals within the community. In that case, it's like a beehive or an ant colony, where the hive or the colony continues to exist as an entity, but the individual bees or ants don't really matter—they just keep dying and being replaced. When the Bible makes promises of future restoration of the people of Israel and says that "all Israel will be saved," I think it means much more than that the nation will continue to exist and that some future representatives of the nation will experience the blessings. I think God really will save "all Israel." For the time being, Israel is hardened and the Gentiles are coming in, but then the Jews will be grafted in again: "how much more readily will the natural branches be grafted into their own olive tree!"

Try reading Romans 9–11 through a restoration framework—it solves many of the dilemmas with that passage! "Just as you [Gentiles] who were at one time disobedient to God have now received mercy as a result of their [the Jews'] disobedience, so they too have now become disobedient in order that they too may now receive mercy as a result of God's mercy to you. For God has bound all men over to disobedience *so that he may have mercy on them all*" (Rom. 11:30–32). God's rich mercy is an essential part of His nature that He continues to display throughout the ages. He will be extending mercy as long as there are creatures who need it!

As you read all of God's promises, especially in the prophets, think about how extensive He intended them to be. Consider a few examples:

Comfort, comfort my people,
  says your God.
Speak tenderly to Jerusalem,
  and proclaim to her
that her hard service has been completed,
  that her sin has been paid for,
that she has received from the Lord's hand
  double for all her sins.
A voice of one calling:
  "In the desert prepare the way for the Lord;
Make straight in the wilderness
  a highway for our God.
Every valley shall be raised up,
  every mountain and hill made low;
The rough ground shall become level,
  the rugged places a plain.
And the glory of the Lord will be revealed,
  and **all mankind together will see it**.
For the mouth of the Lord has spoken." (Is. 40:1–5)

You have burdened me with your sin
  and wearied me with your offenses.
I am he who blots out your transgressions, for my own sake,
  and remembers your sins no more. (Is. 43:24b–25)

But Zion said, "The Lord has forsaken me,
  the Lord has forgotten me."
"Can a mother forget the baby at her breast
  and have no compassion on the child she has borne?
Though she may forget,
  I will not forget you!
See, I have engraved you on the palms of my hands." (Is. 49:14–16)

[3]Talbott, Thomas. *Universal Salvation: The Current Debate.*

# 27

# CALVINISM VS. ARMINIANISM:
# IT'S NOTHING NEW

George Whitefield, a famous preacher and evangelist, and John and Charles Wesley, founders of the Methodist movement, disagreed vigorously about election and predestination. Whitefield was a staunch Calvinist, and the Wesleys were equally committed Arminians. They spoke very strong words defending their own positions and criticizing the opposing views, but those of us on all sides today can learn from their graciousness toward one another.

In 1740, John Wesley preached a sermon entitled "Free Grace," to which Whitefield responded with a long letter to his "very dear brother," defending the Calvinist doctrine of election. In it he says,

> I desire therefore that they who hold election would not triumph, or make a party on one hand (for I detest any such thing)—and that they who are prejudiced against that doctrine be not too much concerned or offended on the other.
>
> Known unto God are all his ways from the beginning of the world. The great day will discover why the Lord permits dear Mr. Wesley and me to be of a different way of thinking.

Wesley wrote in return:

> My dear Brother,
> I thank you for yours, May the 24th. The case is quite plain. There are bigots both for predestination and against it. God is sending a message to those on

either side. But neither will receive it, unless from one who is of their own opinion. Therefore, for a time you are suffered to be of one opinion, and I of another. But when his time is come, God will do what man cannot, namely, make us both of one mind. Then persecution will flame out, and it will be seen whether we count our lives dear unto ourselves, so that we may finish our course with joy. I am, my dearest brother, Ever yours, J. Wesley

Although their differences caused tension in their relationship, they always considered one another brothers and fellow believers in the Lord. In the end they were united in love, and Wesley preached at Whitefield's memorial service. When asked if he thought he would see Whitefield on the Last Day, Wesley replied, "I fear not." Then he explained, "for George will be so much nearer the throne of grace."

John Wesley's brother Charles, a hymn writer, expressed his views poetically; he wrote the words for nearly 9,000 hymns, many of which are still beloved today. One of his poems, "O Horrible Decree," speaks against the Calvinist doctrine of limited atonement. It sparked heated reactions then and still does today. For example, the website "False Teachers Exposed" calls it "a blasphemous hymn by Charles Wesley against God's particular efficacious atonement." I will reprint the poem here so you can make you own assessment:

**O Horrible Decree!**
by Charles Wesley

Ah! Gentle, gracious Dove,
And art thou grieved in me,
That sinners should restrain thy love,
And say, "It is not free:
It is not free for all:
The most thou passest by,
And mockest with a fruitless call
Whom thou hast doomed to die."

They think thee not sincere
In giving each his day,
"Thou only draw'st the sinner near
To cast him quite away,
To aggravate his sin,
His sure damnation seal:
Thou show'st him heaven, and say'st, go in
And thrusts him into hell."

O Horrible Decree
Worthy of whence it came!
Forgive their hellish blasphemy
Who charge it on the Lamb:
Whose pity him inclined
To leave his throne above,
The friend, and Saviour of mankind,
The God of grace, and love.

O gracious, loving Lord,
I feel thy bowels yearn;
For those who slight the gospel word
I share in thy concern:
How art thou grieved to be
By ransomed worms withstood!
How dost thou bleed afresh to see
Them trample on thy blood!

To limit thee they dare,
Blaspheme thee to thy face,
Deny their fellow-worms a share
In thy redeeming grace:
All for their own they take,
Thy righteousness engross,
Of none effect to most they make
The merits of thy cross.

Sinners, abhor the fiend:
His other gospel hear —
"The God of truth did not intend
The thing his words declare,

He offers grace to all,
Which most cannot embrace,
Mocked with an ineffectual call
And insufficient grace.

"The righteous God consigned
Them over to their doom,
And sent the Saviour of mankind
To damn them from the womb;
To damn for falling short,
Of what they could not do,
For not believing the report
Of that which was not true.

"The God of love pass'd by
The most of those that fell,
Ordained poor reprobates to die,
And forced them into hell."
"He did not do the deed"
(Some have more mildly raved)
"He did not damn them — but decreed
They never should be saved.

"He did not them bereave
Of life, or stop their breath,
His grace he only would not give,
And starved their souls to death."
Satanic sophistry!
But still, all-gracious God,
They charge the sinner's death on thee,
Who bought'st him with thy blood.

They think with shrieks and cries
To please the Lord of hosts,
And offer thee, in sacrifice
Millions of slaughtered ghosts:
With newborn babes they fill
The dire infernal shade,
"For such," they say, "was thy great will,
Before the world was made."

How long, O God, how long
Shall Satan's rage proceed!
Wilt thou not soon avenge the wrong,
And crush the serpent's head?
Surely thou shalt at last
Bruise him beneath our feet:
The devil and his doctrine cast
Into the burning pit.

Arise, O God, arise,
Thy glorious truth maintain,
Hold forth the bloody sacrifice,
For every sinner slain!
Defend thy mercy's cause,
Thy grace divinely free,
Lift up the standard of thy cross,
Draw all men unto thee.

O vindicate thy grace,
Which every soul may prove,
Us in thy arms of love embrace,
Of everlasting love.
Give the pure gospel word,
Thy preachers multiply,
Let all confess their common Lord,
And dare for him to die.

My life I here present,
My heart's last drop of blood,
O let it all be freely spent
In proof that thou art good,
Art good to all that breathe,
Who all may pardon have:
Thou willest not the sinner's death,
But all the world wouldst save.

O take me at my word,
But arm me with thy power,
Then call me forth to suffer, Lord,
To meet the fiery hour:

In death will I proclaim
That all may hear thy call,
And clap my hands amidst the flame,
And shout, — HE DIED FOR ALL.

Whatever you think of Whitefield and the Wesleys and their ideas, let's remember that all of us who are in Christ are just foolish, fallible sinners who were bought by His blood. I try to keep in mind the fact that *nobody*, including myself, is right about everything, and I keep looking for those areas where I'm wrong so I can fix my beliefs. There's no shame in changing your mind—in fact, it is very honorable to admit you've been wrong and take a new course!

One way we can all come together is by singing praises to God. Calvinists sing many of Wesley's hymns wholeheartedly. And although I thoroughly disagree with Augustus Toplady's assessment of John Wesley—"the most rancourous hater of the gospel system that ever appeared in England...blind to the doctrines of God"—Toplady's "Rock of Ages" is one of my favorite hymns:

Rock of Ages, cleft for me,
Let me hide myself in Thee;
Let the water and the blood,
From Thy wounded side which flowed,
Be of sin the double cure,
Save from wrath and make me pure.

Not the labor of my hands
Can fulfill Thy law's demands;
Could my zeal no respite know,
Could my tears forever flow,
All for sin could not atone;
Thou must save, and Thou alone.

Nothing in my hand I bring,
Simply to Thy cross I cling;
Naked, come to Thee for dress;
Helpless, look to Thee for grace;

Foul, I to the fountain fly;
Wash me, Savior, or I die.

While I draw this fleeting breath,
When my eyes shall close in death,
When I rise to worlds unknown,
And behold Thee on Thy throne,
Rock of Ages, cleft for me,
Let me hide myself in Thee.

And who has not been moved by Charles Wesley's "And
Can It Be"?

And can it be that I should gain
An interest in the Savior's blood?
Died He for me, who caused His pain—
For me, who Him to death pursued?
Amazing love! How can it be,
That Thou, my God, shouldst die for me?
Amazing love! How can it be,
That Thou, my God, shouldst die for me?

'Tis mystery all: th'Immortal dies:
Who can explore His strange design?
In vain the firstborn seraph tries
To sound the depths of love divine.
'Tis mercy all! Let earth adore,
Let angel minds inquire no more.
'Tis mercy all! Let earth adore;
Let angel minds inquire no more.

He left His Father's throne above
So free, so infinite His grace—
Emptied Himself of all but love,
And bled for Adam's helpless race:
'Tis mercy all, immense and free,
For O my God, it found out me!
'Tis mercy all, immense and free,
For O my God, it found out me!

Long my imprisoned spirit lay,
Fast bound in sin and nature's night;
Thine eye diffused a quickening ray—
I woke, the dungeon flamed with light;
My chains fell off, my heart was free,
I rose, went forth, and followed Thee.
My chains fell off, my heart was free,
I rose, went forth, and followed Thee.

No condemnation now I dread;
Jesus, and all in Him, is mine;
Alive in Him, my living Head,
And clothed in righteousness divine,
Bold I approach th'eternal throne,
And claim the crown, through Christ my own.
Bold I approach th'eternal throne,
And claim the crown, through Christ my own.

Amazing love! How can it be,
That Thou, my God, shouldst die for me?
Amazing love! How can it be,
That Thou, my God, shouldst die for me?

# 28

# BEING THE CHOSEN CHILD

I come from a family of five children. I have always known that my parents loved all of us. As a kid, I might have wanted to be the favored child or I might have fancied myself to be the favored child, but as an adult and a parent myself, I know that good parents love all their children equally—not identically because each one is unique, but not unequally.

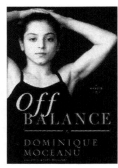

Photograph by Annie Leibovitz

Those who believe that God chooses only a fraction of humanity to be His own try to tell me I should feel great assurance of His love by the fact that He *chose me*. But I'm not convinced. What confidence can I have that His heart is truly loving if there are many more He did *not* choose? Is His love not great enough to take in more people?

Not long ago it was revealed that there was a shocking secret in the life of Dominique Moceanu, the pixie gymnast who captivated the world with her astonishingly skillful and artistic routines. Dominique's father invested everything in his golden child, who became the youngest gymnast ever to win the U.S. National Championship and was a member of the "Magnificent Seven" at the 1996 Summer Olympics.

When Dominique was 26 and about to become a mother herself, she learned that she had a younger sister who had been given up for adoption at birth. The sister, Jennifer Bricker, did not meet the father's standards—she was born with no legs. Not only would she never be an Olympic star, but she would also consume resources needed for the career of the talented young Dominique, reasoned the father.

Thankfully Jennifer was adopted into a loving family and accepted unconditionally along with her three brothers. She developed into a highly accomplished athlete herself, playing softball and volleyball, rollerskating on her hands, and competing in the Junior Olympics in tumbling. She now works as an aerialist with a performing arts group at Universal Studios. She credits her parents with providing the environment where she could realize her potential in spite of the disability that made her unacceptable to her biological father.

Photograph from
Disabled Online

And what of Dominique? When she found out about her sister who had been given up so her parents could lavish all their attention on *her*—the promising young athlete—did she feel grateful to be the chosen one? You can read about her relationship with her parents and her reaction to the news in her memoir, *Off Balance*, but you can guess that the revelation of a lost sister did not produce gratitude toward her parents.

How is it different with our heavenly Father? Should we feel thankful that God chose *us* and *not* someone else? Can I be confident of His love for *me* if He rejects those I love?

Among all the images for God in the Bible—including Shepherd, Judge, King, Lamb, Lion, Father, Brother, Savior, Priest, Light—one of the most potent is "Father." Not only can one learn how to be a good father by observing how our Heavenly Father treats His children, but we can also learn more about Him by watching how good human fathers interact with their children. In fact, our initial and perhaps most enduring images of God come from our own parents, particularly our fathers.

The image of God as Father is even more than an analogy; it goes beyond analogy to reality. By virtue of creating us in His image, He is truly our Father. As Malachi says, "Have we not all one Father? Has not one God created us?" (2:10). And Paul says that every family—or all fatherhood—has its source in God the Father (Eph. 3:14–15). So it is perfectly right to draw comparisons between human fathers and our heavenly Father and to say that no good father—human or heavenly—would cast off his own children forever.

No, God will not abandon the children He created. Yes, some are "chosen," but not to be the *exclusive* recipients of God's grace. Just as Israel was chosen to be a light to the nations, we are chosen *in order* to declare God's praises so that others might also be drawn to His wonderful light:

I, the LORD, have called you in righteousness;
    I will take hold of your hand.
I will keep you and will make you
    to be a covenant for the people
    and **a light for the Gentiles** (Isa. 42:6)

It is too small a thing for you to be my servant to restore the tribes of Jacob and bring back those of Israel I have kept. I will also make you a light for the Gentiles, **that my salvation may reach to the ends of the earth**" (Isa. 49:6).

For this is what the Lord has commanded us: "I have made you a light for the Gentiles, **that you may bring salvation to the ends of the earth**" (Acts 13:47).

But you are **a chosen people**, a royal priesthood, a holy nation, God's special possession, **that you may declare the praises of him who called you out of darkness into his wonderful light** (1 Pet. 2:9).

Yes, we should be eternally grateful that we are "God's special possession." So let's go out and declare the praises of him who called us out of darkness into His wonderful light so that others may also come into the light!

## 29

# "REAL MEN READ PINK"

If you had to take your best guess, what percentage of all the people who have ever lived will be in heaven? Obviously, the numbers are known only to God, but you probably have some sense of whether it's about half, only a minority, or a majority. A friend posted the following meme, and a discussion ensued about what proportion of mankind is saved.

> To argue that God is "trying His best" to save all mankind, but that the majority of men will not let Him save them, is to insist that the will of the Creator is impotent, and that the will of the creature is omnipotent (A. W. Pink).

Arthur Walkington Pink was an English Bible scholar who was not well known during his lifetime (1886–1952) but whose writings sparked a resurgence of Calvinism after his death. Now there is a Facebook page called "Real Men Read Pink." Apparently the idea is that Pink's theology is robust and vigorous and manly, not for the faint-hearted (or tender-hearted). For example, Pink believes that God does *not* love all people but actually hates those who are not His sheep, which is a hard truth to swallow for anyone with a tender and loving nature.

This particular quote by Pink argues against the idea that the will of man can override the will of God. Like all good Calvinists, Pink affirms that it is impossible for men to thwart God's will and that it is wrong for us to put limitations on God's sovereignty. They preserve His sovereignty by saying that He is *not trying* to save all of mankind—only His lost sheep—and He accomplishes that goal just as He decreed. Arminians would counter that it is wrong to put limitations on God's love; He loves all and wants all to be saved, but He allows people to reject His offer.

The *real problem* here is that both Calvinists and Arminians believe that *God's salvation is limited.* Calvinists believe that His atoning work is limited to the elect. Arminians believe that it is limited to those who choose to put their trust in Jesus. Either way, they are putting limitations on God's saving grace. In other words, it is partial, incomplete, not fully executed. Whatever the reason—whether because God never intended to save more than the elect, or because some choose to reject Him—the result is the same: God does not achieve the complete restoration of His creation.

And not only is God's work of redemption incomplete in that way of thinking—most Calvinists and Arminians alike believe that *not even half* of the world will be saved. Pink complains about the Arminians' belief that "the majority of men will not let Him save them," while he himself believes that the majority of men are unsaved by reason of the fact that they are sinners and God has not chosen to save them from their sin. In other words, Satan is more successful in getting people on his side than Jesus is in getting people on His side! Do we not demean both the grace and the justice of God by saying either that God is not able to save more or God is not willing to save more? Whether the percentage of the saved is 50% or 5% or 95%, it's still a fraction of humanity—1/2 or 1/20 or 19/20—not the 100% success that He desires. The Good Shepherd is not content even with 99%, but goes after that one last lost sheep.

Some try to tell us that the salvation of a few people or even *one* person is proof of God's grace because *no one* deserves it. As one commenter put it, "I am in awe that He would save anyone. We all deserve punishment for our sin…. I look at it that God didn't have to save any of us because of our rebellion and He was graceful enough to save some."

Let's examine that logic. What kind of "grace" is it that is handed out sparingly? Is God stingy with His love? Suppose a multi-billionaire decides to help needy families by building houses for them. He chooses three families and builds a fabulous home for each one. Those families are thrilled and grateful, and the rich man is praised by the media. But consider the fact that the man had the means to help a thousand families but chose to help only three. Is he really a generous person? Does he really deserve the accolades?

And we are told that God *has* to condemn some because He is holy and just. But He sent His Son to die precisely *in order to justify sinners without violating His own justice.* If He can justify one sinner without compromising His justice, why not two? And if two, why not twenty? And if twenty, why not twenty thousand or twenty billion? No one would presume to give a figure for the number of the redeemed, but the fact is that both Calvinists and Arminians say there is a cap, a limit to the number of people God will save.

In the essay "Does God Love Everybody?" (#15), I quoted a Calvinist who expressed a sentiment similar to Pink's: To die for the world and fail to redeem all is an epic failure. He is quite right. But to die for the world and *succeed* in redeeming all is an epic success.

Mr. Pink, you are right that the will of the Creator is greater than the will of the creature. But you err in thinking that God had no intention of saving all mankind. Yes, Calvinists are right about the sovereignty of God, but they malign the character of God by limiting His love. Arminians are right about the love of God but malign His character by limiting His sovereignty. We honor God only by affirming His limitless sovereignty AND His limitless love, which leads inescapably to limitless salvation for all His creatures!

> ## What kind of "grace" is it that is handed out sparingly?

# 30

# CAN YOU SEE BEYOND?

Think of someone who is hostile to the gospel—maybe a cynical scoffer or a hardcore atheist or a militant Muslim. What is your attitude toward these enemies of the cross of Christ?

Now suppose that God laid one of these people on your heart and gave you assurance that the person would eventually come to the cross and become a brother or sister in Christ. Would your attitude be different? How would you treat the person? What would you say to him or her? How would you respond to the person's hostility? How would you pray?

Could you look into that enemy of the cross and see the lost sheep inside? And do you have the faith to look beyond the lost sheep to see a future fellow believer and citizen of heaven? Can you see past the person's present condition of being dead in trespasses and sins and envision his future as a redeemed child of the heavenly Father, alive in Christ and taking his place in the family of God?

Now imagine for a moment that everyone who comes across your path—whether close family member, good friend, belligerent foe, slight acquaintance, or anonymous stranger—is destined to be raised up with Christ and to become a son or daughter of God and fellow servant with you. Would it have a positive or negative effect on your relationships with them? On your love for them? On your witnessing to them?

I challenge you to look with the eyes of faith beyond present realities to see what God is doing in people's hearts and one day will accomplish fully—when all mankind will know His name and fear Him and be blessed by Him.

For the earth will be filled with the knowledge of the
glory of the Lord as the waters cover the sea
(Hab. 2:14).

# 31

# FALSE HOPE, TRUE HOPE /
# FALSE FEAR, TRUE FEAR
# PART 1

"You're just giving false hope; UR[1] is nothing more than wishful thinking." This objection is often raised to the idea that God will ultimately redeem all people. The concern is that if people think they will end up in heaven no matter what, they won't feel the need to make a commitment to Christ and live for Him on earth. Furthermore, Christians will feel less urgency to share the gospel and call people to make a decision for Christ now. And they will have a false sense of peace about their loved ones who die without knowing the Lord. In other words, not only is UR unbiblical, but by taking away the fear of eternal hell it removes the urgency of coming to Christ in this life, it gives license to live loosely or violently with impunity, and it gives a false sense of security to the lost and those who love them. Here are some typical comments:[2]

> UR is not good news it is bad news. It deceives people, gives them false hope, and the people who fall for it will end up in hell if God doesn't intervene, brings truth to them, and saves them through the convicting power of God.

> [A]ccording to the only Book that really matters, the Word of God you both a peddling untruth that gives people a false hope and gives believers an excuse not to share God's only plan of salvation for the lost.

As a universalist you are offering people false hope for not only them but for their lost loved ones who have died already. You basically say to them you can live your life anyway you want, party on with no holds barred since after all a day will come when God will save all of us.... [Y]ou are preaching/teaching a false and cheap gospel.

I am more concerned about you promoting a false doctrine that is totally contrary to the Word of God and that offers people a false hope about their loved ones who refused to repent and gives unbelievers the false idea that even if they never come to accept Christ before they die they will eventually go to heaven.

[Y]ou offer people a false hope that they will be reunited with their loved ones who died without making a genuine profession of faith and/or the false hope that there is no need for a person to repent in this life since eventually one day we'll all be in heaven. You inadvertently give people permission to continue to live in sin since all will eventually be saved.

By promoting the false belief that all people will eventually be saved you present a false gospel which can give believers a false hope that unsaved loved ones will eventually be saved, can lead believers to become lazy in their evangelistic efforts..., and worse of all can give the unsaved permission to live in sin since after all eventually all will be saved.

Jerry Newcombe thinks that disbelief in hell contributes to the violence in our society:

I keep reading these stories of some unhappy person blowing away a bunch of people—it even happened recently at a Christian college in California. Where's the fear of God in our society? I don't think people would do those sorts of things if they truly understood the reality of Hell.

And in a review of Francis Chan's *Erasing Hell,* Aaron Armstrong says,

> The Terror of False Hope: One of the big questions in the *Love Wins* controversy centers on whether or not Christian universalism and the opportunity for post-mortem salvation is defensible from Scripture.... Chan's horror that anyone would offer the possibility of post-mortem salvation without explicit biblical reference is palpable, particularly when some passages explicitly speak against this view (see Luke 13:22–30, Hebrews 9:27 among others).

To the question, "Does the promise of ultimate restoration for all allow Christians to slack off on sharing the gospel and give non-Christians an excuse to keep on living without regard for God?" the short answer is the same as Paul's answer to similar questions: "By no means!" "Absolutely not!" (Rom. 6:1–2; 15). On the contrary, the hope of restoration for all gives Christians a greater delight in sharing their faith and offers unbelievers a much more powerful and joyful message. And the motivation to share the gospel or to accept it is not just fear. Here is an illustration I have given of why universal redemption does not take away the urgency of sharing the gospel:

> Suppose you know that your child will be in a terrible fire and suffer horrible burns, but you know he will not die. Within twenty years he will recover completely and be fine. Does the knowledge that he will not die take away the incentive to warn him about the fire? Not at all! You still feel great urgency, just not absolute desperation and hopelessness. Similarly, those who do not come to Christ in this life will face judgment for their sins, and although they will not suffer forever, those who love them feel the urgency to warn them about the judgment to come and to offer them joy and peace now.

Moreover, the gospel of ultimate restoration truly is *good news!* Sharing the traditional gospel means eventually revealing the dark secret that the non-elect/unrepentant are being tormented forever (or else are annihilated and go into oblivion), with no possibility of being reunited with believers. Consider this scenario: Suppose you were to go as a missionary to an unreached people group in a remote region of the world. With the traditional gospel, you can offer these people the good news about Jesus. But what happens when they ask about their loved ones who have died— "What about my grandpa?" "Aunt Lola?" "My friend?" For them the traditional "gospel" has only bad news—in fact, the worst news imaginable: If they died in their sins without knowing Christ as their Savior, they are now paying the ultimate penalty for those sins. At best, you can offer only a vague assurance that God is fair.

This "gospel" is burdensome to bear and unappealing to hear. Does any missionary want to have to tell people that their loved ones are burning in hell because they have offended the "loving" God he is trying to tell them about? Will people be drawn to a "Savior" if He fails to save their loved ones who never had a chance to know Him? Such a message creates ambivalence in the hearers—they may desire to know Jesus themselves but may be repulsed by the idea that He would condemn their loved ones. They may resist coming to Him if they know it means being eternally separated from everyone they have cared about.[3]

But what if you go with the good news of ultimate restoration for all? Then when someone says, "What about Grandma? She never heard about Jesus," you can say, "She's getting her chance to see Him face to face and hear about how He died for her. Her sins have to be dealt with, but she can come to the cross and ask Jesus to cover them with His blood, just as you can. If you believe in Jesus, you can be together forever *and* experience His blessings now."

This news of eternal hope is *truly good news*. It in no way gives people license to live however they want, thinking they'll make it in the end anyway. Rather, it calls people to come to Christ *now* and experience His forgiveness and blessings now and forever. And although it does not carry the threat of eternal damnation, it does hold a very strong view of judgment: God must deal severely with sin in order to purify us and prepare us for living in His Kingdom. (See Part 2, #32.)

Perhaps even more than people who have never heard the gospel, unbelievers who have been exposed to Christianity are often put off by the idea that anyone who does not accept Jesus is condemned to eternal perdition. In fact, it may be the single greatest objection to the gospel in the postmodern world. Many people automatically reject Christianity if they believe that it excludes the majority of people who have ever lived.[4] The following comments are somewhat extreme, but they reflect the sentiments of many unbelievers. Even Christians may have similar but unspoken thoughts.

> So your loving bible god has found it necessary to torture billions simply because they don't "believe". I gotta tell you, your "loving" bible god is a petty, vindictive, bullying, monomaniacal tyrant.

> The pain inflected by the shooting [Colorado movie massacre] nothing in comparison to the evil of The Bible God Eternal Torture Kamp and Molten Sulfur lake of Fire Spa the loving bible god has arraigned for billions of its creation. The irony here, Holmes may join Jesus Fan Klub in prison as so many lifers do and have his ticket punched to eternal bliss in heaven. In the meantime, those non Jesus Fan Klub members he killed have been dispatched to torture kamp.

Some would dismiss these words as the rantings of an angry agnostic. But if we want to honor Christ, we should be prepared to make a defense to anyone who asks the reason for our hope, and it should be done with gentleness and respect (1 Pet. 3:15). We need to give reasonable answers to people who question and even mock our faith—not just blow them off or give stock answers. There will always be resistance to the gospel, but the doctrine of eternal damnation can make the resistance much worse. Perhaps the "Sinners in the Hands of an Angry God" approach does scare some people into heaven, but I suspect that many more are turned away by it. The fear of exquisite, everlasting torture might drive some to their knees, but others will simply be driven away from a God who would do such a thing.

We should be able to give answers not only to skeptics and atheists, but also to those who grieve. Sadly, there have been many young people in our community who have died from accidents, illness, drug overdose, or suicide. (I wrote about one young man in the first chapter of this book.) As bearers of the gospel of Jesus Christ, we above all should be able to bring good news and hope for grieving families. One pastor who believes in eternal damnation said, "I know of no truly compassionate believer who would tell a family in mourning that well tough luck since your son did not make a profession of faith in Christ he's gone to hell." As I replied,

> That's exactly what promoters of eternal damnation are communicating to everyone, including mourning families—not in so many words, but that's the message: "If you don't put your faith in Christ before you die, you go to hell and suffer forever." People can figure it out: "Since my loved one didn't put his faith in Christ before he died, he must be suffering forever."

Does the "good news" of the gospel come with so much bad news baggage? NO! We cannot gloss over the reality of judgment—we must be honest about the severity of the judgment to come—but we don't have to leave people with desperation over those who have not yet come to Christ or despair for those who have already died without Him. The doctrine of ultimate restoration does not offer false hope—it offers true hope. When the whole gospel is clearly understood, it gives a healthy fear of judgment and provides powerful incentive for turning to the One who not only judges but also offers eternal hope for us and all our loved ones.

Whenever judgment comes,
it comes on love's errand,
if it comes from God.
—Thomas Allin

*The promise of ultimate restoration offers true hope, while the threat of eternal damnation gives false fear—an unwarranted terror of something that will not happen. However, there is a true fear that should grip all of us, believers and unbelievers alike. Part 2 of this series will examine the difference between false fear and true fear.*

---

[1]UR = ultimate/universal redemption/reconciliation/restoration

[2]All comments are quoted verbatim.

[3]For a withering assessment of the damage that can be done by missionaries taking the "gospel" of eternal damnation to the lost, see Barbara Kingsolver's novel *The Poisonwood Bible* (1998). It is the story of a hellfire-and-brimstone preacher who takes his wife and four daughters to the Belgian Congo to save the natives. Nathan Price's message of damnation was certainly not the only problem with his missionary efforts, but it contributed to his failure to reach the people and it had destructive effects in his own family.

[4]One notable person who renounced Christianity at least partly, if not primarily, because of the doctrine of eternal damnation was Charles Darwin. In his own words: "Thus disbelief crept over me at a very slow rate, but was at last complete.... I can indeed hardly see how anyone ought to wish Christianity to be true; for if so, the plain language of the text seems to show that the men who do not believe, and this would include my Father, Brother and almost all of my friends, will be everlastingly punished. And this is a damnable doctrine."

# 32

# FALSE HOPE, TRUE HOPE / FALSE FEAR, TRUE FEAR PART 2

*In Part 1 (#31) I tried to show that you do not need to be terrified of unending torment for yourself or anyone else, because God does not inflict pointless suffering. Nevertheless, we do need to fear the judgment of God. He hates sin, not only because it is antithetical to His character, but also because it ruins His good creation and destroys the people He loves. Therefore He will do whatever it takes to root out sin from our lives and ultimately eradicate it from the universe entirely.*

The Bible speaks of the wrath of God against *all* unrighteousness, but here I would like to focus primarily on God's judgment of His own people. Some Christians think believing in Jesus means that you will waltz right into heaven when you die and live happily ever after. They picture salvation as a ticket to heaven, and if you have your ticket in hand when you meet Jesus, you're good to go. Others think it's possible to lose your ticket, so they believe you have to make an effort to hang onto it. So which is it? Once you get your ticket, do you keep it forever? Or can you lose it? Or…does the whole "ticket" paradigm need to be re-examined? Are both complacency about our salvation and fear about losing it misplaced? Where is the false hope? The true hope? What fears can be put to rest? What *should* we fear?

Let me begin by affirming some fundamental Scriptural truths. Nothing I say should be construed to contradict these truths. First, salvation is by grace through faith. It is the gift of God, not a reward for something we do:

For by grace you have been saved through faith. And this is not your own doing; it is the gift of God, not a result of works, that no one may boast (Eph. 2:8–9).

Second, those who are in Christ do *not* need to fear condemnation:

There is therefore now no condemnation for those who are in Christ Jesus (Rom. 8:1).

Not only do we not need to fear condemnation, but on the positive side we have peace with God, access into His grace, and hope of experiencing His glory:

Therefore, since we have been justified by faith, we have peace with God through our Lord Jesus Christ. Through him we have also obtained access by faith into this grace in which we stand, and we rejoice in hope of the glory of God (Rom. 5:1–2).

So what is there to worry about? Why should Christians have any fear of judgment?

The Old Testament has many instances of God's judgment against unbelieving nations, cities, and individuals—the Flood, Sodom and Gomorrah, Egypt, the Canaanites, Nebuchadnezzar, Assyria, Edom, to name just a few. But just as often, God judged *His own people*. He had to deal severely with them to get them back on track, often using pagan nations—the very ones who were also under His judgment—as His instruments. When wooing His people by His lovingkindness and patience did not work, He arrested them in their tracks so they would return to Him. They would fall away again, but He kept calling them back by whatever means were necessary.

Similarly in the New Testament, we see God's opposition to all unrighteousness, as in Romans 1 and throughout Revelation. In the words of Paul,

For the wrath of God is revealed from heaven against all ungodliness and unrighteousness of men, who by their unrighteousness suppress the truth (Rom. 1:18).

Christians sometimes comfort themselves with the thought that their own sins are already covered by the blood of Christ and that God's judgment is only for unbelievers. *But God's people are not exempt from judgment.* In fact, Peter says,

It is time for judgment to begin with the family of God (1 Pet. 4:17).

He goes on to say, "if it begins with us, what will the outcome be for those who do not obey the gospel of God?" In other words, it will be more severe for those who do not obey the gospel, but do not think that a profession of faith will enable you to escape God's judgment.

So what does this judgment look like? What is its purpose? What is its end result? God's judgment could be the topic of many volumes of writing, but I will offer some passages from Scripture and a few comments of my own, and let readers draw their own conclusions.

With regard to judgment, there are some passages that seem to draw a distinction in the status of individuals strictly on the basis of belief or unbelief.

Whoever believes in him [God's Son] is not condemned, but whoever does not believe is condemned already, because he has not believed in the name of the only Son of God (Jn. 3:18).

Whoever believes in the Son has eternal life; whoever does not obey the Son shall not see life, but the wrath of God remains on him (Jn. 3:36).

Truly, truly, I say to you, whoever hears my word and believes him who sent me has eternal life. He does not come into judgment, but has passed from death to life (Jn. 5:24).

I am the resurrection and the life. Whoever believes in me, though he die, yet shall he live, and everyone who lives and believes in me shall never die (Jn. 11:25–26).

Passages like these suggest that belief is the sole criterion for undergoing or escaping judgment. Yet consider the many passages that speak of judgment based on righteousness or unrighteousness, godliness or ungodliness, obedience or disobedience. Jesus says the Father has given all judgment to the Son (Jn. 5:22). He will judge not only on the basis of belief (5:24), but also on the basis of doing good or evil (5:29):

> And he [the Father] has given him [the Son] authority to execute judgment, because he is the Son of Man. Do not marvel at this, for an hour is coming when all who are in the tombs will hear his voice and come out, those who have *done good* to the resurrection of life, and those who have *done evil* to the resurrection of judgment (Jn. 5:27–29).

Paul speaks of the judgment of works in Romans 2:

> We know that the judgment of God rightly falls on those who practice such things. Do you suppose, O man—you who judge those who practice such things and yet do them yourself—that you will escape the judgment of God? Or do you presume on the riches of his kindness and forbearance and patience, not knowing that God's kindness is meant to lead you to repentance? But because of your hard and impenitent heart you are storing up wrath for yourself on the day of wrath when God's righteous judgment will be revealed. **He will render to each one according to his works**: to those who by patience in well-doing seek for glory and honor and immortality, he will give eternal life; but for those who are self-seeking and do not obey the truth, but obey unrighteousness, there will be wrath and fury. There will be tribulation and distress for every human being who does evil, the Jew first and also the Greek, but glory and honor and peace for everyone who does good, the Jew first and also the Greek. (Rom. 2:2–11)

Paul is not teaching works salvation here, but he is warning us that the way we live now will have a profound effect on how we are judged later. The declaration that God "will render to each one according to his works" means that our good and bad works will affect how God deals with us.

In Romans 14 and 2 Corinthians 5, Paul clearly teaches that we will undergo judgment:

> For *we will all stand before the judgment seat of God*; for it is written, "As I live, says the Lord, every knee shall bow to me, and every tongue shall confess to God." So then *each of us will give an account of himself to God.* (Rom. 14:11–12).

> For *we must all appear before the judgment seat of Christ*, so that each one may receive what is due for what he has done in the body, whether good or evil (2 Cor. 5:10).

He also speaks of the judgment of Christians in 1 Corinthians 3. There he explains that the only foundation is Jesus Christ, but on the Day of Judgment our works will be revealed and we will be evaluated and punished or rewarded depending upon how we have built upon the foundation:

> No one can lay a foundation other than that which is laid, which is Jesus Christ. Now if anyone builds on the foundation with gold, silver, precious stones, wood, hay, straw—each one's work will become manifest, for the Day will disclose it, because it will be revealed by fire, and the fire will test what sort of work each one has done. If the work that anyone has built on the foundation survives, he will receive a reward. If anyone's work is burned up, he will suffer loss, though he himself will be saved, but only as through fire (1 Cor. 3:11–15).

In 1 Corinthians 11, Paul warns Christians that they are in danger of judgment and discipline if they take the Lord's Supper in an unworthy way:

Whoever, therefore, eats the bread or drinks the cup of the Lord in an unworthy manner will be guilty concerning the body and blood of the Lord. Let a person examine himself, then, and so eat of the bread and drink of the cup. For anyone who eats and drinks without discerning the body eats and drinks judgment on himself. That is why many of you are weak and ill, and some have died. But if we judged ourselves truly, we would not be judged. But when we are judged by the Lord, we are disciplined so that we may not be condemned along with the world (1 Cor. 11:27–32).

Paul is also speaking to Christians in Galatians 6, where he warns that we will reap what we sow—whether corruption by sowing to the flesh, or life in the age to come by sowing to the Spirit:

Do not be deceived: God is not mocked, for *whatever one sows, that will he also reap*. For the one who sows to his own flesh will from the flesh reap corruption, but the one who sows to the Spirit will from the Spirit reap eternal life. And *let us not grow weary of doing good*, for in due season we will reap, if we do not give up. So then, as we have opportunity, let us do good to everyone, and especially to those who are of the household of faith (Gal. 6:7–10).

The writer of Hebrews uses the rebellion of the people of God in the Old Testament as a warning to believers not to miss out on God's blessing because of disobedience and unbelief:

Take care, brothers, lest there be in any of you an evil, unbelieving heart, leading you to fall away from the living God. But exhort one another every day, as long as it is called "today," that none of you may be hardened by the deceitfulness of sin…. And to whom did he swear that they would not enter his rest, but to those who were disobedient? So we see that they were unable to enter because of unbelief. Therefore, while the promise of entering his rest still stands, let us fear lest any of you should seem to have failed to reach it (Heb. 3:12–13; 18–19; 4:1).

Here the writer sees a real danger that Christians might fall away from the living God and come under His judgment, through disobedience or unbelief, so he warns them against having an unbelieving heart, falling away from the living God, and being hardened by the deceitfulness of sin. Later he also warns against falling into the sin of Esau and missing the grace of God:

> Strive for peace with everyone, and for the holiness without which no one will see the Lord. See to it that no one fails to obtain the grace of God; that no "root of bitterness" springs up and causes trouble, and by it many become defiled; that no one is sexually immoral or unholy like Esau, who sold his birthright for a single meal (Heb. 12:14–16).

And in the same passage where he encourages believers that they can have "confidence to enter the holy places by the blood of Jesus" (10:19) and "the full assurance of faith" (10:22), the writer of Hebrews also warns them of the very real possibility of "a fearful expectation of judgment":

> For if we go on sinning deliberately after receiving the knowledge of the truth, there no longer remains a sacrifice for sins, but a fearful expectation of judgment, and a fury of fire that will consume the adversaries.... How much worse punishment, do you think, will be deserved by the one who has trampled underfoot the Son of God, and has profaned the blood of the covenant by which he was sanctified, and has outraged the Spirit of grace? For we know him who said, "Vengeance is mine; I will repay." And again, "The Lord will judge his people." It is a fearful thing to fall into the hands of the living God (Heb. 10:26–31).

This judgment is upon those who know God. It is possible for those who have received the knowledge of the truth and professed faith to "profane the blood of the covenant by which [they were] sanctified" and to "outrage the Spirit of grace." They, like unbelievers, ought to fear falling into the hands of the living God and experiencing His punishment.

In Matthew 18, 24, and 25, Jesus tells three stories about wicked servants and one about virgins waiting for the bridegroom. In each instance, you could make a case that Jesus is talking about those who belong to Him. In chapter 18, the servant has been forgiven of an enormous debt, only to turn around and refuse to forgive his fellow servant. The master deals with him severely:

> Then his master summoned him and said to him, "You wicked servant! I forgave you all that debt because you pleaded with me. And should not you have had mercy on your fellow servant, as I had mercy on you?" And in anger his master delivered him to the jailers, until he should pay all his debt. So also my heavenly Father will do to every one of you, if you do not forgive your brother from your heart (Mt. 18:32–35).

Notice the hints that Jesus is talking about a believer (master/servant, "I forgave you all that debt," "I had mercy on you," "your brother"). Then in chapter 24, one servant is put in charge of all the servants in the "household." If he starts living loosely and treating his fellow servants badly, he will be sent to a place of weeping and gnashing of teeth:

> If that wicked servant says to himself, "My master is delayed," and begins to beat his fellow servants and eat and drink with drunkards, the master of that servant will come on a day when he does not expect him and at an hour he does not know and will cut him in pieces and put him with the hypocrites. In that place there will be weeping and gnashing of teeth (Mt. 24:48–51).

The servant in chapter 25 has been given one talent but instead of investing it wisely, he hides the talent in the ground. The master is not pleased:

> But his master answered him, "You wicked and slothful servant! You knew that I reap where I have not sown and gather where I scattered no seed? Then you ought to have invested my money with the bankers, and at my coming I should have received what was my own with interest.

> "So take the talent from him and give it to him who has the ten talents. For to everyone who has will more be given, and he will have an abundance. But from the one who has not, even what he has will be taken away. And cast the worthless servant into the outer darkness. In that place there will be weeping and gnashing of teeth (Mt. 25:26–30).

In the parable of the ten virgins in chapter 25, five of the virgins are not prepared when the bridegroom arrives, and they are excluded from the wedding banquet:

> And while they [the foolish virgins] were going to buy oil, the bridegroom came, and those who were ready went in with him to the marriage feast, and the door was shut. Afterward the other virgins came also, saying, "Lord, lord, open to us." But he answered, "Truly, I say to you, I do not know you" (Mt. 25:10–12).

The context in each case indicates that Jesus is talking about His own people—a servant whom He has forgiven or put in charge of His household or blessed with a talent, or virgins who are invited to His marriage banquet. All of them face judgment not because they have never exercised faith, but because of their actions. The people in these passages who are weeping and gnashing their teeth are believers!

Then in Matthew 25:31–46, Jesus describes the judgment of the sheep and the goats. Despite all attempts to make this passage say that Jesus is dividing people into two groups based on whether or not they believe in Him, what He actually says is that the criterion is how they treat others. Did they feed the hungry? Give drink to the thirsty? Welcome strangers? Clothe the naked? Visit the sick and those in prison? Those who do these things are blessed by the Father and will inherit His Kingdom and gain life in the age to come. Those who do not will go away into punishment in the age to come.

So what are we to make of these passages and others like them? Clearly believers are not exempt from judgment, both here on earth and after death. But if Jesus died to forgive our sins and take our punishment for us, why do we still get judged? It is true that we do not have to fear condemnation, but we will have to give an account for the way we have lived. God will evaluate our lives and deal with us accordingly. Our sins that have been brought to the cross are forgiven, forgotten, and buried in the deepest sea. The works we have done in service to the Lord will be rewarded, and we will receive the blessing of the treasures we have laid up in heaven.

But what of our bad works? God's intention is not to get back at us for what we have done wrong; rather, He desires to make us fit to live in His Kingdom, which will require His continued work in our lives. What that work will look like and how long it will take, I cannot say. The passages presented here indicate that the judgment of believers may be very tough, like going through a fire. But like discipline here on earth, the end result will be a harvest of righteousness and peace (Heb. 12:11). We will be thoroughly purified and fit for the Kingdom of God, resulting in praise, glory, and honor to Jesus Christ (1 Pet. 1:7).

You might think that accepting Jesus as your Savior will keep you from ever experiencing God's judgment, but I urge you *not* to be complacent. The people of God must not rest in the *false hope* that they are immune to judgment; the sins of the Church and of individual believers must be exposed so we can be purified and refined. The false prophets were rebuked for not exposing the sins of the people of God but rather filling them with the false hope that all was well when it was not:

Your prophets have said so many foolish things, false to the core. They did not save you from exile by pointing out your sins. Instead, they painted false pictures, filling you with false hope (Lam. 2:14, NLT).

They offer superficial treatments for my people's mortal wound. They give assurances of peace when there is no peace (Jer. 6:14, NLT).

Thus says the Lord of hosts: "Do not listen to the words of the prophets who prophesy to you, filling you with vain hopes. They speak visions of their own minds, not from the mouth of the Lord. They say continually to those who despise the word of the Lord, 'It shall be well with you'; and to everyone who stubbornly follows his own heart, they say, 'No disaster shall come upon you'" (Jer. 23:16, ESV).

So what are we to do? For those Christians who are quick to point out that unbelievers will face God's judgment, I urge you to look first to yourselves. We are not to panic, but we should make a sober assessment of our lives. Are we living in such a way as to be fit for citizenship in the Kingdom of God? Are we following the Kingdom principles outlined in the Word of God? Are we practicing the Beatitudes? Are we filled with the fruit of the Spirit, which will be in full bloom in the Kingdom? Are we, as God's chosen ones, putting on "compassionate hearts, kindness, humility, meekness, and patience," bearing with one another and forgiving each other, and above all putting on love (Col. 3:12–14)?

In some respects God is like the judge of an athletic competition, such as gymnastics or diving, who evaluates a performance and determines whether it is worth gold, silver, or bronze or no medal at all. Both now and at the judgment seat of Christ we receive blessings and rewards for serving Him well. But in another sense, God is more like a coach who evaluates the performance and then says, "OK, how can we turn this 7.3 into a perfect 10?" He longs to sanctify us through and through, and He uses whatever means are necessary, which will vary according to our response. Are we humbly and obediently allowing God to do His work of sanctification in us *now*? We ought to be cooperating with Christ in the process of cleansing us and making us holy, with the goal "that he might present the church to himself in splendor, without spot or wrinkle or any such thing, that she might be holy and without blemish" (Eph. 5:26–27). The more we let ourselves be purified now, the less refining we will need later.

Do you harbor a spirit of bitterness or unforgiveness? Do you have a broken relationship that needs to be healed before you can spend eternity with the other person? Are you living for the pleasures of this world? Do you seek to control rather than to serve? Are you laying up for yourself treasures on earth instead of treasures in heaven? Do you take the bread and the cup unworthily? Then take heed now, and bring those sins to the cross and let God do His sanctifying work in you now. Otherwise, even if you have made a profession of faith, you may face a terrifying expectation of judgment.

Certainly we are to be warning the world about God's judgment. It is our responsibility to share the good news of the gospel and the reality of judgment, and to call people to come to Christ now and repent that they might not be condemned. *Today* is the day of salvation (2 Cor. 6:2); we should never give the idea that it's fine to put off that decision—nor to put off godly living. Hebrews 3 and 4 reiterate multiple times that *today* is the day for repentance and salvation (3:7, 13, 15; 4:7). We should be diligent in calling unbelievers *and* believers to repentance and godliness. We should be examining our own lives to see if there is anything that is incompatible with citizenship in God's Kingdom.

Throughout the Old Testament are promises of blessing now and in the future for those who do what is good and right. For example,

> Whoever pursues righteousness and kindness will find
> life, righteousness, and honor (Prov. 21:21).

And Paul's words to the rich about how to lay a good foundation for the future apply to all of us:

> As for the rich in this present age, charge them not to be haughty, nor to set their hopes on the uncertainty of riches, but on God, who richly provides us with everything to enjoy. They are to do good, to be rich in good works, to be generous and ready to share, thus storing up treasure for themselves as a good foundation for the future, so that they may take hold of that which is truly life (1 Tim. 6:17–19).

The good news is that, one way or another, He who began a good work in us will surely carry it on to completion (Phil. 1:6) and sanctify us fully:

> God is able to keep us from falling and to present us before His glorious presence without fault and with great joy (Jude 24).

Some Christians seem to know just what will happen after death and in what order and to what classes of people. I do not. But Scripture does reveal enough that we can be thoroughly warned and fully reassured:

> Do NOT be in bondage to the **false fear** that you or anyone else will be tormented endlessly.

> Do NOT hold the **false hope** that you can live however you want and still escape God's righteous judgment.

> DO live your life in the **true fear** of God's holiness and the expectation that He will do whatever it takes to root out the sin in your life.

> DO rejoice in the **true hope** that God will fully accomplish His purpose for sending Jesus to die on the cross. He will eradicate sin from His entire creation and make *everything* right!

# 33

# HEIR OF ALL THINGS

The grand sweep of God's purposes for His creation is shown in Colossians 1:15–20. (See "Reconciliation: the Heart of God's Grand Plan for Creation," #7) Speaking of "the Son he [the Father] loves," Paul says,

He existed before all things.
He created all things.
He holds all things together.
He will reconcile all things.

Another passage that shows the whole scope of God's plan for all creation is Hebrews 1:1–4:

In the past God spoke to our forefathers through the prophets at many times and in various ways, but in these last days he has spoken to us by his Son, whom he appointed heir of all things, and through whom he made the universe. The Son is the radiance of God's glory and the exact representation of his being, sustaining all things by his powerful word. After he had provided purification for sins, he sat down at the right hand of the Majesty in heaven. So he became as much superior to the angels as the name he has inherited is superior to theirs.

As the first chapter of Colossians shows the supremacy of the Son, so the first chapter of Hebrews also shows His superiority. Notice the parallels in the person and work of Christ in these two passages:

| Colossians 1: The Supremacy of the Son | Hebrews 1: The Superiority of the Son |
| --- | --- |
| The Son is the image of the invisible God (15) | The Son is the exact representation of God's being (3) |
| God was pleased to have all his fullness dwell in the Son (19) | The Son is the radiance of God's glory (3) |
| God made peace through the blood of the Son, shed on the cross (20) | The Son provided purification for sins (3) |
| The Son is before all things; He is the head of the body, the church (17, 18) | The Son is seated at the right hand of the Majesty in heaven (3) |
| In the beginning, all things were created by the Son (16) | In the beginning, God made the universe through His Son (2) |
| In the present, all things hold together in the Son (17) | In the present, the Son sustains all things by His powerful word (3) |
| In the end, God through the Son will reconcile to Himself all things (20) | In the end, the Son will become heir of all things (2) |

Meditate on these passages. Dare we say that God will do any less than restore His entire creation to the perfection that He intended all along? He will give a *good* inheritance to His Son—all the nations of the earth, with each person bowing the knee to Him, proclaiming Him as Lord, and being reconciled to Him and to one another. Full atonement—can it be? Hallelujah! What a Savior!

# 34

# LIMITED ATONEMENT:
# INTRODUCTION

Don Bell (I'm sure he'd be quick to say no relation to Rob[1]) asks this rhetorical question, which is quoted on Michael Jeshurun's website:

> Which exalts Christ more and demonstrates more the value and efficacy of Christ's atonement: That which effectually secures the actual salvation of every one for whom it was made OR that which ends in the great majority of those for whom He shed His precious blood being eternally punished in hell?[2]

I believe he would say the first exalts Christ more. (I took the hint from the banner on Michael Jeshurun's website: "Smashing Arminian Lies and Everything Else That Opposes the Absolute Sovereignty of the Mighty Jehovah.")

I would pose a rhetorical question for Don and Michael. Actually, it's not rhetorical, because I would like an answer.

> Which exalts Christ more and demonstrates more the value and efficacy of Christ's atonement: That which effectually secures the actual salvation of a small fraction of humanity OR that which effectually secures the actual salvation of all of humanity?

By any reasonable measure the most sensible answer is "the second." No matter how you count, 100% of 100% is greater than 100% of anything less.[3] And if God is glorified by the salvation of one, it stands to reason that He will not be *less* glorified by the salvation of two, but rather *more* glorified.

Don and Michael will tell me that you can't use ordinary logic here but just have to believe the Scriptures, which teach that not all

> **Behold, the Lamb of God, who takes away the sin of about 5% of the world!**

will be saved. I would contend that logic confirms what the Scriptures themselves teach: that God will be maximally glorified by the complete redemption of His entire creation, which is, in fact, exactly what He has purposed to do.

In the next two chapters we will look more closely at the Calvinist doctrine of "limited atonement," the idea that Christ's work on the cross had a definite purpose—the certain salvation of all those whom God chose to save. It stands in contrast to the Arminian belief that Jesus died for all but salvation depends upon a person's response to God's grace. We will try to show that God intended all along to completely defeat sin and death and to restore His whole creation, and that He will fully accomplish His will, for His own glory and our good.

---

[1]Former megachurch pastor Rob Bell wrote the book *Love Wins*, which challenges the traditional Christian understanding of hell. He is not actually a Universalist, but he raised questions that made people suspect him to be. The book created a firestorm in conservative Christian circles, and Bell became an outcast in the evangelical world. As a disclaimer, I will say that I don't align with Bell's beliefs on this subject (partly because I'm not exactly sure what they are), but I do appreciate the fact that he raised questions we should be thinking about and that he sparked an important dialog that continues to this day.

[2]michaeljeshurun.wordpress.com

[3]For those who are mathematically inclined, let $x$ be the percentage of the saved out of all humanity. Calvinists say that God saves 100% of a fraction of humanity (the "elect"): $100\% \times x\% = x\%$. Arminians say He saves a fraction of all humanity: $x\% \times 100\% = x\%$. Not so different really. If $x < 100$, then God falls short of full redemption in either the Calvinist equation or the Arminian equation.

## 35

# LIMITED ATONEMENT: SLEIGHT OF WORD?

William G. T. Shedd was a nineteenth-century Presbyterian theologian. One chapter of his *Dogmatic Theology* was devoted to limited atonement, the idea that God's purpose in sending His Son to die on the cross was to secure the redemption of those He had predetermined to save—

the elect. Shedd's defense of the doctrine falls short, not due to lack of scholarship or effort but, in my opinion, because the doctrine is indefensible.

Shedd opens his argument for limited atonement using semantics to dance around the real problems (pp. 739 ff). His 11-page section entitled "The Extent of the Atonement" begins with nearly two pages analyzing the word *extent*. He notes the two senses of the word in English usage: the "passive meaning" that is equivalent to "value," and the "active signification" that denotes "the act of extending." With these definitions, he can say that the atonement is unlimited in value but limited in application:

> In this use of the term [extent = value], all parties who hold the atonement in any evangelical meaning would concede that the "extent" of the atonement is unlimited. Christ's death is sufficient in value to satisfy eternal justice for the sins of all mankind. If this were the only meaning of "extent," we should not be called upon to discuss it any further....

The word also has an active signification. It denotes the act of extending. The "extent" of the atonement, in this sense, means its personal application to individuals by the Holy Spirit. The extent is now the intent. The question "what is the extent of the atonement?" now means: To whom is the atonement effectually extended?

Certainly we need to look closely at the meanings of words used in the Bible, but "the extent of the atonement" isn't even a biblical term, and my impression of Shedd's discussion here is that it serves to deflect attention from the fact that he is indeed putting limitations on the atonement. He can say that it is limited in its application but still maintain that it has "infinite value" ("Being an infinite atonement, it has infinite value") so as not to appear to demean it. To me it seems that he is using fancy footwork to get around the fact that he is putting limitations on the work of Christ on the cross, in other words, trying to defend this doctrine without making God look bad.

Shedd turns next to a discussion of the preposition *for* (pp. 741ff).

> One theologian asserts that Christ died "for" all men, and another denies that Christ died "for" all men. There may be a difference between the two that is reconcilable, and there may be an irreconcilable difference.

He says that whether the statement "Christ died for all men" is true or not depends upon how you define the word *for*.

> The preposition *for* denotes an intention of some kind. If, in the case under consideration, the intention is understood to be the purpose on the part of God both to offer and apply the atonement by working faith and repentance in the sinner's heart, by the operation of the Holy Spirit, then he who affirms that Christ died "for" all men is in error....

But he who asserts that Christ died "for" all men may understand the intention signified by the preposition to be the purpose on the part of God only to offer the atonement, leaving it to the sinner whether it shall be appropriated through faith and repentance…. When the word *for* is thus defined, the difference between the two parties is reconcilable. The latter means by *for* "intended for offer or publication"; the former means "intended for application."

Again, the preposition *for* is sometimes understood to denote not intention, but value or sufficiency. To say that Christ died "for" all men then means that his death is sufficient to expiate the guilt of all men. Here, again, the difference is possibly reconcilable between the parties. The one who denies that Christ died "for" all men takes "for" in the sense of intention to effectually apply. The other who affirms that Christ died "for" all men takes "for" in the sense of value.

Shedd himself believes that the most proper use of the word *for* is to convey "the notion of intention rather than of sufficiency or value," in other words, that Christ's death actually will be effectually applied to those for whom He died. But then he takes a text like Hebrews 2:9, Christ "tasted death for every man" and says it is explained by the term "many sons" in 2:10; therefore tasting death "for every man" really means "for many sons." And similarly, Christ giving Himself as "a ransom for all" (1 Tim. 2:6) means that His death is effectually applied not to absolutely all, but to all those who will be sons.

Again it seems to me that with all these many words, Shedd is using semantics to try to affirm the biblical principle that Christ died for all without affirming that all will actually be redeemed. All that he can say conclusively is what amounts to this rather roundabout and unenlightening statement:

Christ died for all those for whom He died.

Shedd goes on to talk more about "the distinction between the 'sufficiency' of the atonement and its 'extent' in the sense of 'intent' or effectual application" (pp. 742ff). He quotes the old dictum that Christ died "sufficiently for all, but efficiently only for the elect." As I have commented before on this saying, "Makes for a nice little aphorism, but to say it is efficient only for the elect is just a euphemism for saying it is *not* efficient for everyone else." In other words, it *doesn't work* for them. In my opinion, we demean the work of Christ on the cross if we suggest that it is inefficient in any sense.

Shedd then quotes Puritan theologian John Owen (1616-1683), whose work *The Death of Death in the Death of Christ* is a classic defense of the Calvinist understanding of the atonement. Shedd quotes from Owen's *Against Universal Redemption*:

> It was the purpose and intention of God that his Son should offer a sacrifice of infinite worth, value, and dignity, sufficient in itself for the redeeming of all and every man, if it had pleased the Lord to employ it for that purpose.... Sufficient we say, then, was the sacrifice of Christ for the redemption of the whole world and for the expiation of all the sins of all and every man in the world.... That it did formally become a price for any is solely to be ascribed to the purpose of God intending their purchase and redemption by it.

There is a big *if* in these words! Christ's sacrifice was sufficient for the redemption of all and every man *if it had pleased the Lord to employ it for that purpose*. (Unstated implication: it did *not* please Him to employ it for that purpose.) Like Shedd, Owen tries to defend the infinite value of the atonement without saying it will actually have unlimited application.

Next, Shedd distinguishes atonement from redemption:

> The latter term includes the application of the atonement. It is the term *redemption*, not *atonement,* that is found in those statements that speak of the work of Christ as limited by the decree of election.

He quotes some passages from the Westminster Confession, for example: "to all those for whom Christ has purchased redemption, he does certainly and effectually apply and communicate the same" (8.8). In other words, if Christ has died *for* you in the sense of application, then His work will certainly be applied *to* you (which really doesn't say anything at all). Again, it seems to me that these arguments are like the work of a magician; he confuses you by showing you one thing and making you think you are seeing another—"sleight of word," so to speak.

Shedd elaborates on the distinction between atonement and redemption by saying "the Scriptures limit redemption, as contradistinguished from atonement, to the church," and he quotes verses like Ephesians 2:9 ("faith is the gift of God"), 1 Corinthians 3:5 ("you believed, even as the Lord gave to every man"), Acts 13:48 ("as many as were ordained to eternal life believed"), Hebrews 2:17 ("Christ makes reconciliation for the sins of his people"), Ephesians 1:14 ("the redemption of the purchased possession"), and Hebrews 9:15 ("by means of his death they which are called might receive an eternal inheritance"), as well as some Old Testament verses. He concludes that when God is called "*our* Savior," it means "Savior of the church," by which I understand him to be saying that any references to "saving us" or "redeeming all" mean "us" in the sense of "the church" or "all" in the sense of "the whole body of Christ." For all the elaborate explanations, I can't get around the fact that he is putting gigantic limitations on the work of Christ on the cross.

To summarize his discussion of atonement vs. redemption, Shedd suggests using the following terminology:

> The use of the term *redemption,* consequently, is attended with less ambiguity than that of "atonement," and it is the term most commonly employed in controversial theology. Atonement is unlimited, and redemption is limited. This statement includes all the scriptural texts: those which assert that Christ died

for all men, and those which assert that he died for his people. He who asserts unlimited atonement and limited redemption cannot well be misconceived. He is understood to hold that the sacrifice of Christ is unlimited in its value, sufficiency, and publication, but limited in its effectual application.

One question that springs to mind is how Shedd's view of "unlimited atonement" is different from the Arminian view of "unlimited atonement." I know that they differ in their *application*: Calvinists believe that salvation is wholly the work of God in ordaining people to eternal life, while Arminians believe, as Shedd puts it, "that personal faith in Christ's atonement is necessary to salvation, but that faith depends partly upon the operation of the Holy Spirit and partly upon the decision of the sinful will."[1] Either way, they both would say that the atonement is unlimited in value but limited in application (for whatever reason). Again it seems to me that it is an exercise in using semantics and splitting hairs with little profit.

Some prefer the term "particular atonement" to indicate that Christ's atonement is intended, by design, for those whom God has chosen. Shedd says that the idea of particular redemption means that "the number of persons to whom it is effectually applied is a fixed and definite number. The notion of definiteness, not of smallness, is intended." He admits that "in common speech, if anything is 'limited,' it is little and insignificant in amount," but he tries to say that this is not the idea when it comes to Christ's redemptive work. Substituting the word *particular* is one way to get rid of the word *limited*, with its connotation of being restricted or constrained or circumscribed or somehow less than or inferior to *unlimited*. But it doesn't eliminate the *fact* that such a doctrine *does* put limitations on the work of Christ! (And it messes up the TULIP acronym.[2] ☺)

Shedd then takes up the matter of election.[3] He says, "The tenet of limited redemption rests upon the tenet of election, and the tenet of election rests upon the tenet of the sinner's bondage and inability." His point is that since fallen man is bound in sin and has no power even to believe, then his salvation is entirely dependent on the grace of God, and "redemption is limited by election," as taught, for example, in Romans 9:16: "It is not of him that wills nor of him that runs, but of God that shows mercy." He explains that, in the Arminian view, "the Holy Spirit does not overcome a totally averse and resisting will, which is the Calvinistic view, but he influences a partially inclining will."

So Calvinists believe that the total inability of man to save himself is most consistent with Scripture, as is the fact that God is "independent and sovereign in bestowing faith and salvation." Synergism—the idea that man can contribute even partially to his own salvation—has the same effect as "plenary ability" (coming to faith being entirely man's choice) in terms of making God dependent upon man to "do his part" before God can do His.

I am in agreement with Calvinists on some key principles regarding our salvation:

> Salvation does not depend on our choosing God but on God choosing us.
> No one can come to Jesus unless the Father enables and draws him.
> Belief in Jesus does not come from within a person but is granted by God.
> Jesus will not lose any of those He died for and has determined to save.

In other words, we agree that the Arminian concept of "free will"[4] is not biblical. I think John 1:12–13 perfectly captures the interplay between human responsibility and God's sovereign will:

> But to all who did receive him, who believed in his name, he gave the right to become children of God, who were born, not of blood nor of the will of the flesh nor of the will of man, but of God.

We have the responsibility to receive Jesus and believe in His name, but in the final analysis, as the end of verse 13 makes very clear, becoming children of God is *not* by the will of man but by the will of God.

I also believe in irresistible grace, and I think that Calvinist explanations of irresistible grace are accurate descriptions of how God sovereignly works in the heart of man. (See "Irresistible Grace," #43.) However, there is a key difference in our understanding of irresistible grace: I believe *nobody* can forever resist God's grace. Sooner or later, His effectual grace will do its work in every single human being. We long for it to be sooner, so we share the gospel with them. But we do not despair if it is later, because we know that God's will that all come to repentance cannot be thwarted.

So I agree with Shedd that it doesn't make sense that the Son of God would die for the sin of the world, "leaving it wholly or in part to the sinful world to determine all the result of this stupendous transaction." But while he believes that the Father "determined that this sacrifice should be appropriated through faith by a definite number of the human family," I believe that He determined that Christ's sacrifice should be appropriated through faith by *every* member of the human family. Both positions are logically sound; both can be supported by Scripture. But only one recognizes the full value and power of "this stupendous transaction."

A biblical case *can* be made for salvation being only for a portion of humanity, "the elect." Shedd quotes a number of verses to show that redemption is not for all, but for "the sheep" (Jn. 10:15), "friends" (Jn. 15:13), "the children of God" (Jn. 11:52), "the church" (Eph. 5:23, 25), "his people" (Mt. 1:21, Heb. 2:17), the ones "chosen in Christ before the foundation of the world" (Eph. 1:4), the ones "given to Christ by the Father" (Jn. 10:29). There are others he might have cited as well, like John 17:6, 9: "I have manifested your name to the people whom you gave me out of the world.... I am praying for them. I am not praying for the world but for those whom you have given me, for they are yours." It also could be pointed out that the epistles are for the church, not the world, so the promises there apply to believers.

But there is another huge set of verses that indicate the universality of Christ's work. He is "the Savior of the world" (1 Jn. 4:14) who came for the purpose of saving the world (Jn. 3:17, 12:47). He is the propitiation for the sins of the whole world (1 Jn. 2:2). He is "the Lamb of God who takes away the sin of the world" (Jn. 1:29). In Christ God was "reconciling the world to Himself" (2 Cor. 5:19). "As in Adam all die, so in Christ all are made alive" (1 Cor. 5:22). "By the righteousness of one the free gift came upon all men unto justification of life" (Rom 5:18). It is God's good pleasure to reconcile all to Himself through the cross (Col. 1:20). "All have sinned and fall short of the glory of God, and are justified by his grace as a gift, through the redemption that is in Christ Jesus" (Rom. 3:23–24).

So what are we to do if some parts of Scripture seem to conflict with others? I agree with Shedd that "Scripture must be explained in harmony with Scripture." Shedd makes reference to some of the verses I just named and says, "Texts that speak of the universal reference of Christ's death must, therefore, be interpreted in such a way as not to exclude its special reference." He believes that the election of only a portion of humanity is a given fact of Scripture, and verses that suggest otherwise must be interpreted in light of that given fact. I would say, "Texts that speak of the special reference of Christ's death must be interpreted in such a way as not to exclude its universal reference." In other words, I see the redemption and restoration of God's entire creation as a theme running throughout Scripture, from Genesis to Revelation, so verses that seem to limit that restoration should be interpreted in light of the given big picture.

As an example, Shedd and I agree that the word *world* can have different meanings in Scripture, and for any particular verse we each take the meaning that best fits our overall view. Shedd says that the word sometimes refers to "the world of believers," and he gives it that meaning when it fits his theology: "The bread of God is he which gives life to the world [of believers]" (Jn. 6:33, 51); Abraham is "the heir of the world [the redeemed]" (Rom. 4:13); "if the fall of them be the riches of the world,... if the casting away of them be the reconciliation of the world" [the church] (Rom. 11:12, 15). You can guess how I would interpret these verses.

Similarly, Shedd says that "the word *all* sometimes has a restricted signification, denoting all of a particular class." So when Paul says, "As in Adam all die, so in Christ shall all be made alive" (1 Cor. 15:22), Shedd says, "the 'all' in Adam is a larger aggregate than the 'all' in Christ, because Scripture teaches that all men without exception are children of Adam and that not all without exception are believers in Christ." I readily acknowledge that the word *all* does not always mean "absolutely all," but here it certainly cannot be restricted in such a way as to say that the fall of Adam is more powerful in its effect than the work of Christ! Again in 2 Corinthians 5:14 ("If one died for all, then all died"), Shedd says that "the 'all' here denotes the body of believers, as it does in Romans 5:18" ("As the judgment came upon all men to condemnation, even so the free gift came upon all men unto justification"). (But see "By the Righteousness of One," #19.)

So we recognize that the word *all* in Scripture does not always mean "absolutely all." But in Paul's magnificent declaration about the person and work of Christ from eternity past to eternity future in Colossians 1:15–20, which of the "alls" does not mean "absolutely all"? The word *pan* (παν) in all its forms does mean "all without exception" in each of the eight instances where it is used:

The firstborn over all (πάσης) creation (15)
By Him all things (τὰ πάντα) were created (16)
All things (τὰ πάντα) were created by Him and for Him (16)
He is before all things (πάντων) (17)
In Him all things (τὰ πάντα) consist (17)
In all things (πᾶσιν) He might have supremacy (18)

God was pleased to have all (πᾶν) His fullness dwell
in Him (19)
God was pleased through Him to reconcile to
Himself all things (τὰ πάντα) (20)

Shedd concludes with a section entitled "Universal Offer
of the Atonement," in which he tries to answer the question
"If the atonement of Christ is not intended to be universally
applied, why should it be universally offered?" It is a necessary question, because given that a predetermined group of
people will be saved through God's set decree (and the rest
will necessarily be lost), it doesn't make sense that anything
we do would make any difference.

The first reason given for making the gospel offer to all
men (because "it is the divine command") is reason enough
for a believer to obey. But the fact that Shedd spends nearly
five pages giving a total of twelve reasons why we ought to
share the gospel with all is for me a red flag that hints that the
reasons for doing it will take some heavy-duty convincing. I
agree that it is an act of obedience first of all, but the hope
and conviction that God will fully accomplish His work of
redemption gives far greater and more sensible and compelling motivations for sharing the gospel, as I will try to explain.

Let's look first at a few points regarding Shedd's reasons.
As I implied above, the sheer volume of the words suggests
that the reasons will be somewhat convoluted and difficult to
grasp, and I did find them to be so. I won't try to recap them
all, but they are related to his arguments for limited atonement, which I also find hard to understand. I will comment
on a few of them.

In point #4 Shedd says, "God opposes no obstacle to the
efficacy of the atonement in the instance of the nonelect. He
exerts no direct efficiency to prevent the nonelect from
trusting in the atonement. The decree of reprobation is per-
missive. God leaves the nonelect to do as he likes." To me
this type of argument seems to be an attempt to get God off
the hook for the damnation of the masses; He doesn't

prevent their being saved—He just lets them go their own way. But whether their reprobation is by direct decree (God actively causes their damnation and suffering) or by default (He allows it to happen), the result is the same—they are born with absolutely no ability to come to Christ, and they die with absolutely no hope of ever being rescued.

In point #5 Shedd says we should offer the atonement to all because "God desires that every man would believe in it"—i.e., because the salvation of sinners is pleasing to God. He quotes Turretin who says that God "delights in the conversion and eternal life of the sinner, as a thing pleasing in itself and congruous with his infinitely compassionate nature." What strikes me is that God wants sinners to be saved, which means He does *not* want sinners to remain unsaved. But if most do remain unsaved, then God does *not* get what He wants—and we cannot truly say that His nature is "infinitely compassionate." If, as Shedd says, "God decides not to overcome by special grace the obstinate aversion which resists common grace," then His desire for the sinner's repentance is not strong enough to move Him to overcome by special grace the sinner's aversion.

Point #6 is similar: "It is the nonelect himself, not God, who prevents the efficacy of the atonement." What jumps out at me here is that human beings are able to "prevent the efficacy of the atonement," that is, to thwart God's desire for their salvation—sounds very un-Calvinistic! Shedd explains that "the real reason of the inefficacy of Christ's blood is impenitence and unbelief.... The nonelect himself...is the responsible cause of the inefficacy of Christ's expiation." If the unbeliever is "the responsible cause" of his own damnation, then he has the power to thwart God's desire that he be saved! And it really troubles me to hear the word "inefficacy" in the same breath as "Christ's blood" or "Christ's expiation," just as it troubles me to hear "limited" in the same breath as "atonement." Shedd believes that "nonprevention is not causation," and he gives the analogy of a man who throws himself into the water and drowns, saying that "a spectator on the bank cannot be called the cause of that man's death." But what about a trained lifeguard with the ability and the equipment and the opportunity to make the rescue—would *he* bear no responsibility for failing to rescue the man?

People ask the Calvinist, "Why bother sharing the gospel if it is already predetermined who will be saved?" People ask the Universalist, "Why bother sharing the gospel if everybody is going to be saved anyway?" For both it is a matter of obedience. But beyond that, the Universalist's reasons, unlike the Calvinist's, are simple, sensible, satisfying, and compelling—and it doesn't take a Ph.D. to explain or understand them. For one thing, it is a great delight to tell about this awesome God who will right all wrongs, redeem all suffering, and reunite all loved ones. I no longer have to worry about someone asking the question, "Why does a loving God allow people to suffer forever?"—a good question for which I had no good answer. Now I have the answer—He doesn't! Now I can call people to repentance and faith in a truly loving God. The offense of the gospel itself is still there, but not the unnecessary offense of a repugnant tradition of men (eternal conscious torment). Believing that God loves all people, I now personally have greater love for all people and a greater desire for them to come to Christ. And just because the judgment is finite does not mean it is not awful and terrifying. It is very real and very terrible, but also very purposeful and effective, completely in keeping with God's loving character. I don't want anyone to stand before God without being clothed in the righteousness of Christ, but rather to come to the cross now and experience the blessings of knowing Him now.

If you have had trouble following Shedd's arguments— join the club! My overall impression of his piece is that he goes to great lengths to explain that Christ's work on the cross is, but really is not, for the whole world. He spills a lot of ink to say that Christ died for all the people He died for. He goes through logical contortions to contend that God sovereignly chooses whether or not to rescue an individual from the sin that he is powerless to escape—that He decrees whether or not to grant faith that the individual otherwise has no ability to exercise—yet that He bears no responsibility for the damnation of the wicked.

As R. C. Sproul[5] says, "Unless you are a universalist, you must agree that the Atonement is limited in some sense." Right! Both Calvinists and Arminians limit the atonement—Calvinists by the decree of God, and Arminians by the free will of man. But if you are a Universalist, you *don't* agree that the atonement is limited in any way! And by any reasonable measure, unlimited is better than limited: There is no getting around the fact that "some" is less than "all," that a fraction of humanity is less than the whole of humanity, that saving a subset of all people is not as great as saving the whole set of people who have ever lived. And changing the name of the doctrine to "particular atonement," "actual atonement," "intentional atonement," or "definite atonement" does not change the fact that it *limits* the efficacy of Christ's work!

Shedd says, "Since redemption implies the application of Christ's atonement, universal or unlimited redemption cannot logically be affirmed by any who hold that faith is wholly the gift of God and that saving grace is bestowed solely by election." Not true! Thankfully, we are not left with the insoluble Calvinist vs. Arminian dilemma that either God is sovereign *or* He is loving; there is a way to maintain that God is fully sovereign *and* fully loving. One can believe that faith is wholly the gift of God *and* that the atonement is unlimited *if* one believes that God has chosen to grant faith to all and thus redeem all. The purpose of the cross was to show God's righteousness, "that he might be just *and* the justifier of the one who has faith in Jesus" (Rom. 3:26)—i.e., that He might save sinners while maintaining His own righteousness. It is no more a violation of His holiness or His justice to redeem *all* through the death of His Son than to redeem some, and it is a far greater reflection of His love.

On the one hand, we will *never* fully comprehend all the depth and richness of the atonement. On the other hand, *It's not complicated*:[6]

Jesus died to be the atoning sacrifice for the sins of the whole world.

His death will fully accomplish its purpose of redeeming the whole world.

---

[1]Calvinists say the atonement is unlimited in value but limited by God's sovereign choice. Arminians say the atonement is unlimited in value but limited by human free will. Either way, the bottom line is that it is limited in some way. As the website gotquestions.org puts it, "Both the Arminian and the Calvinist believe in some sort of limited atonement. The Arminian limits the effectiveness of the atonement in saying Christ died for all people but not all people will be saved. His view of the atonement limits its power as it only makes salvation a possibility and does not actually save anyone. On the other hand, the Calvinist limits the intent of the atonement by stating that Christ's atonement was for specific people (the elect.... So, all Christians believe in some sort of limited atonement." (Note: This analysis of Calvinist and Arminian beliefs is correct, but the final statement is not true!)

[2]TULIP is an acronym for the five major points of Calvinism:
T = total depravity
U = unconditional election
L = limited atonement
I = irresistible grace
P = perseverance of the saints

[3]The whole question of the meaning of election is another huge discussion for another day. Here we will just touch on it and I will simply suggest that election is not about heaven and hell but rather about being chosen by God for His purposes. (See footnote 3 in chapter 24.)

[4]Many Christians are insistent that our salvation hinges on our choosing to trust Christ, but in the matter of free will, I think Calvinists hold the more biblical position. To say that we determine our eternal destiny by the choices we make is to ascribe too much power to human beings and not enough to God. ("He has saved us and called us to a holy life—*not because of anything we have done but because of his own purpose* and grace" 2 Tim. 1:9). Watching a documentary about Aaron Hernandez, the New England Patriots football player who murdered his friend and then took his own life in prison, reminded me that our circumstances are largely out of our control.

[5]"Particular Atonement," R.C. Sproul, www.ligonier.org. Dr. Sproul, a champion of Reformed Theology, passed away in December, 2017.

[6]Occam's razor seems to apply here: the simplest explanation is probably correct.

# 36

# LIMITED ATONEMENT:
# A BACKWARD ARGUMENT?

The previous chapter, "Limited Atonement: Sleight of Word?" (#35), is a response to W. G. T. Shedd's discussion of the extent of the atonement in his *Dogmatic Theology*, first published in 1888. Here we look at Wayne Grudem's treatment of the same subject in his *Systematic Theology*, published a century after Shedd's book. Some of the same observations apply to both, but Grudem takes a little different approach.[1]

Dr. Grudem frames the question about the extent of the atonement this way: "When Christ died on the cross, did he pay for the sins of the entire human race or only for the sins of those who he knew would ultimately be saved?" (p. 594). He explains that non-Reformed people argue that in Scripture the gospel is repeatedly offered to all people, and in order for the gospel offer to be genuine, the payment for sins must actually be available for all people. Furthermore, they say, "if the people whose sins Christ paid for are limited, then…the offer of the gospel cannot be made to all mankind without exception" (p. 594).

Reformed people, on the other hand, argue that if the atonement actually paid for the sins of all people, then God could not condemn anyone to eternal punishment because that would be demanding double payment for the same sins, which is unjust. *We* do not know who will come to Christ, so we have to offer the gospel to all. Furthermore, all God's purposes are certainly fulfilled; therefore, what is actually accomplished is exactly what God intended to accomplish.

Then Grudem cites Scripture passages used to support the Reformed view[2] and others used to support the non-Reformed view. Like Shedd, he notes that the Scriptures speak of Christ dying for "his people"—"the sheep" (Jn. 10:15), "the church of God" (Acts 20:28), "God's elect" (Rom. 8:33, 34), and "her," i.e., "the church" (Eph. 5:25). Christ spoke of those whom the Father gave Him (Jn. 6:37–39; Jn. 17:9, 20)—a group of people whom He specifically prayed for and who would be raised up at the last day, not one of whom would be cast out or lost. When the Bible talks about what Christ did for "us" or for "our sake" through His death, it is referring specifically to those who would believe (e.g., Rom. 5:8, 10; 2 Cor. 5:21; Gal. 3:13; Eph. 1:3–4).

For each of the five doctrinal points of Calvinism, Grudem "attempts to point out the arguments in favor of an opposing position and to provide an appropriate bibliography representing both views," which I really appreciate. In this case, he mentions some of the Scripture passages used to support "general redemption" or "unlimited atonement," noting that they indicate "that in some sense Christ died for the whole world" or that they "appear to speak of Christ dying for those who will not be saved." Then he goes on to explain why the Calvinist position is more true to Scripture.

But first he mentions some points of agreement between the Reformed and non-Reformed views. First on the list is that both sides agree that "not all will be saved." Since Calvinists and Arminians agree on this point, he doesn't even consider the possibility that all might be saved. He simply assumes that not all are saved and builds his argument on that basic assumption.

Here, I believe, is a serious problem with his argument. His logic may be sound (and I believe that it is), but if he starts with a premise that is not true, then his conclusion may not be true. And if he considers only two possibilities, he may be missing a third position that even better explains all that has been revealed in Scripture. And it seems to me that he is working backward to arrive at limited atonement. Let me explain.

Grudem's arguments[3] in favor of the Reformed view of particular atonement assume that not all people are saved. (Not that he assumes out of thin air, but he believes it has already been established as fact.) Since he also believes in the sovereignty of God (that God will surely accomplish all that He purposes to do), Grudem logically has to conclude that God did *not* purpose to save all through Christ's death. The logic might be stated as follows:

> If God intended to save all, He would save all.
> God does not save all.
> Therefore, God did not intend to save all.
> $P \rightarrow Q \quad \sim Q \rightarrow \sim P$

In Grudem's words,

> Reformed people argue that God's purposes in redemption are...certainly accomplished. Those whom God planned to save are the same people for whom Christ also came to die, and to those same people the Holy Spirit will apply the benefits of Christ's redemptive work.... What God the Father purposed, God the Son and the Holy Spirit agreed to and surely carried out.

The implication is that since some people are not saved, then God did not *plan* to save them and the Son did not die for them. The logic itself is sound, but if the premise is not true, then we cannot have confidence in the conclusion.

To me it seems backwards to start with the premise that not all are saved. Rather than taking it as a given, I think we should start by determining what Scripture says about Jesus' work on the cross and from there determine whether or not all will saved. In this approach we would harmonize the apparent damnation passages with the apparent universal ones, rather than the other way around.

From another angle, Grudem believes that if Jesus actually paid for everyone's sins, then everyone's sins would be forgiven and everyone would be saved (and I agree). Since not everyone is saved, Jesus did not pay for everyone's sins:

> If Jesus paid for everyone's sins, then everyone would
> be saved.
> Not all are saved.
> Therefore, Jesus did not pay for everyone's sins.

As Grudem puts it,

> Reformed people argue that if Christ's death actually
> paid for the sins of every person who ever lived, then
> there is no penalty left for *anyone* to pay, and it
> necessarily follows that all people will be saved,
> without exception.

His logic is fine, but since he believes that not all people are
saved, he has to conclude that Christ's death did *not* actually
pay for the sins of every person who ever lived. However,
notice what he is saying: *If* the atonement is unlimited, then
all people will be saved (i.e., universalism is true).[3] If only he
would explore this possibility!

Grudem's other points supporting limited atonement also
assume that not all people are saved.[4] Like Shedd, he takes
verses that seem to teach unlimited atonement and interprets
them in light of his belief that eternal punishment is true.[5]
Here are some examples of how he interprets such verses:

> The fact that Christ is the Lamb of God who takes
> away the sin of the world (John 1:29) does not mean
> (on anybody's interpretation) that Christ actually
> removes the sins of every single person in the world,
> for both sides agree that not all are saved (p. 598).
> [My note: In reality, some people *do* believe that all
> will be saved and that Christ actually *does* remove the
> sins of every single person in the world!]

> Jesus said that "the bread of God is that which comes
> down from heaven, and gives life to the world" (John
> 6:33). This may be understood in the sense of
> bringing redeeming life into the world but not
> meaning that every single person in the world will
> have that redeeming life (p. 598).

When Jesus says, "The bread which I shall give *for the life of the world* is my flesh" (John 6:51), it is in the context of speaking of himself as the Bread that came down from heaven, which is offered to people and which they may, if they are willing, receive for themselves (p. 598).

The fact that God was in Christ reconciling the world to himself (2 Cor. 5:19) does not mean that every single person in the world was reconciled to God, but that sinners generally were reconciled to God (p. 598).

When Paul says that Christ "gave himself as a ransom *for all*" (1 Tim. 2:6), we are to understand this to mean a ransom available for all people (p. 599).

When Paul says that God "is the Savior of all men, especially of those who believe" (1 Tim. 4:10),... surely Paul does not mean that every single person will be saved (p. 599). [My note: Or maybe that is, in fact, precisely what Paul means!]

When John says that Christ "is the propitiation for our sins, and not for ours only but also for the sins of the whole world" (1 John 2:2, author's translation), he may simply be understood to mean that Christ is the atoning sacrifice that the gospel now *makes available for* the sins of everyone in the world (p. 598).

When the author of Hebrews says that Christ was made lower than the angels "so that by the grace of God he might taste death for every one" (Heb. 2:9),[6] the passage is best understood to refer to every one of Christ's people, every one who is redeemed.... The Greek word *pas*, here translated "every one," is also used in a similar sense to mean "all God's people" in Hebrews 8:11 and 12:8 (p. 599).

So Grudem, like Shedd, goes to great lengths to interpret verses in such a way as to support limited atonement. If only he would give a hearing to the idea of unlimited atonement coupled with the sovereignty of God! I do agree with him that the Arminian concept of unlimited atonement (which is not coupled with a full recognition of God's sovereignty) is in error.[7] The following analogy occurred to me:

> Suppose a little girl is drowning and a man jumps in to save her. If in the process he himself drowns, we can truly say that "he died for her." But if she drowns too, then his saving effort was ineffective. Arminianism says something similar: Christ died for all; He gave His life in an attempt to rescue all. But the sad fact is that many perish anyway.

However, if the man *succeeded* in rescuing her and died in the process, then truly he gave his life for her *and* his sacrifice was completely effective. Similarly, if Christ died for all and succeeds in saving all, then the atonement is "for" all in every sense, God's purpose is fully accomplished, and every person for whom Christ died (i.e., the whole world) will be saved.

Another thing I do appreciate about Dr. Grudem is that he takes a pastoral approach when presenting his position (which is not always the case with Calvinists). In a section entitled "Points of Clarification and Caution Regarding This Doctrine," he acknowledges that "we can rightly object to the way in which some advocates of particular redemption have expressed their arguments."

He also looks at "the pastoral implications for this teaching." For example, it is easy for non-Reformed people to hear the sentence "Christ died for his people only" and see it as a threat to the free offer of the gospel to every person. Therefore, Reformed people should be cautious about making that statement:

> Reformed people who hold to particular redemption should recognize the potential for misunderstanding that arises with the sentence "Christ died for his people only," and, out of concern for the truth and

out of pastoral concern to affirm the free offer of the gospel and to avoid misunderstanding in the body of Christ, they should be more precise in saying exactly what they mean. The simple sentence, "Christ died for his people only," while true in the sense explained above ["Christ died to actually pay the penalty for all the sins of his people only"], is seldom understood in that way when people unfamiliar with Reformed doctrine hear it, and it therefore is better not to use such an ambiguous sentence at all (p. 601).

Yet as I have noted before, it is problematic to use semantics to get around the implications of a doctrine.

Grudem also says that Reformed people should not object to the statement "Christ died for all people," because Scripture uses that kind of language and because it can be consistent with the Reformed belief that "Christ died to make salvation available to all people." He warns against splitting theological hairs:

It really seems to be only nit-picking that creates controversies and useless disputes when Reformed people insist on being such purists in their speech that they object any time someone says that "Christ died for all people" (p. 602).

Why not consider the possibility that if Scripture uses language like "Christ died for all people," maybe that's precisely what it means!

Grudem also tries to bring together those who hold to particular redemption and those who hold to general redemption by noting the key points where they agree:

- Both sincerely want to avoid implying that people will be saved whether they believe in Christ or not.

- Both sides want to avoid implying that there might be some people who come to Christ for salvation but are turned away because Christ did not die for them.

- Both sides want to avoid implying that God is hypocritical or insincere when he makes the free offer of the gospel.

I would add that Universalists also agree on these key points.

Finally, Grudem cautions that Reformed people should not make belief in particular redemption "a test of doctrinal orthodoxy," and it should not become divisive:

> It would be healthy to realize that Scripture itself never singles this out as a doctrine of major importance, nor does it once make it the subject of any explicit theological discussion. Our knowledge of the issue comes only from incidental references to it in passages whose concern is with other doctrinal or practical matters.... A balanced pastoral perspective would seem to be to say that this teaching of particular redemption *seems* to us to be true, that it gives logical consistency to our theological system, and that it can be helpful in assuring people of Christ's love for them individually and of the completeness of his redemptive work for them; but that it also is a subject that almost inevitably leads to some confusion, some misunderstanding, and often some wrongful argumentativeness and divisiveness among God's people—all of which are negative pastoral considerations (p. 603).

Grudem's pastoral emphasis is a welcome relief from some of the more strident Calvinists. But I can't help thinking that, no matter what you call it or how you define it or how you explain it, limited atonement is just an awful doctrine. Worst of all, it diminishes Christ's magnificent work on the cross, limiting its efficacy to only a fraction of humanity. How could we ever say that the efficacy of His work is anything less than perfect and complete? And if we allow ourselves to think about it using the sense of reason, compassion, and justice that God has given us, we find it *un*reasonable, *un*loving, and *un*just that God would bring people into the world in total bondage to sin and then leave many (if not most) with no real possibility of escaping from that bondage. The natural aversion that many feel to that idea is not because they are bleeding-heart liberals who have no concept of God's holiness; rather, they are using their God-given mind, heart, and conscience. Let the words of the Westminster Confession sink in, and ask God if they really express His gracious and loving and sovereign purposes:

> VI. As God has appointed the elect unto glory, so has He, by the eternal and most free purpose of His will, foreordained all the means thereunto. Wherefore, they who are elected, being fallen in Adam, are redeemed by Christ, are effectually called unto faith in Christ by His Spirit working in due season, are justified, adopted, sanctified, and kept by His power, through faith, unto salvation. Neither are any other redeemed by Christ, effectually called, justified, adopted, sanctified, and saved, but the elect only.

> VII. The rest of mankind God was pleased, according to the unsearchable counsel of His own will, whereby He extends or withholds mercy, as He pleases, for the glory of His sovereign power over His creatures, to pass by; and to ordain them to dishonor and wrath for their sin, to the praise of His glorious justice.

*The rest of mankind God was pleased to pass by; and to ordain them to dishonor and wrath for their sin, to the praise of His glorious justice.* Are these statements consistent with what you know about the God who redeemed you? Does "passing by" His creatures and ordaining them to dishonor and wrath bring praise to "His glorious justice" or to His loving character?

And while it does give logical consistency to the Reformed theological system, the fact that God specifically chooses some does *not*, in my opinion, assure people of Christ's love for them individually. How can we be certain of God's love for *us* if He does not in the same way love those whom we love? Is love really part of His essential character, or is it a selective love that chooses to love some enough to save them and others not? (For a look at this question from a more devotional angle, see "Being the Chosen Child," #28.)

Here I will remind you of John Piper's words to show where the doctrine of limited atonement leads when it goes from dry theology to personal application. His sons are now grown, but when they were little he wrote:

> I have three sons. Every night after they are asleep I turn on the hall light, open their bedroom door, and walk from bed to bed, laying my hands on them and praying. Often I am moved to tears of joy and longing. I pray that Karsten Luke become a great physician of the soul, that Benjamin John become the beloved son of my right hand in the gospel, and that Abraham Christian give glory to God as he grows strong in his faith.

> But I am not ignorant that God may not have chosen my sons for his sons. And, though I think I would give my life for their salvation, if they should be lost to me, I would not rail against the Almighty. He is God. I am but a man. The potter has absolute rights over the clay. Mine is to bow before his unimpeachable character and believe that the Judge of all the earth has ever and always will do right.

*God may not have chosen my sons for his sons.* Piper said that he himself would give his life for their salvation, but he could not be sure that Jesus had died for them! While I admire the faith that would allow him to continue to trust God in the face of the possible damnation of his children, I think it is utterly tragic that a dad would have to live with the uncertainty of whether or not Jesus had died for his children.

Looking back at Grudem's original question—"When Christ died on the cross, did he pay for the sins of the entire human race or only for the sins of those who he knew would ultimately be saved?"—I think the answer is that those two groups are one and the same! Jesus gave His life for the entire human race, and ultimately all will be saved.

I do take seriously Grudem's caution not to nit-pick about the finer points of doctrine. But I think we *must* recognize and proclaim the full power of the work of Christ on the cross—that He saves the world not just partially (as Calvinists maintain) and not just potentially (as Arminians believe), but perfectly and completely and gloriously. And I do believe there is a way to harmonize the most important doctrines of both Calvinism and Arminianism—*if* they both let go of one doctrine they agree on: that not all will be saved. Then we can maintain with the Arminians that God is infinitely loving and with the Calvinists that God is absolutely sovereign—and therefore that He both *desires* to redeem all of humanity and He will *accomplish* the redemption of all humanity.

---

[1] For a comprehensive treatment of definite atonement, see *From Heaven He Came and Sought Her: Definite Atonement in Historical, Biblical, Theological, and Pastoral Perspective* (2013), by David Gibson with contributions by many contemporary Reformed scholars. David Wells calls it "the definitive study."

[2] Grudem mentions that what he calls the "Reformed view" is often referred to as "limited atonement," but the preferred term is *particular redemption,* which means that Christ died for particular people and foreknew each of them individually.

[3] Grudem's arguments can be summarized as follows:

- "People who are eternally condemned to hell suffer the penalty for all of their own sins, and therefore their penalty could not have been fully taken by Christ" (p. 597).

- Through particular redemption, Christ "completely earned our salvation, paying the penalty for all our sins. He did not just redeem us potentially, but actually redeemed us as individuals whom he loved" (p. 598).

- "Several passages that speak about 'the world' simply mean that sinners generally will be saved, without implying that every single individual in the world will be saved" (p. 598).

- "The passages that speak about Christ dying 'for' the whole world are best understood to refer to the free offer of the gospel that is made to all people" (p. 598).

- "To say that Jesus came to offer eternal life to the world (a point on which both sides agree) is not to say that he actually paid the penalty for the sins of everyone who would ever live" (p. 598).

- 1 John 2:2 "may simply be understood to mean that Christ is the atoning sacrifice that the gospel now *makes available for* the sins of everyone in the world" (p. 598).

- 1 Timothy 2:6 means that "a ransom [is] available for all people, without exception" (p. 599).

- Verses that speak about what Christ has done for all (e.g., Heb. 2:9) "refer to every one of Christ's people, every one who is redeemed" (p. 599).

[4]Arminians would not agree with the statement "If the atonement is unlimited, then all people will be saved." They contend that a person can choose to reject the sacrifice that was made for him.

[5]As Grudem says about "the narrow point of the question of the extent of the atonement,... the specific scriptural texts on that point are too few and can hardly be said to be conclusive on either side. One's decisions on these passages will tend to be determined by one's view of the larger question as to what Scripture as a whole teaches about the nature of the atonement and about the broader issues of God's providence, sovereignty, and the doctrine of election. Whatever decisions are made on those larger topics will apply specifically to this point, and people will come to their conclusions accordingly" (p. 601). Here we are in agreement that all of us come to our conclusions about the meaning of specific passages by interpreting them in light of our view of the big picture.

[6]Grudem justifies a narrow interpretation of Hebrews 2:9 ("everyone" = "all God's people") by giving a narrow interpretation to Hebrews 8:11 and 12:8.
2:9—"Jesus...suffered death, so that by the grace of God he might taste death for *everyone*."
8:11—"No longer will a man teach his neighbor, or a man his brother, saying, 'Know the Lord,' because they will *all* know me, from the least of them to the greatest."
12:8—"If you are not disciplined (and *everyone* undergoes discipline), then you are illegitimate children and not true sons."

[7]Grudem says, "Reformed people argue that it is the other view [non-Reformed, or Arminianism] that really limits the power of the atonement because on that view the atonement does not actually guarantee salvation for God's people but only makes salvation possible for all people. In other words, if the atonement is not limited with respect to the number of people to which it applies, then it must be limited with respect to what it actually accomplishes."

# 37

# HERETIC!

Since I went public with the fact that I believe in the ultimate restoration of all mankind, a number of people have said or implied that I am a heretic, and I'm sure others think it. I have to say that my belief does fit the dictionary definition of *heresy*:

heretictshirts.com

> dissent or deviation from a dominant theory, opinion, or practice; adherence to a religious opinion contrary to church dogma (Merriam-Webster)

> opinion or doctrine at variance with the orthodox or accepted doctrine, especially of a church or religious system; any belief or theory that is strongly at variance with established beliefs, customs, etc. (dictionary.com)

> A belief or teaching considered unacceptable by a religious group (The American Heritage® New Dictionary of Cultural Literacy)

Yes, the belief that God will ultimately redeem all mankind (not just the "elect" or not just those who trust Christ before they die) does go contrary to centuries of church dogma and is considered by the majority of evangelical Christians in our day to be a deviation from accepted doctrine.

But let's go a little deeper. The term *heresy* is a loaded word, so let's look very carefully at what it means, what it implies, and what our response should be. What does the Bible say about heresy? What has the word come to mean? Who is a heretic? How should such a person be treated?

The words *heresy* (αἵρεσις, *hairesis*) and *heretic* (αἱρετικός, *hairetikos*) come from a root meaning "to choose." In the New Testament the word *hairesis* often refers to a religious sect or party that has separated itself from the mainstream, like the sect of the Sadducees (Acts 5:17), the party of the Pharisees (Acts 15:5; 26:5), the Nazarene sect (Acts 24:5), or the Christians (Acts 28:22).

Paul himself was part of a group considered to be a "heresy":

> However, I admit that I worship the God of our ancestors as a follower of the Way, which they call a sect (*hairesin*). I believe everything that is in accordance with the Law and that is written in the Prophets (Acts 24:14, NIV).

Paul was deemed a "heretic" by the religious leaders of his day, though he believed "everything that is in accordance with the Law and that is written in the Prophets"! And lest anyone accuse me of leaving out the rest of his words, let me be the first to quote the whole passage:

> .... I believe everything that is in accordance with the Law and that is written in the Prophets, and I have the same hope in God as these men themselves have, that there will be a resurrection of both the righteous and the wicked. So I strive always to keep my conscience clear before God and man (Acts 24:14–16).

Someone might say, "Aha! He believes in the resurrection of both the righteous and the wicked. You don't believe that the wicked will rise to face eternal condemnation." No, I don't believe that the wicked will be forever damned, but I do believe there will be a resurrection of both the righteous and the wicked. I want to be the kind of "heretic" Paul was— someone who worships God as a follower of the Way, who believes everything in accordance with Scripture, who hopes in God, who looks forward to the final resurrection, and who strives to keep a clear conscience before God and man.

But sometimes the word *heresy* or *heretic* is used in a more negative way. Paul included heresies among the acts of the flesh, which disqualify a person from inheriting the kingdom of God:

> The acts of the flesh are obvious: sexual immorality, impurity and debauchery; idolatry and witchcraft; hatred, discord, jealousy, fits of rage, selfish ambition, dissensions, factions (αἱρέσεις) and envy; drunkenness, orgies, and the like. I warn you, as I did before, that those who live like this will not inherit the kingdom of God (Gal. 5:19–21).

Paul also warned Titus about heretical men (divisive or factious people) in strong terms:

> But avoid foolish controversies, genealogies, dissensions, and quarrels about the law, for they are unprofitable and worthless. As for a person who stirs up division (*hairetikon anthropon,* αἱρετικὸν ἄνθρωπον), after warning him once and then twice, have nothing more to do with him, knowing that such a person is warped and sinful; he is self-condemned (Tit. 3:9–11).

He calls such people warped and sinful and self-condemned, and told Titus to have nothing to do with them. In this context it seems that "heretics" are those who cause division in the body of Christ. They undermine the message that Paul was trying to emphasize in the preceding verses:

> But when the goodness and loving kindness of God our Savior appeared, he saved us, not because of works done by us in righteousness, but according to his own mercy, by the washing of regeneration and renewal of the Holy Spirit, whom he poured out on us richly through Jesus Christ our Savior, so that being justified by his grace we might become heirs according to the hope of eternal life. The saying is trustworthy, and I want you to insist on these things,

so that those who have believed in God may be careful to devote themselves to good works. These things are excellent and profitable for people (Tit. 3:4–8).

Second Peter connects the idea of heresies with the false prophets and false teachers who introduce them, so we should also look at the biblical teaching on false prophets and teachers.

But there were also false prophets among the people, just as there will be false teachers among you. They will secretly introduce destructive heresies (αἱρέσεις), even denying the sovereign Lord who bought them— bringing swift destruction on themselves. Many will follow their depraved conduct and will bring the way of truth into disrepute. In their greed these teachers will exploit you with fabricated stories. Their condemnation has long been hanging over them, and their destruction has not been sleeping (2 Pet. 2:1–3).

These people are guilty of following "depraved conduct," bringing "the way of truth into disrepute," and acting with greed and deception. And it seems that there is a critical doctrinal issue that characterizes false prophets: as Peter puts it, "denying the sovereign Lord who bought them," i.e., denying the work of Christ on the cross that purchased our redemption. Jude expresses it in a similar way:

They are ungodly people, who pervert the grace of our God into a license for immorality and *deny Jesus Christ our only Sovereign and Lord* (Jude 4).

Jesus said to watch out for false prophets because they might look like sheep but inwardly they are ferocious wolves (Mt. 7:15). He said that in the end times many false prophets would appear and would deceive many people (Mt. 24:11). John also warned of them and told how to recognize them:

Dear friends, do not believe every spirit, but test the spirits to see whether they are from God, because many false prophets have gone out into the world.

This is how you can recognize the Spirit of God: Every spirit that acknowledges that Jesus Christ has come in the flesh is from God; every spirit that does not acknowledge Jesus is not from God. This is the spirit of the antichrist, which you have heard is coming and even now is already in the world (1 Jn. 4:1–3).

Again we see a doctrinal issue about the person of Christ that identifies a false prophet: failing to acknowledge that Jesus is from God.

It seems that false teachers were a problem in Timothy's church, because Paul mentions them several times in his letters to the young pastor, beginning with the opening of 1 Timothy 1:

As I urged you when I went into Macedonia, stay there in Ephesus so that you may command certain people not to teach false doctrines any longer or to devote themselves to myths and endless genealogies. Such things promote controversial speculations rather than advancing God's work—which is by faith. The goal of this command is love, which comes from a pure heart and a good conscience and a sincere faith. Some have departed from these and have turned to meaningless talk. They want to be teachers of the law, but they do not know what they are talking about or what they so confidently affirm (1 Tim. 1:3–7).

The Spirit clearly says that in later times some will abandon the faith and follow deceiving spirits and things taught by demons. Such teachings come through hypocritical liars, whose consciences have been seared as with a hot iron (1 Tim. 4:1–2).

If anyone teaches otherwise and does not agree to the sound instruction of our Lord Jesus Christ and to godly teaching, they are conceited and understand nothing. They have an unhealthy interest in contro-versies and quarrels about words that result in envy, strife, malicious talk, evil suspicions and constant friction between people of corrupt mind, who have been robbed of the truth and who think that godliness is a means to financial gain (1 Tim. 6:3–5).

Timothy, guard what has been entrusted to your care. Turn away from godless chatter and the opposing ideas of what is falsely called knowledge, which some have professed and in so doing have departed from the faith (1 Tim. 6:20–21).

But mark this: There will be terrible times in the last days. People will be lovers of themselves, lovers of money, boastful, proud, abusive, disobedient to their parents, ungrateful, unholy, without love, unforgiving, slanderous, without self-control, brutal, not lovers of the good, treacherous, rash, conceited, lovers of pleasure rather than lovers of God— having a form of godliness but denying its power. Have nothing to do with such people…. [T]hese teachers oppose the truth. They are men of depraved minds, who, as far as the faith is concerned, are rejected (2 Tim. 3:1–8).

As the introduction to 1 Timothy in the ESV Study Bible points out, "false teachers are the primary occasion for the letter," but the exact nature of the false teaching is not identified. What really matters is the fruit:

Paul's real concern is with the results of the false teaching—for example promoting speculations (1:4; 6:4), arrogance (6:4), and greed (6:5–10). Paul addresses the content of the false teaching only in passing but focuses on the fact that true Christianity is evidenced by lifestyles shaped by the gospel. Those whose lives are not shaped by the gospel show that they have turned away from the faith (ESV Study Bible, p. 2322).

With these passages and observations in mind, how can we recognize heresy? One tip-off as to whether a teaching is false is that it maligns the name of Christ and His work on the cross. Another is that it produces ugly fruit in one's life. Not all heretics, false teachers, and false prophets will have all of the characteristics, but here are some red flags: denial that Jesus has come in the flesh, rejection of His work on the cross, divisiveness, immorality, foolish quarrels, depraved conduct, lack of love, seared conscience, arrogance, slander, selfishness, greed, exploitation, maliciousness, hypocrisy, deception.

So how can we evaluate Evangelical Universalism against the biblical understanding of heresy? I have already acknowledged that I fit the dictionary definition of a heretic, and I *want* to be a "heretic" in the same way that Paul was. But am I a heretic in the biblical sense of one who has departed from the faith and bears bad fruit? Like most Evangelical Universalists, I hold a very high view of Scripture, a very high view of the character of God, a very high view of the Person of Christ, a very high view of the cross, a very strong view of sin and judgment, a very strong desire to live a godly life, and a very strong desire to share the gospel. I have made every effort to base my beliefs not on my own thoughts or wishes but on God's revealed Word.

As Robin Parry has stated, the debate between those who hold to a traditional view of eternal damnation and those who believe that God will reconcile all to Himself

> is not a debate between Bible-believing Christians (traditionalists) and "liberals" (universalists). It is, to a large extent, a debate between two sets of Bible-believing Christians on how best to understand scripture.

Holding to a different interpretation of a biblical doctrine does not make a person a heretic. Hunting down brothers and sisters in Christ who have different opinions has done far more harm than good throughout church history. And don't forget the meaning of the word *heresy* as "divisiveness" and of *heretic* as "a divisive person," and the strong scriptural admonitions against creating disunity in the Body of Christ. Could it be that some accusations of heresy are themselves divisive and "heretical"?

St. Ignatius of Antioch, a student of John the Apostle, was very concerned about heresy in the early Church, but he knew that "heresy" is not just wrong belief. He said,

> Heretics are those who have
> no care for love,
> none for the widow,
> none for the orphan,
> none for the afflicted,
> none for the prisoner,
> none for the hungry or thirsty.

---

**Summary:**

One key to recognizing heretics or false prophets is that they malign the person and work of Christ: they fail to acknowledge that Jesus Christ has come in the flesh and they deny the sovereign Lord who bought them. However, the biblical descriptions of heretics, false prophets, and false teachers focus primarily on their life and character. Before giving anyone these labels, please consider carefully whether or not they actually fit these descriptions:

**Matthew:**
ravenous wolves
bear bad fruit

**1 Timothy:**
controversial speculations
departed from a pure heart, good conscience, and
    sincere faith
meaningless talk
abandon the faith
follow deceiving spirits
hypocritical liars
seared conscience
do not agree to sound instruction and godly teaching

puffed up with conceit
understand nothing
unhealthy interest in controversies and quarrels
envy, strife, malicious talk, evil suspicions, constant
    friction
corrupt mind
think that godliness is a means to financial gain
departed from the faith

## 2 Timothy:

have a form of godliness but deny its power
oppose the truth
depraved minds

## Titus:

unprofitable and worthless dissensions and quarrels
warped and sinful

## 2 Peter:

depraved conduct
bring the way of truth into disrepute
greed, exploit with fabricated stories
unrighteous, follow the corrupt desire of the flesh
despise authority
bold and arrogant
heap abuse on celestial beings
blaspheme in matters they do not understand
unreasoning animals
creatures of instinct
do harm
carouse in broad daylight
blots and blemishes
revel in their pleasures
eyes full of adultery
never stop sinning
seduce the unstable
experts in greed
have left the straight way

springs without water and mists driven by a storm
mouth empty, boastful words
appeal to the lustful desires of the flesh
entice by sensual passions
slaves of depravity
entangled in defilements of the world
ignorant and unstable
twist the Scriptures

**Jude:**
pervert the grace of God into a license for immorality

# 38

# INFERNO

Like millions of other people, I watched in horror as the fires raged after the explosion in West, Texas in April 2013. Less than three weeks later, it was the horrific fire in the limo carrying nine young women for a bachelorette party. The bride-to-be and four of her friends, all nurses, perished in the flames. The limo tragedy particularly hit home as it happened one week before my own daughter's wedding. As we anticipated our happy day, I could not begin to imagine the grief of the family and friends of the bride-not-to-be who would never see her own wedding day.

If standard evangelical theology is true, then all those who died in these fires without knowing Christ as their personal Savior will go into an inferno that is infinitely worse and never-ending. We've all heard the rationales for the doctrine of eternal damnation; they have been so drilled into us that even if we don't like them we accept them uncritically because we think we *have* to in order to be faithful to Scripture.

Brothers and sisters, *think* about what you are affirming! If even a little part of your sanctified conscience whispers that something is wrong with this picture, do not ignore that still, small voice; it could be the prompting of the Holy Spirit. If you wonder how our Heavenly Father could do something that no halfway decent earthly father would ever dream of doing, maybe the answer is that He does *not* do it.

There are those who will say I'm just appealing to human reasoning or emotion, which cannot be trusted, or that my understanding of God's holiness is deficient. Of *course* my view of God's holiness is deficient, but that is *not* the problem here! And living by faith does *not* mean checking common sense and compassion at the door! God gives us a mind, a heart, and a conscience, which He expects us to use. He does not expect us to blindly believe something that violates every sense of reason, compassion, and justice that He has implanted in us.

Allow yourself to imagine fully what it would be like to burn forever. The limo fire erupted in 90 seconds, and the women were gone in minutes. Picturing even those few moments of searing heat, choking smoke, roasting flesh, and desperate attempts to escape fills a merciful person with anguish. Can you imagine your own loved ones going through it? What would it be like to endure that intense torture for an hour...a day...a week...a year...a lifetime...an eternity?

God will certainly not let the guilty go unpunished. But will He allow them to be tormented forever? Punishment that goes on endlessly either has no purpose or fails to accomplish its purpose. Once punishment achieves its goal, it ends; continuing ad infinitum means it has not achieved its goal (its end) or else it has no real purpose.

If you feel even a tiny twinge of doubt about eternal damnation—or a twinge of hope that maybe God in Christ will actually redeem and restore His entire creation—then *please* keep exploring it more. You do not have to deny *any* of Scripture in order to embrace the belief that God will reconcile *all* to Himself through Christ. God sent His Son into the world to save the world, Jesus is the Savior of the world, and He *will* save the world. He is the atoning sacrifice for the sins of the whole world, and He will not fail to accomplish His purpose for coming into the world.

# 39

# WHAT IS HELLFIRE? PART 1

If you believe in hell as a fiery place of afterlife punishment, where do you think it came from? Who created hell? When did it come into existence? Did God conceive and design and create hell? Did Satan have a hand in it? Did hell come into being at the time the rest of the universe was created? At the foundation of the world? Or even before that time, in anticipation of the fall of Satan and then humanity? If God looked at everything He made and proclaimed it "very good," then is hell good? In what sense? Or was hell created after the fall, as a consequence of it? Does hell mean separation from God? If so, where could it possibly be? Where can one go to be out of the presence of God? Will hell ever go out of existence? And finally, how does hell fit into God's eternal purposes, conceived in His mind before the world came into being?

Now reread the questions in the first paragraph and try to formulate answers to them. (Really give some thought to how you would articulate your answers!) If you are having trouble coming up with sensible, biblical answers, maybe it is because we are asking the wrong questions. The idea of "hell" as a literal place of never-ending torment or as a state of eternal separation from God is fraught with logical and biblical problems, as you can see if you have attempted to give coherent answers to the questions above. It is worth at least considering a different picture of what may happen to unbelievers when they die. Let's think about what we do know from Scripture, and then try to put it all together. Here are some principles to keep in mind as we explore these questions.

## The Omnipresence of God

We know that it is impossible to escape from the presence of God. God is omnipresent—He is present everywhere, and everything is in His presence. David asked where He could go to get away from the Spirit of God. The answer is nowhere—neither in the heavens nor in the depths:

> Where shall I go from your Spirit?
>     Or where shall I flee from your presence?
> If I ascend to heaven, you are there!
>     If I make my bed in Sheol, you are there!
> (Ps. 139:7–8, ESV)

## Fire as a Symbol of the Presence of God

We know that fire signifies the presence of God: He appeared to Moses in flames of fire from within the burning bush (Ex. 3:2). He accompanied His people in the pillar of fire during the wilderness wanderings (Ex. 13:21). He descended on the mountain in fire to give the Ten Commandments (Ex. 19:18; Deut. 4:11–12). He revealed His presence in the fire that burned up the sacrifice of Elijah (1 Ki. 18:38–39). He baptizes with the Holy Spirit and with fire, imparting His indwelling presence (Mt. 3:11; Luke 3:16). His Holy Spirit was present in the tongues of fire that came down on Pentecost (Acts 2:3–4). Jesus will be "revealed from heaven in blazing fire" (2 Thess. 1:7). And God Himself is a fire:

> The Lord your God is a consuming fire (Deut. 4:24a).

> Let us offer to God acceptable worship, with reverence and awe, for our God is a consuming fire (Heb. 12:28b–29).

## Fire as a Symbol of Judgment

Fire is also a symbol of judgment: Isaiah said that those who rejected the Holy One and His word would be destroyed as fire destroys dry grass (5:24). He also said, "See, the Name of the Lord comes from afar, with burning anger and dense clouds of smoke; his lips are full of wrath, and his tongue is a consuming fire" (30:27). John the Baptist speaks of judgment when he says of Jesus, "His winnowing fork is in his hand, and he will clear his threshing floor, gathering his wheat into the barn and burning up the chaff with unquenchable fire" (Mt. 3:12). Jesus' words in Matthew 25 are a statement of judgment against those who failed to show His compassion:

> Depart from me, you who are cursed, into the eternal fire prepared for the devil and his angels. For I was hungry and you gave me nothing to eat, I was thirsty and you gave me nothing to drink, I was a stranger and you did not invite me in, I needed clothes and you did not clothe me, I was sick and in prison and you did not look after me (vv. 41–43).

Paul speaks of God's judgment/punishment in 2 Thessalonians 1:

> All this is evidence that God's judgment is right.... God is just: He will pay back trouble to those who trouble you and give relief to you who are troubled, and to us as well. This will happen when the Lord Jesus is revealed from heaven in blazing fire with his powerful angels (5–7).

The writer of Hebrews says that those who rebel against God face "a fearful expectation of judgment and of raging fire that will consume the enemies of God" (10:27). Jude warns of "the punishment of eternal fire" on the great day of judgment (Jude 9). Revelation is full of images of fire symbolizing judgment, and Peter speaks of the destruction of the heavens and earth by fire on the day of the Lord.

> But the day of the Lord will come like a thief. The heavens will disappear with a roar, the elements will be destroyed by fire, and the earth and everything in it will be laid bare.... That day will bring about the destruction of the heavens by fire, and the elements will melt in the heat (2 Pet. 2:10, 12).

## Fire Associated with Light

Fire is associated with light, both literal and metaphorical. The pillar of fire provided a literal light to guide the people of Israel and show them the way to take:

> By day the Lord went ahead of them in a pillar of cloud to guide them on their way and by night in a pillar of fire to give them light, so that they could travel by day or night (Ex. 13:21).

> Because of your great compassion you did not abandon them in the wilderness. By day the pillar of cloud did not fail to guide them on their path, nor the pillar of fire by night to shine on the way they were to take (Neh. 9:19).

Metaphorically, God Himself is represented as a light, a fire, and a flame:

> The Light of Israel will become a fire, their Holy One a flame (Is. 10:17a).

The "true light that gives light to every man" (John 1:9) came into the world in the person of Jesus Christ:

> I am the light of the world. Whoever follows me will never walk in darkness, but will have the light of life (John 8:12)

And lamps blazing with light represent the seven-fold Spirit of God:

> Before the throne, seven lamps were blazing. These are the seven spirits of God (Revelation 4:5b).

## Fire as a Symbol of Purification

Another purpose of fire is purification. God's words are pure, like silver refined in a fiery furnace:

> The words of the Lord are flawless, like silver refined in a furnace of clay, purified seven times (Ps. 12:6).

The law required purification by fire, for example, when men came back from battle:

Gold, silver, bronze, iron, tin, lead and anything else that can withstand fire must be put through the fire, and then it will be clean (Num. 31:22–23).

The Lord speaks of refining and testing us through a "furnace" of suffering:

See, I have refined you, though not as silver; I have tested you in the furnace of affliction (Is. 48:10).

The prophet Malachi says that God Himself is like a refiner's fire:

But who can endure the day of his coming? Who can stand when he appears? For he will be like a refiner's fire or a launderer's soap. He will sit as a refiner and purifier of silver; he will purify the Levites and refine them like gold and silver. Then the Lord will have men who will bring offerings in righteousness (3:2–3).

There seems to be an element of purification in the winnowing that happens when Jesus burns up the chaff with unquenchable fire (Mt. 3:12). The chaff may represent the sin in our lives; Jesus will purify us by getting rid of all that is worthless in our lives. This understanding is supported by Paul's description of judgment in 1 Corinthians 3:

[A man's work] will be shown for what it is, because the Day will bring it to light. It will be revealed with fire, and the fire will test the quality of each man's work. If what he has built survives, he will receive his reward. If it is burned up, he will suffer loss; he himself will be saved, but only as one escaping through the flames (vv. 13–15).

Peter gives the image of a fiery furnace where we are refined by fire as gold is. The outcome is that our faith is proved genuine and Jesus Christ is glorified:

These [trials] have come so that your faith—of greater worth than gold, which perishes even though refined by fire—may be proved genuine and may result in praise, glory and honor when Jesus Christ is revealed (1 Pet. 1:7).

This idea of purification is also in view in "the words of the Amen, the faithful and true witness":

I counsel you to buy from me gold refined in the fire, so you can become rich; and white clothes to wear, so you can cover your shameful nakedness; and salve to put on your eyes, so you can see (Rev. 3:18).

## The Character of God

What else do we know from Scripture that might give us insight into the nature and purpose of hell? We know that God can do nothing that would violate His own character. Since He is perfectly holy, righteous, loving, merciful, and true, He can do nothing that is unholy, unrighteous, unloving, unmerciful, or inconsistent with truth. Since He is good, we can be confident that all His purposes are good. He is the one to define what "good" is, and He helps us understand what He means by "good." Whatever hell is, we can be confident that if God made it, then it is good and has a good purpose.

## Summary

We might summarize these observations as follows:

- Unless hell has existed since eternity past, it came or will come into being at some point.

- It is unlikely that hell existed with the Father, Son, and Holy Spirit in eternity past.

- If hell was created, it must have had a designer and creator, either God or Satan.

- Hell must have come into being before, during, or after the creation of the universe.

- Since God is omnipresent, it is impossible to be out of the presence of God.

- "Hell" is typically characterized by fire.

- Fire can represent the presence of God.

- Fire can be a symbol of judgment.

- Fire is associated with light.

- Fire can be for purification or refinement.

- God never violates His own holiness, love, mercy, truth, or goodness.

- If God is responsible for hell, then it has a good purpose, however God defines "good."

*Part 2 will describe various explanations that have been offered for the concept of hell.*

# 40

# WHAT IS HELLFIRE? PART 2

In Part 1 (#39) we examined Scripture to find principles that can help us understand what hell is. Here in Part 2 I present some possible explanations that can be supported by Scripture. Consider which of these scenarios is most consistent with what we know about God and His purposes, or whether there might be another explanation that is better still.

## The Inferno?

So what is hell? Is it the lake of fire, where Satan, the Beast, the False Prophet, and those whose names are not written in the Book of Life are tormented forever? Is it Dante's Inferno, where the lost suffer endless torments and are forced to abandon all hope? Is it the place imagined by Jonathan Edwards, where "Your bodies...will remain to roast through eternity"?[1] Is it the place envisioned by Charles Spurgeon, "where beds of flame are the fearful couches upon which spirits groan,...where the only music is the mournful symphony of damned spirits; where howling, groaning, moaning, wailing and gnashing of teeth make up the horrid concert,...where soul and body endure as much of infinite wrath as the finite can bear"?[2]

For anyone who believes that the Bible is the Word of God, "hell" means whatever Jesus and the authors of Scripture meant it to mean. Does the depiction of hell by Dante, Edwards, Spurgeon, Calvin, Augustine, and others with similar ideas throughout church history accurately portray what Jesus and the writers of Scripture had in mind? Or have people extrapolated beyond what Scripture teaches to come up with this notion of eternal conscious torment (ECT)? Does ECT sound like the work of the God of the Bible, or more like the work of Satan, or a pagan notion or a bad dream or a medieval doom painting?[3] If all of God's purposes are good, what is the good purpose of creating billions of people who will end up being tormented forever? As a personal question, have you ever been horribly burned in a fire or experienced chronic, unremitting, excruciating pain? What purpose did it serve? Try to imagine how God might bring good from billions of people suffering such pain endlessly.

## Separation from God?

The idea of hell as eternal separation from God is a popular way to soften the teaching of eternal conscious torment. It may not include the unbearable physical pain of being continually burned without being consumed, but it can still be described as torment because the person is forever separated from God and from all that is good—there will be no beauty, no friendship, no love, no peace, no joy, no comfort, no hope. People will experience the utter despair of knowing that they have missed their opportunity for repentance and there is no possibility of ever finding relief from their condition.

Could hell be a state of separation from God? Here is some evidence from the Bible. The people of Israel were thrust out of the presence of God for their sin:

> So the Lord was very angry with Israel and *removed them from his presence....* The Lord rejected all the people of Israel; he afflicted them and gave them into the hands of plunderers, until he thrust them from his presence (2 Ki. 17:18, 20).

The separation that Isaiah speaks of in this life could become permanent in the next: "Your iniquities have *separated you* from your God; your sins have hidden his face from you, so that he will not hear" (Is. 59:2).

And Jesus makes some similar statements to that effect:

> Not everyone who says to me, "Lord, Lord," will
> enter the kingdom of heaven, but only the one who
> does the will of my Father who is in heaven. Many
> will say to me on that day, "Lord, Lord, did we not
> prophesy in your name and in your name drive out
> demons and in your name perform many miracles?"
> Then I will tell them plainly, "I never knew you. *Away
> from me*, you evildoers!" (Mt. 7:21–23).

> *Depart from me*, you who are cursed, into the eternal
> fire prepared for the devil and his angels (Mt. 25:41).

In 2 Thessalonians 1:8–9, Paul says, "He will punish those
who do not know God and do not obey the gospel of our
Lord Jesus. They will be punished with everlasting destruction and shut out from the presence of the Lord and from the
majesty of his power." (But see Passage 14 in Chapter 5,
"Presuppositions and Interpretations," for a different translation and interpretation.)

But what are we to do with the fact that God is omnipresent? As Solomon acknowledges, heaven and earth cannot
contain God: "The heavens, even the highest heaven, cannot
contain you" (1 Ki. 8:27). There is nowhere that anyone can
go to be out of the presence of God. Therefore the verses
above may refer to separation from God in the sense of
distance in their *relationship* but not in their *location*. To be
separated from God in this sense would mean that a person
would never experience His love and friendship.

## Annihilation?

Another way to soften the idea of ECT is to say that the
unbelieving will cease to exist. Some who find the idea of
everlasting suffering unbearable have opted for "annihilation," or "conditional immortality," the idea that people are
not inherently immortal but are granted immortality if and
only if they receive the gift of eternal life through Christ.

Those who fail to accept the gift will be judged and punished and eventually destroyed. To incorporate the idea of "eternal" punishment, some suggest that the "everlasting destruction" might be an "asymptotic" process where a person's existence diminishes but never reaches the limit of non-existence. It could also be said that annihilation is "eternal" because the consequences of going out of existence last forever.

The idea of annihilation is more palatable than thinking of people suffering endlessly, but is it correct? Eminent Christians like John Stott have considered the doctrine of endless hell emotionally intolerable and have found support in Scripture for annihilation. They point to the fact that the immortality of the soul is a Greek concept, not a biblical one, and that eternal life is granted to a person when he receives it through faith in Christ, before which time he is only potentially immortal. The language of "destruction" also supports the idea that people will be completely consumed and will no longer exist. For example, Matthew 10:28 makes it sound as if both soul and body will be snuffed out in hell:

> Do not be afraid of those who kill the body but cannot kill the soul. Rather, be afraid of the One who can destroy both soul and body in hell.

This position also allows for punishment in proportion to the crime: people are punished for a longer or shorter time depending on the degree of their sin. This view would seem to be more compatible with the justice of God than never-ending suffering/separation for all the unredeemed alike; if it is infinite for all, there is no distinction between degrees of evil. The doctrine of *conditional* immortality is also consistent with the fact that the gospel is an *offer* of eternal life (immortality), which we do not have apart from Christ:

> I am the living bread that came down from heaven. Whoever eats this bread will live forever. This bread is my flesh, which I will give for the life of the world (John 6:51).

Christ Jesus has destroyed death and brought life and immortality to light through the gospel (2 Tim. 1:10).

So each of these positions on hell—ECT, separation from God, annihilation—accounts for some truths in Scripture regarding the eternal state. Yet each is also lacking in some way. Is there an alternative?

*Part 3 will continue this series by offering another picture of "hellfire"—one that I believe is more consistent with the truths discussed in Part 1 and with all that we know about God's character and purposes.*

---

[1]Jonathan Edwards, "The Eternity of Hell Torments," 1739. He goes on to say, "Do but consider what it is to suffer extreme torment forever and ever: to suffer it day and night from one year to another, from one age to another, and from one thousand ages to another (and so adding age to age, and thousands to thousands), in pain, in wailing and lamenting, groaning and shrieking, and gnashing your teeth –with your souls full of dreadful grief and amazement, [and] with your bodies and every member full of racking torture; without any possibility of getting ease; without any possibility of moving God to pity by your cries; without any possibility of hiding yourselves from him; without any possibility of diverting your thoughts from your pain; without any possibility of obtaining any manner of mitigation, or help, or change for the better."

[2]Rev. Charles H. Spurgeon, "Profit and Loss," 1856.

[3]It is revealing to explore the development of the concept of eternal damnation in both Christian and non-Christian cultures. A study of the history of the doctrine of hell is not a focus of this book and in fact could be an entire book in itself. For an overview, read "How & When the Idea of Eternal Torment Invaded Church Doctrine" (http://sumo.ly/e1ID). Author Jacob McMillen contends that the doctrine of eternal torment "was not a pillar of church doctrine for the first 5 centuries after Christ" and that St. Augustine was largely responsible for making a never-ending hell part of Christian "orthodoxy." Ilaria Ramelli's *The Christian Doctrine of Apokatastasis* is a scholarly work on beliefs regarding hell and restoration in the early centuries of the Church. The website hopebeyondhell.net also has resources on this topic and links to other websites.

# 41

# WHAT IS HELLFIRE? PART 3

P art 1 laid the groundwork for this series by identifying some biblical principles that have a bearing on our understanding of hell. Part 2 gave three pictures of what hell might be, each of which finds support in Scripture. Here in Part 3 I attempt to put it all together to formulate an alternate view of "hellfire" that is more consistent with the revelation we have of God's character and purposes.

## Caution about Assumptions

Before attempting to answer the question "What is hellfire?" we really should examine the assumptions that are implicit in the question. Many English Bibles have taken four different biblical words (*Hades, Sheol, Gehenna,* and *Tartarus*) and translated them with the same English word (hell). That word is invested with a meaning that the original speakers and writers never intended. Detailed studies of these four words and of the origins of the concept of hell have been done by many people more capable than I. For example, a number of nineteenth-century writers have written in-depth discussions of these words and traced the origins of the prevailing notion of hell.[1] Contemporary writers have come to many of the same conclusions: George Sarris[2] devotes two chapters to a discussion of the words translated as "hell" in *Heaven's Doors: Wider Than You Ever Believed!* and John Noe[3] has written a thoroughly researched and documented exploration of the whole concept of hell. I will not attempt to convey all their conclusions, but let me say that we need to be very careful not to make unwarranted assumptions.

For example, we should not make the mistake of equating *Hades* and *Gehenna*—an easy mistake to make if both are translated with the same word. *Sheol* and *Hades* are the Hebrew and Greek words, respectively, that refer to the place of the dead (both the righteous and the wicked). Neither should we assume that when Jesus was talking about *Gehenna,* He was referring to "hell" as we commonly conceive of it—a place or state of after-death punishment for the wicked. In His day, *Gehenna* was known as the accursed place outside Jerusalem where children had been sacrificed to pagan gods and where dead bodies were dumped without a proper burial. As John Noe points out, *Gehenna* "was and still is a proper noun and the name of a real, literal, familiar, this-world place." This fact and certain Old Testament prophecies "render as highly suspect our modern-day concept of Jesus' *Gehenna* being a metaphorical, other-worldly, afterlife place of eternal conscious punishment and torment that we have come to know as 'hell.'"[4] Rather, Jesus was speaking of a literal, impending, this-world judgment resulting in suffering and death.

Nor should we assume that "the lake of fire" is equivalent to hell. In Scripture, the lake of fire is never identified with any of the words translated as "hell." (In fact, *Hades* is thrown "into" the lake of fire, indicating that they are not the same.) Rather than attempting to translate the four "hell" words with equivalent English words, which do not exist, I believe it would be better to transliterate the words and then explain what they meant in the minds of the original speakers, writers, hearers, and readers.

With these considerations in mind, let's look at how we might understand the biblical references to "hell" and after-death judgment.

## "Hellfire" as the Presence of God

Western Christians tend to think of "hell" as a place of torment or a state of being separated from God. But the teaching of Orthodox Christianity may be closer to the truth in this regard: that all will be in the direct, intense presence of

God, but each one will experience it differently depending upon his or her relationship with God. For example, some contemporary Orthodox scholars put it this way: "Those theological symbols, heaven and hell, are not crudely understood as spatial destinations but rather refer to the experience of God's presence according to two different modes."[5] An analogy might be the blazing fire that instantly destroyed Nebuchadnezzar's soldiers. It not only failed to harm Shadrach, Meshach, and Abednego, but it gave them an astounding, unforgettable experience of intimacy with God, because they worshiped Him alone and refused to bow to any other.

Isaiah understood that the presence of God is like a fire. He asks, "Who among us can dwell with the consuming fire?" Answer: "He who walks righteously and speaks uprightly" (Is. 33:14–15). Only the righteous can stand in the direct presence of God without being burned; their eyes "will behold the king in his beauty" (v. 17)

Gregory of Nazianzus, who lived in the fourth century, believed that God Himself is both paradise and punishment. He spoke of "the Judgment and the Reward according to the righteous scales of God":

> This will be Light to those whose mind is purified (that is, God—seen and known) proportionate to their degree of purity, which we call the Kingdom of heaven; but to those who suffer from blindness of their ruling faculty, darkness, that is estrangement from God, proportionate to their blindness here.[6]

Those who know God and are right with Him will see His blazing holiness and feel reverent fear but will experience His presence as a state of joy and light. They will bow before their King, be received by Him, and have intense intimacy with Him.

On the other hand, those who are in rebellion against Him will have a very different experience. They will stand naked before the Judge of all the earth, with no robes of righteousness, not pleading the name of Jesus. They will fully experience what the writer of Hebrews was talking about:

A fearful expectation of judgment and of raging fire that will consume the enemies of God (10:27).

It is a dreadful thing to fall into the hands of the living God (10:31).

Our God is a consuming fire (12:29).

Imagine having all your sins laid bare before the King and Judge of the universe! Think of the worst thing you have ever done and the most important person you have offended, and remember the deep regret, the knot of anxiety in the pit of your stomach, the despair—and multiply it all a million times over. There will be weeping and gnashing of teeth, agonizing guilt, and bitter anguish. Even those who once did evil with a seared conscience will now, in the presence of an infinitely holy God, be fully aware of the depth of their depravity. When they see God face to face, every deep recess of their hearts will be exposed. Their consciences will be made acutely aware of the heinousness of their sins, and they will feel the torment of their own utter ruin. They will see God in all His burning holiness and will experience the terror of His consuming fire.

Consider this passage describing the dedication of Solomon's temple. It catches a glimpse of what it is like to be in the presence of our holy God—both the terror and the glory:

> When Solomon finished praying, fire came down from heaven and consumed the burnt offering and the sacrifices, and the glory of the Lord filled the temple. The priests could not enter the temple of the Lord because the glory of the Lord filled it. When all the Israelites saw the fire coming down and the glory of the Lord above the temple, they knelt on the pavement with their faces to the ground, and they worshiped and gave thanks to the Lord, saying, He is good; his love endures forever (2 Chron. 7:1–3).

Daniel also used the image of fire (not a "lake of fire" but a "river of fire") as he struggled to try to describe his vision of the presence of God in all His majesty:

As I looked, thrones were set in place, and the Ancient of Days took his seat.... His throne was flaming with fire, and its wheels were all ablaze. A river of fire was flowing, coming out from before him... (Dan. 7:9–10).

The writer of Hebrews describes the contrast between being in the presence of God without a mediator and being in His presence with Jesus as our Mediator:

You have not come to a mountain that can be touched and that is burning with fire; to darkness, gloom and storm; to a trumpet blast or to such a voice speaking words that those who heard it begged that no further word be spoken to them, because they could not bear what was commanded: "If even an animal touches the mountain, it must be stoned to death." The sight was so terrifying that Moses said, "I am trembling with fear."

But you have come to Mount Zion, to the city of the living God, the heavenly Jerusalem. You have come to thousands upon thousands of angels in joyful assembly, to the church of the firstborn, whose names are written in heaven. You have come to God, the Judge of all, to the spirits of the righteous made perfect, to Jesus the mediator of a new covenant, and to the sprinkled blood that speaks a better word than the blood of Abel....

Therefore, since we are receiving a kingdom that cannot be shaken, let us be thankful, and so worship God acceptably with reverence and awe, for our "God is a consuming fire" (12:18–24, 28–29).

With these images in mind, we can see that a "lake of fire" is an apt metaphor for total immersion in God. It describes the intensity of being in His direct presence and captures both the terror and anguish experienced by the wicked in His presence, as well as the holiness and light experienced by the righteous. How much more reasonable than a literal lake with literal burning sulfur!

So I would suggest that none of the biblical words and images commonly assumed to refer to hell actually describes a place of never-ending conscious torment in the afterlife: *Sheol/Hades* is the place of the dead, *Gehenna* represents a terrible national judgment in this world, and the lake of fire is the intense presence of God. Part 4 will look at some of the hard passages in Revelation that speak of "everlasting torment with burning sulfur" and will suggest a purpose for "hell" that is consistent with the observations we have made about the character of God and the nature of His judgment.

---

[1]J. W. Hanson, "The Bible Hell," 1888, on tentmaker.org. Thomas B. Thayer, "The Biblical Doctrine of Hell," from *The Origin and History of the Doctrine of Endless Punishment*, 1855, on auburn.edu.

[2]George W. Sarris, *Heaven's Doors: Wider Than You Ever Believed.* 2017.

[3]John Noe, Ph.D., *Hell Yes / Hell No,* 2011.

[4]Ibid., pp 43, 52. See his detailed study of Jesus' use of the word *Gehenna.*

[5]Aristotle Papanikolaou and Elizabeth H. Prodromou, *Thinking Through Faith: New Perspectives from Orthodox Christian Scholars,* 2008.

[6]Gregory of Nazianzus, Oration on Holy Baptism (A.D. 381)

# 42

# WHAT IS HELLFIRE? PART 4

I would be remiss if I ended our study of hellfire without taking a hard look at passages that seem to teach clearly that eternal torment awaits those who finally reject the Savior. We will consider some possible ways to understand these passages and then wrap up our study of hellfire.

The most graphic image of judgment is the lake of fire, which is mentioned five times in Revelation and is also alluded to in 14:10. The way these passages are generally translated and interpreted, it would seem conclusive that unbelievers, along with the devil, the beast, and the false prophet, are destined for a state of horrific, never-ending torment:

> A third angel followed them and said in a loud voice: "If anyone worships the beast and his image and receives his mark on the forehead or on the hand, he, too, will drink of the wine of God's fury, which has been poured full strength into the cup of his wrath. He will be tormented with burning sulfur in the presence of the holy angels and of the Lamb. And the smoke of their torment rises for ever and ever. There is no rest day or night for those who worship the beast and his image, or for anyone who receives the mark of his name" (14:9–11).

> But the beast was captured, and with him the false prophet who had performed the miraculous signs on his behalf. With these signs he had deluded those who had received the mark of the beast and worshiped his image. The two of them were thrown alive into the fiery lake of burning sulfur (19:20).

And the devil who deceived them was thrown into the lake of burning sulfur, where the beast and the false prophet had been thrown. They will be tormented day and night for ever and ever" (20:10).

Then death and Hades were thrown into the lake of fire. The lake of fire is the second death (20:14)

If anyone's name was not found written in the book of life, he was thrown into the lake of fire (20:15).

But the cowardly, the unbelieving, the vile, the murderers, the sexually immoral, those who practice magic arts, the idolaters, the idolaters and all liars— their place will be in the fiery lake of burning sulfur. This is the second death (21:8).

These verses seem to seal the case for the eternal torment of the wicked. Revelation 20:10 says that the devil, the beast, and the false prophet were thrown into the lake of burning sulfur and will be tormented day and night for ever and ever, and verse 20:15 indicates that this will be the fate not just of the devil, the beast, and the false prophet, but also of all those whose names are not found written in the book of life.

But let's take a closer look at what these verses could mean.[1] The book of Revelation can be approached in a variety of ways, both within a traditional framework and within a universalist framework. The way these passages are translated and interpreted will depend on one's whole approach to eschatology, indeed on one's entire outlook on the character and purposes of God, but let me put forward some ideas to be thinking about. We will focus on Revelation 20:10, which says that the devil, the beast, and the false prophet are thrown into the lake of burning sulfur where they will be tormented for ever and ever, which will also be the fate of the wicked.

First, what is "the lake of fire and brimstone," or "the lake of burning sulfur" (τὴν λίμνην τοῦ πυρὸς καὶ θείου, *tēn limnēn tou pyros kai theiou*)? The word *pyros* is usually translated "fire" and can mean a literal or figurative fire. As we have seen, the image of fire is often associated with judgment and also with testing or the divine presence. Another important function of fire is purification, as in burning up chaff, refining gold to remove the dross, or burning up a person's worthless works. The dictionary definition of "brimstone" is just "sulfur," a nonmetallic element that burns with a strong odor. The Greek word is *theion* (θεῖον), related to the word *theios* (θεῖος), meaning "divine." Sulfur was used in ancient times for purification, and even today sulfur compounds are used in modern medicine to fight infection and treat illness. As Friberg's Analytical Lexicon states, *theion* was "anciently regarded as divine incense to purify and prevent contagion."

The word for "will be tormented" is the Greek *basanisthēsontai* (βασανισθήσονται) from *basanizō* (βασανίζω). The meaning of *basanizō* is to test metals by using a touchstone, a *basanos* (βάσανος). A touchstone is a hard black stone that was used to test the purity of silver or gold by observing the color of the marks made on the stone by the precious metals. So a touchstone is a test to determine the quality of something.

The Greek noun *basanos* can mean torture or torment, for example in the judicial examination of a person. Correspondingly, the verb *basanizō* can mean to question by applying torment. Matthew uses the word in 14:24 when he says that the boat was "beaten" or "battered" by the waves, and Peter says that righteous Lot was "tormented" by the wicked behavior of the people around him (2 Pet. 2:8). The word carries the idea of great distress or anguish, not necessarily deliberately inflicted but resulting from the nature of the situation.

The torment or distress is said to last "for ever and ever" (*eis tous aiōnas tōn aiōnōn*, εἰς τοὺς αἰῶνας τῶν αἰώνων). The basic meaning of *aion* is "age," like the English word "eon."[2] It is usually understood to mean an unbroken age, a very long time, or eternity, depending on the subject to which it is applied. The idea of endlessness is not inherent in the word; rather the end is not known. In his *Word Studies in the New Testament*, Marvin R. Vincent defines *aion* as:

a period of longer or shorter duration, having a beginning and an end, and complete in itself.... The word always carries the notion of time, and not of eternity.... Otherwise it would be impossible to account for the plural, or for such qualifying expressions as this age.... The adjective *aionios* in like manner carries the idea of time. Neither the noun nor the adjective, in themselves, carry the sense of endless or everlasting.[3]

What do we do with these observations? Could the fire and brimstone have a purifying function? Could *basanizō* refer to testing for the purpose of revealing and refining rather than torturing for the purpose of causing torment? Could this process be a long but finite period—just long enough to accomplish its purpose? In other words, could this lake of fire be God's means for purifying the wicked so that sin is actually eradicated from the universe, not simply punished forever?

The idea of fire for refining and purifying is a scriptural principle:

> But who can endure the day of his coming, and who can stand when he appears? For he is like a **refiner's fire** and like fullers' soap. He will sit as a **refiner and purifier** of silver, and he will **purify** the sons of Levi and **refine** them like gold and silver, and they will bring offerings in righteousness to the LORD (Mal. 3:2–3).

> For no one can lay a foundation other than that which is laid, which is Jesus Christ. Now if anyone builds on the foundation with gold, silver, precious stones, wood, hay, straw—each one's work will become manifest, for the Day will disclose it, because it will be **revealed by fire**, and **the fire will test what sort of work each one has done**. If the work that anyone has built on the foundation survives, he will receive a reward. If anyone's work is burned up, he will suffer loss, though he himself will be saved, but only as **through fire** (1 Cor. 3:11–15).

The tested genuineness of your faith—more precious than gold that perishes though it is **tested by fire**—may be found to result in praise and glory and honor at the revelation of Jesus Christ (1 Pet. 1:7).

Notice too that the lake of fire and brimstone where the process of *basanizō* takes place is not in some location apart from God; it is "in the presence of the holy angels and of the Lamb" (Rev. 14:10). In fact, as we have noted before, the lake of fire may actually *be* the presence of God. Daniel describes the throne of the Ancient of Days as "flaming with fire," and "a river of fire" flowing out from Him:

His throne was flaming with fire,
    and its wheels were all ablaze.
A river of fire was flowing,
    coming out from before him (Dan. 7:9–10).

Just as the fiery furnace of Daniel 3 destroyed the king's men while the Hebrew children not only were unharmed but had an intense experience of the presence of their God, the lake of fire affects people differently, depending on the condition of their hearts. Greek Orthodox priest Alexandre Kalomiros describes this phenomenon:

"For our God is a consuming fire" (Heb. 12:29). The very fire which purifies gold also consumes wood. Precious metals shine in it like the sun, rubbish burns with black smoke. All are in the same fire of Love.[4]

Another Greek Orthodox priest, Fr. Richard Demetrius Andrews, has a similar description:

Thus, what St. Paul is telling us is that God's fire works in two ways. It can be light, warm and purifying. Or God's fire can be torturous, burning and consuming us. The Church Fathers say that God's fire is actually His love. If we love Him and each other, especially those in need, then we experience God's love positively. If we don't love God and others, including our enemies, then we experience the negative aspect of God's love. The determining factor in how we experience the fire of God's love is the disposition of our heart and the righteousness of our deeds.[5]

In J. Preston Eby's "The Lake of Fire," he explains the purpose of the fire:

> Make no mistake! Our God is a consuming fire!... He will bring you to the foot of the cross of Jesus no matter how hot He has to build the fire around you! Even if long ages of fiery judgment and tormenting darkness fall upon you, they will last no longer than till the Great Fire of God has melted all arrogance into humility, and all that is self has died in the bloody sweat and all-saving cross of the Christ, which will never give up its redeeming power till sin and sinners have no more a name among the creatures of God.[6]

The exposure of our sins in the presence of God's holiness, with the realization of how great our transgressions and failures truly are, will in itself be torment. There will be plenty of weeping and gnashing of teeth. There will be the wailing of regret and the deep sorrow that comes from feeling the full impact of sin. Perhaps the mental anguish will be felt physically. Whatever the exact nature of the suffering, "it is a fearful thing to fall into the hands of the living God!"

The good news, however, is that this recognition of one's own sin is the first step toward receiving God's grace. Once people truly understand their own need, their total inability to fix themselves, and the depth of God's holiness, they are in a position to humbly accept His redemption. The judgment of both Christians and non-Christians will include going through the difficult and painful process of reconciliation, both with God and with all those we have hurt. But like the loving fatherly discipline described in Hebrews 12, the ultimate result will be "our good, that we may share in his holiness" and "a harvest of righteousness and peace" (vv. 10–11).

Will unrepentant sinners be allowed into heaven? Absolutely not! As long as they remain in that condition, they will not enter but will undergo punishment in the lake of fire:

> But as for the cowardly, the faithless, the detestable, as for murderers, the sexually immoral, sorcerers, idolaters, and all liars, their portion will be in the lake that burns with fire and sulfur, which is "the second death" (Rev. 21:8).

> Nothing unclean will ever enter [the city], nor anyone who does what is detestable or false, but only those who are written in the Lamb's book of life (Rev. 21:27).

Is that the end of the story for them? Absolutely not! They must repent and wash their robes so they might enter the city and be blessed:

> Blessed are those who wash their robes, so that they may have the right to the tree of life and that they may enter the city by the gates (Rev. 22:14).

The gates will never be shut and the invitation is always open:

> The Spirit and the Bride say, "Come." And let the one who hears say, "Come." And let the one who is thirsty come; let the one who desires take the water of life without price (Rev. 22:17).

Whenever I sing the line "Through gates of pearl streams in the countless host" from "For All the Saints," I picture vast multitudes of people streaming into the holy city. Among them are "the kings of the earth"—the kings who once were enemies of God. And the nations were once at war with God, but in that day the nations will be healed. As John says, "The leaves of the tree [of life] were for the healing of the nations" (Rev. 22:2).

As we noted at the outset of this book (Chapter 2), the Bible has seemingly contradictory statements and concepts about the final destiny of the human race. Either we live with the tension (which is what many choose to do) or we identify one concept as the fundamental, non-negotiable truth and interpret the apparently contradictory verses in light of that truth.[7] As I try to show in this book, the overwhelming weight of evidence is that God's ultimate purpose is the full redemption of His entire creation. Therefore, those passages that seem to say that the final outcome will be anything less should be understood within the framework of universal salvation. And it is particularly important to be careful when interpreting highly symbolic apocalyptic literature from the ancient Near East; trying to impose modern journalistic standards of accuracy and literalness, which may go against the big truths, can lead us desperately astray.

Knowing that Jesus will draw all people to Himself, we can be sure that He will continue calling them, in this life and the next, until His goal is accomplished. Knowing that Death and Hades will be thrown into the lake of fire (Rev. 20:14), we can rest in the fact that death and hell will have no more power. Knowing that in the end there will be no more death or mourning or pain and that God will surely be all in all, we can be confident that whatever exactly it is, the lake of fire will consume all evil so that the universe can be free of sin.

> Behold, the dwelling place of God is with man. He will dwell with them, and they will be his people, and God himself will be with them as their God. He will wipe away every tear from their eyes, and death shall be no more, neither shall there be mourning, nor crying, nor pain anymore, for the former things have passed away (Rev. 21:3–4).

> And he put all things under his feet and gave him as head over all things to the church, which is his body, the fullness of him who fills all in all (Eph. 1:22–23).

> When all things are subjected to him, then the Son himself will also be subjected to him who put all things in subjection under him, that God may be all in all (1 Cor. 15:28).

---

[1]I have compiled these observations using several tools:

Edward Beecher, *History of Opinions on the Scriptural Doctrine of Retribution,* 1878.

*A Greek English Lexicon of the New Testament and Other Early Christian Literature* 2nd ed. Bauer, Danker, Arndt, and Gingrich. 1979.

*Thayer's Greek-English Lexicon of the New Testament.* Joseph H. Thayer. Hendrickson Publishers, Inc. 1996. Reprinted from the fourth edition, 1896.

*The Analytical Greek Lexicon.* Zondervan Publishing House. 1974.

[2]For a thorough treatment of the word *aiōnios,* see *Terms for Eternity: Aiōnios and Aïdios in Classical and Christian Texts* by Ilaria Ramelli and David Konstan.

[3]Marvin R. Vincent's *Word Studies in the New Testament.* www.auburn.edu

[4]Alexandre Kalomiros, "The River of Fire." St. Nectarios Press. ©1980 blogs.ancientfaith.com

[5]Greek Orthodox priest, Fr. Richard Demetrius Andrews, stgeorgegoc.org

[6]J. Preston Eby. "The Lake of Fire," from *Savior of the World.* Eby gives an illustration of how fire, though it is devastating, can bring about a cleansing and purification. Once the purification is complete, the devastation can end: "More than three centuries ago when the Black Plague swept through London, England, more than 68,000 men, women, and children were sickened with the putrid fever, suffered nameless agonies, passed into delirium, sometimes with convulsions, and then died. Before the end of the terrible nightmare of anguish and death, what was thought to be an even greater tragedy occurred. The city caught fire, the whole heavens were ablaze as the Great Fire destroyed more than 13,200 homes and 89 churches. Most of the city, which was built largely of wood, lay in ashes. Wonder of wonders! As soon as the last dying embers cooled and the smoke cleared, the inhabitants of the city discovered that the Plague had been stayed! Not another person died of the epidemic. The Plague never returned. The fire had killed the bacteria-carrying fleas and rats that caused the Plague. It took a fire to do it!"

[7]As an example of this principle, there are verses you could pull out of the New Testament to make a case that Jesus is just a man, not God. But the preponderance of the evidence is that He is fully God as well as fully man. The verses that seem to indicate otherwise should be interpreted to fit the basic truth that Jesus is God incarnate.

# 43

# IRRESISTIBLE GRACE

Need a gift for the man who has everything? One Internet image suggests Irresistible Grace Cologne for Elect Men, by John Calvin Klein.

All kidding aside, here are some definitions of the Calvinist doctrine of irresistible grace:

> This act of drawing is an act of power, yet not of force; God in drawing of unwilling, makes willing in the day of His power: He enlightens the understanding, bends the will, gives an heart of flesh, sweetly allures by the power of His grace, and engages the soul to come to Christ, and give up itself to Him; he draws with the bands of love.
>
> —John Gill

> All those whom God hath predestinated unto life, and those only, he is pleased, in his appointed and accepted time, effectually to call, by his word and Spirit, out of that state of sin and death in which they are by nature, to grace and salvation by Jesus Christ; enlightening their minds spiritually and savingly to understand the things of God; taking away their heart of stone, and giving unto them an heart of flesh; renewing their wills, and by his almighty power determining them to that which is good, and effectually drawing them to Jesus Christ; yet so as they come most freely, being made willing by his grace."
>
> —Westminster Confession of Faith

Irresistible grace does not mean that God's grace is incapable of being resisted. Indeed, we are capable of resisting God's grace, and we do resist it. The idea is that God's grace is so powerful that it has the capacity to overcome our natural resistance to it. It is not that the Holy Spirit drags people kicking and screaming to Christ against their wills. The Holy Spirit changes the inclination and disposition of our wills, so that whereas we were previously unwilling to embrace Christ, now we are willing, and more than willing. Indeed, we aren't dragged to Christ, we run to Christ, and we embrace Him joyfully because the Spirit has changed our hearts.

—R. C. Sproul

Irresistible Grace is a Reformed teaching that states that when God calls his elect into salvation, they cannot resist. God offers to all people the gospel message. This is called the external call. But to the elect, God extends an internal call and it cannot be resisted. This call is by the Holy Spirit who works in the hearts and minds of the elect to bring them to repentance and regeneration whereby they willingly and freely come to God.

—Matt Slick

According to this doctrine, not a single one of the elect can forever resist God's grace. No matter how hardened their hearts might be initially, the Holy Spirit pursues them with the intent of changing the disposition of their will so that they inevitably come to repentance and embrace Him willingly.

However, according to Calvinists, this irresistible grace is *only* for the elect—the select few who have been chosen by God out of all humanity before the foundation of the world. The corollary is that God's grace *can* be resisted by the non-elect. In fact, it *will be* resisted by the non-elect forever. They will remain in a perpetual state of resistance and rebellion against the Lord. Some Calvinists would defend this doctrine by saying that no, the non-elect do *not* resist God's grace—because it is never offered to them. (As one put it, "In the Calvinist system most people do not resist his grace; His grace is not extended to the reprobate.") If he does not offer saving grace to them, then we can say only that they resist the scraps of common grace that he extends. (Or that he is an inadequate god who doesn't have enough grace to go around or a stingy god who withholds the grace he does have.)

I also believe in irresistible grace. Although we will never be able to comprehend fully the workings of God's grace, I think the explanations above accurately describe how God draws a rebellious and wicked person to repentance and faith—how the Holy Spirit changes a heart of stone to a heart of flesh. Where I differ with the Calvinists is that I believe He extends His grace to all and *nobody* can forever resist it. Sooner or later, His effectual grace will do its work in every single human being. We long for it to be sooner, so we share the gospel with them. But we do not despair if it is later, because we know that God's will that all come to repentance cannot be thwarted.

John 1:12–13 captures the interplay of divine sovereignty and human free will:

> But to all who did receive him, who believed in his name, he gave the right to become children of God, who were born, not of blood nor of the will of the flesh nor of the will of man, but of God.

It is our responsibility to receive Christ and to believe in His name, but *in the final analysis*, it is not by man's will but by God's will.

I invite you to study these explanations carefully and meditate on them prayerfully.

> In which view of Irresistible Grace—that it is for the elect only or that it is for all humanity—is the grace more powerful?

Which view fully eradicates sin from the universe, rather than allowing sin and rebellion to exist forever?

Which view is more consistent with the sovereignty and heart of God as revealed in Scripture?

Which one is more glorifying to God?

# 44

# WHAT DOES IT TAKE
# TO GET INTO HEAVEN?

Y ou may have shared the gospel many times, and I'm sure you care about getting it right. You care about what happens to people after they die, and if you believe that all people will end up either in heaven or in hell, then you want to make sure you present the truth clearly so they can make an informed and wise choice in response to it.

But have you ever tried to formulate a concise, coherent statement of what it takes to get into heaven? Suppose you want to distill the essence of the gospel into its simplest form in order to help people understand what it is they must do or believe in order to get into heaven and stay out of hell. Of course you don't want to stop with the minimum requirements just to squeak into heaven, but let's start at the beginning.

The box $x$ represents what a person *must* believe and/or do in order to be saved; that is, if you do *not* do $x$, you will *not* be saved. Therefore, you have to put the same thing in both $x$ boxes below:

If you believe/do $\boxed{\phantom{xx}}^{\,x}$, you will go to heaven.

If you do *not* believe/do $\boxed{\phantom{xx}}^{\,x}$, you will not go to heaven.

Before reading on, get a paper and pencil. Think about what you would put in the boxes (same thing in both boxes!) and *write it down*. (Don't cheat!) And please don't cop out and say the gospel can't be reduced to a formula, it depends, only God can judge, etc. To this all-important question regarding where they will spend eternity, we ought to be able to give people a clear answer. Furthermore, they long to know what has happened to their loved ones who have died; if we are the bearers of the truth about the ultimate questions of the universe, we should be able to give some decent answers to this question—not the question of what happens to any one person in particular, which we cannot know, but at least what God requires of people in general.

Calvinists would say that our salvation is solely dependent on God's sovereignty, not on anything that *we* choose to do. In this book I challenge Calvinists on some of their beliefs; here is a challenge for Arminians, who hold that human free will is key: You believe that Jesus died for all, but some people go to heaven and some to hell. What is it that sets you apart from your unsaved neighbor? Why do you go to heaven while he does not? (In other words, what is *x*? Try to articulate it carefully!) If *Jesus* has done the same for both of you, then the deciding factor is something *you* do that your neighbor fails to do, even if the "something" is simply receiving the gift. Do you see the problem here?

If you have a good answer to the question of what *x* is, please let me know. I have never heard a coherent explanation of what you need to do to get into heaven, *without* which you go to hell. Every answer is fraught with buts and what-ifs—"But it's not fair!" "But what about those who have never heard the gospel?" "What if the person is mentally challenged or too young to understand?" If we can't come up with a good answer to the question of how to get into heaven, maybe it's time to ask whether it's even the right question. Perhaps we need to take another look at the whole question of heaven and hell and who's where and how you get there—and whether we should even be thinking in those terms.

The standard evangelical concept of the afterlife is that there are two places you can go—one a place of perfect bliss and the other a place of everlasting torment—and that you are locked into one or the other by what you believe and do in this life. You are either "saved" or "unsaved," "born again" or "unregenerate," a "believer" or an "unbeliever." You can repent and get saved any time before you die, but the moment you take your last breath, your fate is sealed and you go to the place where you will spend eternity. There are many variants of this doctrine (see the chart of Christian views of heaven and hell in Appendix C), but they are consistent in that there are two opposite and eternal destinies.

I would like to suggest that Scripture teaches a different view of God's Kingdom and purposes, one that is thoroughly satisfying to our sense of reason, compassion, and justice.

First of all, notice that heaven and hell are never juxtaposed in Scripture; one is never presented as the antithesis of the other. Some passages suggest two different destinies (e.g., John 3:18; Matthew 25:31–46), but these are never identified as "heaven" and "hell." Could it be that we have set up a dichotomy that is not true to the Word of God? Is our definition of "hell" based on the Bible, or on human (or even pagan) ideas of retribution?

It is with caution that I call into question the "orthodox" view that a majority of Christians have held for most of church history, but at the same time, it's healthy to challenge our entrenched ideas and see if they stand up to scrutiny. The majority is not always right! I'm sure that my understanding of what will happen after we die is entirely inadequate, but perhaps it could get us thinking along different lines.

As I suggested above, I believe the idea of exactly two opposite destinies is mistaken. Salvation is not like the Sorting Hat of Hogwarts! Although the Bible speaks of believers/unbelievers, the righteous/the wicked, saved/unsaved, etc., human beings don't divide neatly into two discrete categories. The "two-track" system has enormous problems. For one thing, even if you take into account that there are huge gradations of blessings in heaven and punishments in hell, in the end all that really matters in that model is whether you are united with God or separated from Him for eternity. Does it really matter whether your mansion has ten rooms or fifty, as long as Jesus has prepared a place for you? In hell, will you notice if the fire is only 3000 degrees instead of 5000 degrees?

To give a mathematical analogy, heaven will be so spectacularly wonderful that you might give it an average value of positive one trillion. Because of their service to Christ, some people will experience extra blessings—maybe one trillion, one hundred billion. Those who fail to use their gifts to serve God will suffer loss—maybe only nine hundred billion. Conversely, hell might have a value of negative one trillion. Jesus said it would be more bearable in the judgment for some than for others. So will the people of Sodom be bumped up a few notches so they suffer less than the people of Capernaum? And if the suffering is infinite in duration for all, can it be said that one person has it better or worse than another?

Instead of the two-track approach to our eternal destiny, I submit that we should view all of creation and the entirety of history and eternity as the Kingdom of God. What God does after we die is a continuation of what He has been doing in this world, with the final goal that He will "unite all things in Christ" (Eph. 1:10), "reconcile to Himself all things" (Col. 1:20), and be "all in all" (1 Cor. 1:28). God's mercy endures forever; it doesn't come to a screeching halt the moment a person takes his last breath. He will continue to "work out everything in conformity with the purpose of His will" (Eph. 1:11), which includes wanting "all men to be saved" by "Christ Jesus, who gave himself as a ransom for all men" (1 Tim. 2:4–6). This outworking of His will includes not simply the judgment and punishment of sin, but the eradication of it.

In this understanding, instead of assigning people to one track or the other, God has a tailor-made destiny for every individual, depending upon the person's capacity to understand, what he does or fails to do, what he believes or fails to believe, the knowledge he has received, the experiences he has had, and all the factors that make each of us who we are. God will use His infinite wisdom, justice, and compassion to judge the person in a way that is perfectly fair and perfectly loving. He will remember our idle words and will make us give an account of them in the day of judgment (Mt. 12:36). He will also remember every cup of cold water given for His sake and will reward it (Mt. 10:42). Nothing escapes His notice; He will give rewards and punishments in accordance with His perfect knowledge and justice.

We will all stand before the judgment seat and have to give an account of our lives. People's experience of standing before God will be vastly different, depending on their relationship with Him and how they have lived. Those sins that we have brought to the cross have already been forgiven, buried, and forgotten. Those we refuse to bring to the cross must be dealt with before we will be fit to be in God's presence for eternity. One who has lived for God can expect to hear, "Well done, good and faithful servant." Those who have defied Him and harmed others will find out what a fearful thing it is to fall into the hands of the Living God. Have you ever had to go to court? Did you feel fear clutching at your chest? Even the sight of flashing lights and the sound of a siren closing in behind you on the highway creates a knot in the stomach; imagine that feeling multiplied a million times over when you stand before the Judge of all the earth!

Judgment will bring weeping and gnashing of teeth. I envision the guilty ones feeling enormous regret when they see the infinite compassion they have rejected. I also suspect that they will experience a measure of the suffering they have inflicted on others. Perhaps it will be physical pain, or maybe it will be the mental torment of coming to the full realization of what they have done, like when you realize that you have done some awful thing. Can you imagine what it would be like to kill someone in a car accident? The crimes we have committed against God are far greater! The judgment of the wicked can be likened to searing fire—fire that exposes their evil and causes them to reap the consequences they may have avoided on earth.

Yet that fire is not simply for judgment; it is also for purification. God's desire is not just to punish the sin but to do away with it. The cross of Christ does not lose its power after we die but is still there, calling people to repent and let Jesus take their sins on Himself. There will probably be those who continue to defy and resist God, even in the face of direct judgment, but I believe that ultimately His kindness and His severity will bring even the most hardened to repentance. I think the Calvinists got it right with "irresistible grace"—in the end, *no one* will be able to forever resist God's infinite grace, expressed in both the severity of judgment and in His "kindness, tolerance and patience" (Rom. 2:4). As each of the most wretched sinners finally bows the knee and whole-heartedly proclaims Jesus as Lord and becomes reconciled to God and to everyone they have hurt, the Kingdom of God will have reached the fulfillment of His purpose.

I know that some evangelical feathers have been ruffled by what I have said so far, and now I'll make it worse. The cornerstone of evangelical teaching regarding salvation is that salvation is by grace alone through faith alone, so any mention of "works" in connection with salvation is suspect. But as I suggested above, I think our works play an important role in our destiny—not that we can earn our way to heaven, but that God will consider our works along with our faith as He plans our future.

Recent celebrations of the 500th anniversary of the beginning of the Reformation reminded us that Luther and the Reformers did an important service by rediscovering the truth that "the just shall live by faith." By looking to Scripture and fighting against the abuses of the Church, they helped restore the simple biblical truth that we cannot earn or buy God's favor. We can never be good enough to merit heaven; we can be in right relationship with God only through the merits of Jesus Christ. But in the process I'm afraid the Reformation lost some of the biblical emphasis on works. The Bible actually has a lot more to say about works (how we live) than about faith (what we believe). We get nervous talking about the necessity of works (and Luther even threw out the book of James for its emphasis on works), but we shouldn't shy away from what the Bible says about works.

In Romans 2:6–10, right on the heels of stating that the righteous shall live by faith, Paul says

God "will give to each person according to what he has done." To those who by persistence in doing good seek glory, honor, and immortality, he will give eternal life. But for those who are self-seeking and who reject the truth and follow evil, there will be wrath and anger. There will be trouble and distress for every human being who does evil; first for the Jew, then for the Gentile; but glory, honor and peace for everyone who does good: first for the Jew, then for the Gentile.

Commentators say that yes, God judges according to works, but nobody can persist in doing good anyway, so this passage isn't really promising eternal life for doing good since you can't do it well enough. But I think it means that God *will* take into account what you do, as well as what you believe, as He determines your eternal life (ζωή αἰώνιος, *zoe aionios*)—your life in the age to come. If you are self-seeking and reject the truth and follow evil, you will experience wrath and anger, trouble and distress. But to the extent that you do good, you will experience glory, honor, and peace.

James describes the interaction between faith and works in James 2:14–26. You can go to great lengths to explain that James doesn't really mean that "a person is justified by what he does and not by faith alone" (or you can ditch the whole book, as Luther did)—or you can take James's argument at face value and conclude that our faith and our deeds go hand-in-hand and God will assess both as He evaluates our lives.

As Paul explains, the law itself is powerless to save us—it just highlights our inability to live up to it perfectly and points us to the Savior. Nevertheless, we are expected to follow God's law and obey His Word, and He will not ignore our efforts to do so, however faltering. Doesn't your heart tell you that God will reward good works and punish evil? It's true: goodness and decency, even in those who do not profess faith in Christ, will not go unnoticed and unrewarded; and evil and violence, even (or maybe especially) in those who do profess faith in Christ, will not go unnoticed and unpunished.

In Romans 14 Paul says that Christ died and returned to life so that he might be the Lord of both the dead and the living. Then he states, "we will all stand before God's judgment seat.... Each of us will give an account of himself to God" (vv. 9–12). He is speaking to *believers* here, as he is in 2 Corinthians 5:9–10, where he says, "So we make it our goal to please him.... For we must all appear before the judgment seat of Christ, that each one may receive what is due him for the things done while in the body, whether good or bad." God sees it all, and *both* believers and unbelievers will answer to Him. Those who have put their trust in Christ will be able to plead His blood for their sins, though we all will need some cleansing to be fit for heaven. Those who have not yet trusted Christ will face judgment for the evil they have done, but I believe they will be given opportunity to come to the cross too.

Although you can make a case that the Bible teaches that there are two and only two places where people go after death, and that one's fate is locked in at the time of death, there are massive problems with that view. As you can see from the chart in Appendix C, there is no consensus about who goes where. Some claim that salvation is only for the elect and the rest go to hell. Some think salvation is for those who respond to the light they have; others think you have to profess explicit faith in Christ. Some think there are many in heaven and few in hell, and others think it's the other way around. Some believe in eternal torment and others believe the wicked will go out of existence.

If we can't get our story straight, then maybe we need to re-examine the whole two-track paradigm and see if perhaps we have created a system that is not taught in Scripture. I invite you to offer your own minimum conditions for getting into heaven and staying out of hell. I challenge you to give it some real thought and formulate a coherent statement. If you have trouble defining the conditions for salvation, then consider looking at it through a different framework. Please take it seriously—what could be more important than presenting the truth about people's eternal destiny!

# 45

# LET JUSTICE ROLL ON LIKE A RIVER

As I think about the whole concept of justice, I ask myself, What constitutes true justice? How is human justice similar to and different from divine justice? Will there ever be complete justice?

The dictionary defines *justice* as "the quality of being just; righteousness, equitableness, or moral rightness; the administering of deserved punishment or reward." That which is *just* is "guided by truth, reason, justice, and fairness; in keeping with truth or fact; rightful, equitable; given or awarded rightly; deserved, as a sentence, punishment, or reward."

Our human justice system can give us insight into God's justice, because our sense of justice is derived from the conscience and reason He has given us. He has planted in us a sense of right and wrong, and although it is imperfect, we should pay attention to what it tells us.

What does justice look like in our human legal system? Let's take the case of robbery: a thief breaks into a home and steals a diamond ring. Justice would involve capturing the thief, trying and punishing him, and returning the ring to its rightful owner. What about someone who embezzles an elderly couple's life savings? Again, justice means *making it right*: punishing the perpetrator and forcing him to restore what he has taken unlawfully.

So justice involves at least punishing the wrongdoer and making restitution to those who have been wronged. It would be nice if our legal system could reform criminals and make them into productive members of society, but it is not particularly successful at rehabilitation. It might be able to modify behavior—if you get picked up for speeding and slapped with a $300 fine, you might mind your manners in the future, or if you know you'll get life in prison for murder, you might think twice before killing someone. It can give criminals the punishment they deserve and prevent them from committing future crimes—either by jailing them or putting them to death—but it is powerless to really transform anyone. If our legal system manages to capture a criminal, give him a fair trial, impose a fair sentence, and compel him to make restitution to the victim, it will have done its job.

Even at its best, the human legal system cannot provide perfect justice. Can it restore the peace of mind of the homeowner whose refuge has been violated and whose security has been shattered? Can it restore the health and joy of the elderly couple who worked their whole lives in anticipation of spending their golden years together and now have seen their dreams ruined? Can it restore the trust of an abused child or the virginity of the rape victim?

At its worst, our legal system can make a complete travesty of justice. It can be guilty of the charge Isaiah made in 5:20: "Woe to those who call evil good and good evil, who put darkness for light and light for darkness, who put bitter for sweet and sweet for bitter." Given the limited knowledge of human beings and our inability to discern wisely and our capacity for evil, it is to be expected that complete justice will never be realized in this life.

As Christians we try to comfort ourselves with the fact that God is the Just Judge and will ultimately bring about complete and perfect justice. Every injustice perpetrated in our world will be corrected by the One who judges justly. In His infinite wisdom He knows all the hurts that have been suffered, and He will perfectly execute the components of justice: punishing all the evildoers and making restitution to all who have been wronged, as well as rewarding those who do good.

But how can this be? All of us have been both victims *and* wrongdoers. The sexual predator was probably a victim himself as a defenseless little child. What would justice for him look like? The thief who steals to support his drug habit may have been born of a drug-addicted mother. What is an equitable outcome of such a situation? Even those of us who are not overtly depraved are a complex mixture of good and evil. Yes, our sins are forgiven in Christ, but is that the end of the story? Will there not be final resolution of and restitution for all the injustices in our world?

Most troubling of all, what about murder? How often have family members and friends of a murder victim expressed relief that some measure of justice has been accomplished with the conviction of the murderer, only to add "It will never bring our loved one back." Our human justice system is powerless to bring about full justice in the sense of restoring the lives of those who have been murdered. We can take another life to even the score, but we can't achieve real equity.

But God can! He is fully able to bring about complete restitution for all losses, including bringing murder victims back from the dead to be reunited with their loved ones in heaven. But what if the murder victim is himself an unbeliever? The traditional Christian view says that that person will spend eternity in hell, forever separated from loved ones. His punishment means that justice for his loved ones—i.e., restoration of what was stolen from them—is not achieved.

Is that the best God can do? No! His infinite wisdom and infinite power and infinite righteousness will be able to achieve *perfect* justice, including bringing back from the dead those who have lost their lives unjustly. They themselves will undergo judgment and will have to answer for their own sins, but ultimately they will be not just rehabilitated but fully transformed and restored to those they have been taken from. Only God could weave together the infinite number of factors in the lives of all humanity to bring about perfect justice for all. There is hope! God will punish all evil, reward all good, and restore all that has been lost!

Will not the Judge of all the earth do right?
(Genesis 18:25)

Behold my servant, whom I uphold,
my chosen, in whom my soul delights;
I have put my Spirit upon him;
He will bring forth justice to the nations....
He will faithfully bring forth justice.
He will not grow faint or be discouraged
till he has established justice in the earth;
Is. 42:1–4

# 46

# ETERNAL PUNISHMENT
# BY LEWIS CARROLL

Lewis Carroll is best known for authoring *Alice's Adventures in Wonderland* and its sequel *Through the Looking-Glass,* but he was also a brilliant logician. In some of his writings he used logic to explore religious ideas. If we want to give a reasonable defense of our faith, we should

**Off with their heads!**

not discard the sense of reason that God has given us. There are many mysteries and paradoxes in the faith that are beyond our comprehension, but at the same time there is also a beautiful simplicity that is satisfying to our God-given sense of reason. As Paul did, we can use logic to appeal to people whose minds are so inclined, and also to understand and appreciate the wonderful beauty and coherence of the gospel.

In this piece, Carroll examines the doctrine of eternal punishment. He starts with propositions about the nature and purposes of God and tries to put them together to form conclusions that follow logically. Trying to follow his reasoning is not for the faint-hearted, but it provides a good challenge to your mind and your faith. (I have condensed his argument and added clarifying statements to make it easier to follow, but you might want to read his essay in its entirety.) The more you understand your faith, the better equipped you are "to give an answer to everyone who asks you to give the reason for the hope that you have" (1 Pet. 3:15).

Carroll begins by laying out three propositions, each of which "has, apparently, a strong claim for our assent," but not all of which can be true:

> The most common form of the difficulty, felt in regard to this doctrine, may be thus expressed:

> "I believe that God is perfectly good. Yet I seem compelled to believe that He will inflict Eternal Punishment on certain human beings, in circumstances which would make it, according to the voice of my conscience, unjust, and therefore wrong." This difficulty, when stated in logical form, will be found to arise from the existence of three incompatible Propositions, each of which has, apparently, a strong claim for our assent. They are as follows:

> I. God is perfectly good.
> II. To inflict Eternal Punishment on certain human beings, and in certain circumstances, would be wrong.
> III. God is capable of acting thus.

> One mode of escape from this difficulty is, no doubt, to let the whole subject alone. But to many such a position is a cause of distress; they feel that one of these three Propositions must be false; and yet to regard any one of them as false plunges them into difficulties and bewilderment. The first thing to be done is to settle, as clearly as possible, what we mean by each of these Propositions, and then to settle, if possible, which two of the three rest, in our minds, on the deepest and firmest foundations, and thus to discover which one, of the three, must perforce be abandoned.

To lay the foundation for his argument, Carroll first sets out to define the propositions:

> First, then, let us settle, as clearly as possible, what we mean by each of these Propositions.

I. God is perfectly good. As to the meaning of this word "good," I assume that the Reader accepts, as an Axiom antecedent to any of these three Propositions, the Proposition that the ideas of Right and Wrong rest on eternal and self-existent principles, and not on the arbitrary will of any being whatever. I assume that he accepts the Proposition that God wills a thing because it is right and not that a thing is right because God wills it. Any Reader, of whom these assumptions are not true, can feel no difficulty in abandoning Proposition II, and saying, "If God inflicts it, it will be right." He, therefore, is not one of those for whom I am now writing. I assume, then, that this Proposition means that God always acts in accordance with the eternal principle of Right, and that He is, therefore, perfectly good.

II. To inflict "Eternal Punishment" on certain human beings and in certain circumstances, would be wrong. The word "Punishment" I assume to mean, here, "suffering inflicted on a human being who has sinned, and because he has sinned."... The word "Eternal" I assume to mean "without end." As to the human beings who are here contemplated as the subjects of Eternal Punishment,... we may interpret Proposition II as asserting that it would be wrong to inflict infinite suffering on human beings who have ceased to sin [either because they choose to stop sinning or because they have no power to choose either to sin or to repent, as Carroll identified these human beings previously], as punishment for sins committed during a finite time.

Proposition III does not seem to need any explanation.

So Carroll's three propositions can be stated as follows:

I. God is perfectly good.

II. To inflict infinite suffering on human beings who have ceased to sin, as punishment for sins committed during a finite time, would be wrong.

III. God is capable of acting thus.

Carroll reiterates that not all three propositions can be true: "We know with absolute certainty that one at least of these three Propositions is untrue. Hence, however over-whelming may be the weight of evidence with which each seems to claim our assent, we know that one at least may reasonably be abandoned." Next, Carroll considers the reasons for believing or abandoning each proposition:

Let us now take them, one by one, and consider, for each in turn, what are the grounds on which it claims our assent, and what would be the logical conse-quences of abandoning it. It may be that the Reader will then be able to see for himself which two of the three have the strongest claims on his assent, and which he must, therefore, abandon. First, then, let us consider the Proposition I. "God is perfectly good." The grounds on which this claims our assent, seem to be, first, certain intuitions (for which, of course, no proofs can be offered), such as "I believe that...I am not the outcome of blind material forces, but the creature of a being who has given me Free-Will and the sense of right and wrong, and to whom I am responsible, and who is therefore perfectly good. And this being I call 'God.'" And these intuitions are confirmed for us in a thousand ways by all the facts of revelation, by the facts of our own spiritual history, by the answers we have had to our prayers, by the irresistible conviction that this being whom we call "God" loves us, with a love so wonderful, so beautiful, so immeasurable, so wholly undeserved, so unaccount-able on any ground save His own perfect goodness, that we can but abase ourselves to the dust before Him, and dimly hope that we may be able some day to love Him with a love more like His great love for us. The abandonment of this Proposition would mean practically, for most of us, the abandonment of the belief in a God, and the acceptance of Atheism.

Secondly, let us consider the Proposition II. To inflict infinite suffering, on human beings who have ceased to sin, as punishment for sins committed during a finite time, would be wrong.... We recognise that some proportion should be observed, between the amount of crime and the amount of punishment inflicted: for instance, we should have no hesitation in condemning as unjust the conduct of a judge who, in sentencing two criminals, had awarded the greater punishment to the one whose crime was clearly the lesser of the two.... We cannot believe God to be ignorant of any of the circumstances, or capable of announcing that He will do what He does not really intend to do. We must trust His perfect knowledge of the thoughts of men, for judging who is guilty and who is not, and the only principle of right and wrong that seems reasonably applicable, is the sense that some proportion should be observed between the amount of sin and the amount of the punishment awarded to it. And here comes in the one considera- tion which, as I believe, causes all the difficulty and distress felt on this subject. We feel intuitively that sins committed by a human being during a finite period must necessarily be finite in amount; while punishment continued during an infinite period must necessarily be infinite in amount. And we feel that such a proportion is unjust....

There is another intuition, felt, I believe, by most of us, of which no account has yet been taken. It is that there is some eternal necessity, wholly beyond our comprehension, that sin must result in suffering. This principle is, I believe, enshrouded in, and may to some extent make more credible to us, the unfathomable mystery of the Atonement. And this principle must be allowed for, I think, in considering the present subject. There is also a difficulty that will probably occur to some readers, which ought to be noticed here.... If a man checks the evil wish merely from fear of punishment, and not because it is an evil wish, does he thereby cease to sin?" Here it must be admitted, I think, that the enactment of punishment for evil wishes does not, of itself, produce the love of good as good, and the hatred of evil as evil. Yet surely it may help in that direction? God uses, I believe, such motives as best suit the present need; at one time, perhaps, fear may be the only one that will influence the sinner; later on, when, through fear, some habit of self-restraint has been formed, the evil wish may be checked by the consideration that indulgence of it might lead to acts which the man is beginning dimly to recognise as evil; later still, when this recognition has grown clearer, a higher motive (such as human love) may be appealed to; and later still, the love of good as good, and the love of God as the Being whose essence is goodness. When all this has been considered, its outcome seems to me to be the irresistible intuition that infinite punishment for finite sin would be unjust, and therefore wrong. We feel that even weak and erring Man would shrink from such an act. And we cannot conceive of God as acting on a lower standard of right and wrong. In the words of Dean Church, "Can we be so compassionate and so just, and cannot we trust Him to be so?" To set aside this intuition, and to accept, as a just and righteous act, the infliction on human beings of infinite punishment for finite sin, is virtually the abandonment of Conscience as a guide in questions of Right and Wrong, and the embarking, without compass or rudder, on a boundless ocean of perplexity. In taking this position, we have to face such questions as these: "Why do I accept whatever God does as being right, though my conscience declares it to be wrong? Is it that He is my Maker? What ground have I for holding that the power of creating is a guarantee for goodness? Or is it that He loves me? But I know already that wicked beings can love. No. The only reasonable ground for accepting what He does as being right seems to be the assurance that He is perfectly good. And how can I be assured of this, if I put aside as useless the only guide that I profess for distinguishing between right and wrong, the voice of Conscience?" Such are the difficulties that meet us, if we propose to take the second possible course, and to reject Proposition II.

The third possible course is to accept Propositions I and II, and to reject III. We should thus take the following position. "I believe that God will not act thus. Yet I also believe that, whatever He has declared He will do, He will do. Hence I believe that He has not declared that He will act thus."

The difficulties, entailed by choosing this third course, may be well exhibited in another set of incompatible Propositions, as follows: 1. God has not declared that He will act thus. 2. All that the Bible tells us, as to the relations between God and man, are true. 3. The Bible tells us that God has declared that He will act thus. As these three Propositions cannot possibly be all of them true, the acceptance of (1) necessarily entails the rejection of either (2) or (3). If we reject (2), we are at once involved in all the perplexities that surround the question of Biblical Inspiration. The theory of Plenary Inspiration which asserts that every statement in the Bible is absolute and infallibly true has been largely modified in these days, and most Christians are now, I think, content to admit the existence of a human element in the Bible, and the possibility of human error in such of its statements as do not involve the relations between God and Man. But, as to those statements, there appears to be a general belief that the Bible has been providentially protected from error: in fact, on any other theory, it would be hard to say what value there would be in the Bible or for what purpose it could have been written. The more likely course would seem to be to reject (3). Let us consider what difficulties this would entail. We are now supposed to have taken up the following position: "I do not believe that the Bible tells us that God has declared He will inflict Eternal Punishment on human beings, who are either incapable of sinning, or who, being capable of sinning, have ceased to sin." It is well to remind the Reader that, in taking up this position, he entirely escapes from the original difficulty on account of which we entered on this discussion. And how widely different this is from what we considered as the first of the courses possible to us! That would have involved us in the abandonment of Christianity itself; this entails many difficulties, no doubt: but they all belong to the infinitely less important field of Biblical Criticism. The Reader who is unable, whether from want of time or from want of the necessary learning, to investigate this question for himself, must perforce accept the judgment of others: and all he needs here to be told is that the interpretation of the passages, which are believed to teach the doctrine of "Eternal Punishment," depends largely, if not entirely, on the meaning given to one single word (*aion*). This is rendered, in our English Bibles, by the word "eternal" or "everlasting": but there are many critics who believe that it does not necessarily mean "endless." If this be so, then the punishment, which we are considering, is finite punishment for finite sin, and the original difficulty no longer exists. In conclusion, I will put together in one view the various modes of escape, from the original difficulty, which may be adopted without violating the inexorable laws of logical reasoning.

Having laid out the dilemma, Carroll proceeds to offer the ways to resolve it: One can reject the original proposition I (God is perfectly good) and accept propositions II and III, saying it is wrong to inflict endless punishment for finite sins *and* that God does act thus, meaning He does what is wrong and therefore is not perfectly good. Another might reject proposition II, saying it is *not* unjust for an infinitely holy God to inflict infinite punishment for finite sins. In that case, God can do so and still be good. Yet another could say that God is good and such infliction of punishment is wrong, but the Bible tells us that God does act that way, so the Bible cannot be trusted. Finally, one can maintain that it is indeed wrong to inflict infinite punishment for finite sins but the Bible does *not* say that God acts that way, so the Bible can be trusted and God can be called perfectly good.

So here are Carroll's "modes of escape, from the original difficulty, which may be adopted without violating the inexorable laws of logical reasoning":

They are as follows: (1) "I believe that the infliction, on human beings, of endless punishment, for sins committed during a finite time, would be unjust, and therefore wrong. Yet I cannot resist the evidence that God has declared His intention of acting thus. Consequently I hold Him to be capable of sinning." This would practically mean the abandonment of Christianity. (2) "I believe that God is perfectly good, and therefore that such infliction of punishment would be right, though my conscience declares it to be wrong." This would practically mean the abandonment of conscience as a guide to distinguish right from wrong, and would leave the phrase "I believe that God is perfectly good" without any intelligible meaning.

(3) "I believe that God is perfectly good. Also I believe that such infliction of punishment would be wrong. Consequently I believe that God is not capable of acting thus. I find that the Bible tells us that He is capable of acting thus. Consequently I believe that what the Bible tells us of the relations between God and Man cannot be relied on as true." This would practically mean the abandonment of the Bible as a trustworthy book. (4) "I believe that God is perfectly good. Also I believe that such infliction of punishment would be wrong. Consequently I believe that God is not capable of acting thus. I find that the Bible, in the English Version, seems to tell us that He is capable of acting thus. Yet I believe that it is a book inspired by God, and protected by Him from error in what it tells us of the relations between God and Man, and therefore that what it says, according to the real meaning of the words, may be relied on as true. Consequently I hold that the word, rendered in English as 'eternal' or 'everlasting,' has been mistranslated, and that the Bible does not really assert more than that God will inflict suffering, of unknown duration but not necessarily eternal, punishment for sin." Any one of these four views may be held, without violating the laws of logical reasoning.

Here ends my present task; since my object has been, throughout, not to indicate one course rather than another, but to help the Reader to see clearly what the possible courses are, and what he is virtually accepting, or denying, in choosing any one of them.

If you have made it through this essay to the end, well done—it takes a lot of mental energy! Having read Carroll's treatise, which of his propositions do you think "rest on the firmest and deepest foundations"? Which of the four views do you hold? What are you virtually accepting, or denying, in choosing that view?

# 47

# TRUE JOY

My first book included a four-part series called "Joy Is a Choice," in which I speak of principles for experiencing the joy of the Lord. The principles are sound, but before I understood the all-encompassing grace of God, there was always an uneasy, nagging sense that something wasn't quite right. I couldn't precisely identify the problem, but the deep joy always seemed just out of reach.

Many years ago I wrote a letter to my then-pastor in which I described some of the struggles I was going through. I was trying to verbalize my conflicting thoughts, and I was hoping to get help in sorting out some of the issues that troubled me. Under the heading "Joy" I wrote the following:

> One of the hallmarks of a Christian and perhaps the quality that is most attractive to unbelievers is joy. Part of the secret of joy is keeping things in perspective and seeing them in light of eternity. The prospect of heaven can make sorrows fade into insignificance. For example, if my house and all my possessions were to burn to the ground, I would grieve the loss, but I know that we are just passing through this world and that God is preparing mansions in heaven for us that will make our houses here look like the temporary tents that they are. Similarly, if (or I should say "when") my body breaks down, I will be sad, but I can still have joy. I know that in light of eternity it doesn't really matter what my earthly body is like because I will be getting a new body in heaven.

Remembering that our material possessions and earthly bodies really don't matter can help us maintain joy even in the face of loss. My problem is that there are some things that really *do* matter in light of eternity, like the choices we make, the words we speak, and above all, the eternal destiny of people's souls. Life is deadly serious; our actions now do have eternal consequences, and the choices that our children make will affect them not just temporarily but often eternally. That is what makes me lose joy.... How do I maintain joy not only in the face of trials, but even when the harmful consequences *do* matter for eternity? We're commanded not to worry, and I know I can trust God to provide for my needs and compensate for the loss of any temporal possessions, but how do I learn not to worry when there is *real* cause for worry, i.e., the eternal destiny of souls?

In other words, I believed everything the Bible teaches about keeping earthly trials in perspective by focusing on the heavenly glory to come, but I worried about those who will experience not eternal glory but eternal damnation. I understood the value of suffering to produce positive results in our lives—to refine us, conform us to the image of Christ, give us compassion for others in distress, and make us long for heaven—but most of the suffering in the world is not of that nature; billions of people suffer in this life, die, and then suffer forever. I knew these biblical principles:

> Our light and momentary troubles are achieving for us an eternal glory that far outweighs them all.... We know that if the earthly tent we live in is destroyed, we have a building from God, an eternal house in heaven, not built by human hands (2 Cor. 4:17, 5:1).

> I consider that our present sufferings are not worth comparing with the glory that will be revealed in us (Rom. 8:18).

But I understood that unbelievers face eternal torment that will far outweigh in horror anything they have suffered on earth, and that thought robbed me of joy. Sure, heaven would be great for me personally, but how could I enjoy it knowing that billions of others were experiencing eternal pain and hopelessness? Under the heading "Heaven" I wrote,

> Suppose that you and your spouse are about to go on your dream vacation—the trip of a lifetime. You have planned and saved and anticipated for years, and now it is about to come true. Then you find out that your child has been in a terrible accident and is in a coma near death. Do you still want to go on the vacation? Could you enjoy it? Even seeing other people's poverty puts a damper on a vacation, which is why travel agencies try to shield tourists from slums and begging children.

> I have absolutely no doubt that heaven will be glorious and spectacular beyond our wildest dreams. I believe everything the Bible says about the wonderful place God is preparing for us. I believe that God will wipe away every tear, heal all diseases, and restore all relationships. Yet it is hard for me to fathom how I could ever be completely happy knowing that the majority of people who have ever lived won't experience this glorious place. No matter how I read the Bible, I can't get around the fact that most people don't know God. Although countless multitudes will be in heaven, countless more will spend eternity apart from God. Even if all my children and grandchildren and all the people I care about personally are in heaven, there will be untold numbers of people that *somebody* cares about—*somebody's* children and friends and family—who are *not* there.

> Just knowing that it is well with *my* soul is not enough for me to have joy. Any peace or comfort that I have

for myself is overshadowed by the lack of peace and joy that I know other people are experiencing or will experience forever.

My pastor did not answer my questions. Books I read and sermons I heard did not answer my questions. I didn't know anyone who had good answers to these questions. Some say that in the bliss of heaven we will not remember the wicked. Others say that when we are transformed into the image of God we will have a holy hatred of all that is evil, including all evil-doers. But even if I could convince myself that I would forget about the lost or not care about them, it would not change the fact that *they* would be in torment forever. How could we have a heart for the lost in this life and forget them or turn against them in the next?

I spent several more years wrestling with these questions and not coming to any resolution or peace about them. I wanted to believe that God would somehow mercifully redeem everyone, but I was afraid that believing it would mean that I didn't really believe the Bible or I had a low view of God's holiness or I was resistant to His will and purpose. I tried to delight in the Lord, and I managed to have a generally joyful disposition, but there was always at least an aching distress—sometimes escalating into full-blown horror—about the billions of people who would *never* know the joy of the Lord and on the contrary would live with unending pain and hopelessness.

God graciously answered the cries of my heart when I learned that Christianity has a long history of belief in the ultimate redemption of all creation, going all the way back to the early church and some of the Church Fathers. I am now firmly convinced that God's grace reaches beyond death and He will not leave His beloved creatures to suffer forever with no hope.

Peace comes from the certainty that *God is in control* and that *He is good.* If human beings have the power to determine their eternal destiny by choosing to accept or reject Christ, then I cannot rest in the assurance that God is in complete control. Neither can I have real security and peace if God is in complete control but is not always good. But if God is in control *and* is good to all He has made, then I can experience the true joy that comes from resting in the knowledge that He will certainly accomplish all His good purposes. And I can *choose joy* in the face of sorrow and loss, knowing that one day everything will be made right.

Each time someone is reunited with a loved one after an absence, we get a tiny glimpse of the joy that will be multiplied zillions of times over and magnified to the nth degree. The movie *Lion* tells the true story of a small boy who was separated from his family in India and adopted by a couple in Australia. His reunion with his birth mother more than two decades later made my heart leap for joy!

I can now get excited about heaven because it's not a place where I'm in perfect personal bliss while billions more are on the outside, weeping and gnashing their teeth in their eternal torment. Rather, it's a place where there is great joy over every sinner who repents, right down to the last straggler who comes in on his knees, humbling himself, praising God, being forgiven of every sin, and being received into fellowship with the Lord and His people.

Some say it's too good to be true. I say, Is anything impossible for God? Some say it's wishful thinking. I say, Could I or anyone else even dream up a plan that is better than what God will actually do? Some say I'm trying to make God in my own image. No! It was all His idea, and it's all in the Bible. He wants us to have pure joy, untainted by the fear that some people will experience endless suffering. We can rest in His perfect love that casts out all fear. We can look forward to an unimaginably wonderful future when everything will be made right and the whole creation will be restored to a state even better than before sin corrupted it. Rest assured that Satan will be completely defeated and God will have *complete* victory, with absolutely no sin or suffering to mar the beauty and perfection of His creation. Having full assurance of God's good purposes for *all* people is the source of the most unshakeable joy and peace imaginable!

# 48

# OUR ADVERSARY, THE DEVIL

The introduction to the book of Job in the NIV Study Bible has a good explanation of Satan's goal in afflicting people:

Incapable of contending with God hand to hand, power pitted against power, he is bent on frustrating God's enterprise embodied in the creation and centered on the God-man relationship. As tempter he seeks to alienate man from God (see Ge 3; Mt 4:1); as accuser (one of the names by which he is called, *satan,* means "accuser") he seeks to alienate God from man (see Zec 3:1; Rev 12:9–10). *His all-consuming purpose is to drive an irremovable wedge between God and man, to effect an alienation that cannot be reconciled."*

The question is WILL SATAN SUCCEED?

If the view that billions of people will be eternally separated from God is true, then we must admit that Satan will be wildly successful. Yes, he will be forced to submit to God and will himself be punished forever. But he will be laughing all the way to the pit because he has managed to take so many with him, which was his goal all along. And Satan's success must also be God's failure; He *attempts* to save the world, but falls far short.

Compare the answers to the following questions according to the traditional view that many people, if not most, will be eternally condemned, and the restoration view that God will ultimately redeem all.

| | Eternal Damnation | Ultimate Restoration |
|---|---|---|
| **Will Satan frustrate God's enterprise centered on the God-man relationship?** | Yes. In billions of cases Satan will frustrate God's desire to restore the God-man relationship. | No. Satan cannot forever frustrate God's plans. |
| **Will Satan be successful in alienating man from God and God from man?** | Yes. He will be extremely successful in alienating man from God and God from man forever. | No. Satan experiences some temporary success in this life but cannot alienate us from God forever. |
| **Will Satan drive an irremovable wedge between God and man to effect an alienation that cannot be reconciled?** | Yes. There will be an irremovable wedge; many people will never be reconciled to God, either in this life or in the next. | No. God will override Satan's attempt to effect an alienation that cannot be reconciled. |
| **Will God be 100% successful in thwarting Satan's schemes and bringing about the reconciliation of man to Himself?** | No. He manages to draw a lot of people to Himself but loses more than He wins. | Absolutely! Not one will be lost forever; God will reconcile *all* to Himself through the cross. |

As Job himself said after God spoke to him personally and revealed His true character, "I know that you can do all things; **no plan of yours can be thwarted**" (Job 42:2). John tells us that "the reason the Son of God appeared was **to destroy the works of the devil**" (1 Jn. 3:8). I urge you to examine your own view of the final destiny of all creation and ask yourself these questions: Is God's plan thwarted? Do any of the works of the devil remain in the end? Or does God win? Is His victory complete?

Many are the plans in a man's heart [and in Satan's heart],
but **it is the Lord's purpose that prevails.**
Proverbs 19:21

"I make known the end from the beginning,
from ancient times, what is still to come.
I say: **My purpose will stand,**
**and I will do all that I please.**"
Isaiah 46:10

"So is **my word** that goes out from my mouth:
It will not return to me empty,
but **will accomplish what I desire**
**and achieve the purpose for which I sent it.**"
Isaiah 55:11

And he made known to us the mystery of his will
according to his good pleasure,
which he purposed in Christ, to be put into effect
when the times will have reached their fulfillment—
to bring all things in heaven and on earth together
under one head, even Christ.
In him we were also chosen,
having been predestined according to the plan of him
**who works out everything in conformity**
**with the purpose of his will.**
Ephesians 1:9–11

# 49

# REFLECTIONS ON
# *THE GREAT DIVORCE*

A number of years ago, a friend invited me to read *The Great Divorce*, C. S. Lewis's allegorical journey to Heaven and Hell. I had not read the book since shortly after I became a Christian, so I found our old paperback copy and read it again. As I turned the brittle, yellowed pages they came unglued in my hands until the book was just a pile of pages, but the message is still as powerful as it was when it was written in the mid-twentieth century.

The narrator takes a bus from Hell, "the grey town," to the outskirts of Heaven. During his journey he converses with his fellow travelers, who give a variety of reasons why they refuse to turn away from the darkness and misery of the grey town and embrace the everlasting light and joy of Heaven.

Lewis is a masterful storyteller, and like *The Chronicles of Narnia*, this fantasy tale provides food for thought about how God works in the world and what awaits us after we die. After I read it I shared some of my reflections with my friend:

I finished reading *The Great Divorce*—thanks for recommending it. It was good to read it again—I read it when I first became a Christian but it has been a long time!

I love C. S. Lewis and he does a great job of describing the different forms that rebellion against God can take. But with all due respect, I think he makes the mistake of giving too much power to human free will. I do believe we have true free will—we make real choices with real consequences. In fact, for the sovereign God to grant some measure of true sovereignty to created beings is an astounding exercise of His sovereignty. But our "free" will is not absolutely free; it cannot forever override God's will. Yet one of the characters in *The Great Divorce,* who seems to express Lewis's own opinion, says, "There are only two kinds of people in the end: those who say to God, 'Thy will be done,' and those to whom God says, in the end, '*Thy* will be done.' All that are in Hell, choose it. Without that self-choice there could be no Hell."

In my opinion, it's a mistake to think we have so much power that we can choose our eternal destiny in opposition to God's desire for us. Yes, we can make lots of choices that can ruin our lives and grieve God and thwart His good plans for us. But we cannot forever override His good purposes. As Job learned through his ordeal, "I know that You can do all things, and that no purpose of Yours can be thwarted" (Job 42:2). Although we have the responsibility to receive Christ and believe in His name, John makes it clear that salvation is *not* by the will of man but by the will of God:

> But to all who did receive him, who believed in his name, he gave the right to become children of God, who were born, *not of blood nor of the will of the flesh nor of the will of man, but of God* (1:12–13).

If God desires that all men come to repentance, then it will happen. If God wants all men to be saved, then no force of evil or will of man can prevent their salvation. If Jesus is the Lamb of God who takes away the sin of the world, then He will actually *take it away*. If Jesus came into the world to save the world, then He *will* save the world. If He says He will draw ("drag") all men to Himself, then ultimately none can resist Him. If God purposed to reconcile all to Himself through the cross, then He will do it. If it's His good pleasure to bring all things in heaven and on earth together under Christ, then in His time—when the times have reached their fulfillment—we will see nothing less. If He says that every knee will bow and every tongue confess Jesus as Lord, then I believe every knee will bow in true adoration and every tongue will agree from the heart "Jesus is my Lord."

But some say, if God forces people to love Him, how can it be true love and adoration? I don't think God forces anybody to believe, any more than He forced you and me. Rather, because of His infinite wisdom and knowledge, He knows exactly what will bring us to repentance. Because of His infinite love, He cares enough to pursue us relentlessly. By His kindness *and* His severity He draws each person to the point of willingly bowing the knee and submitting to Him. Many will go to their grave without having done so, and there will be severe judgment, but I don't think physical death is the end of hope. The Hound of Heaven keeps pursuing the lost through death and beyond, by whatever means it takes to secure their salvation. It takes only brute strength to punish sin and destroy the sinner. It takes the power of God to transform a sinner into a saint. Jesus won't let a drop of His blood be wasted, but will make sure that His death fully accomplishes His purpose. It will truly be, in the words of our church's Prayer of Consecration, "a perfect and sufficient sacrifice for the sins of the whole world."

I'm convinced that God will do much more than punish sinners or annihilate them or send them off to some corner of the universe where they can do their own thing and not bother the saved ones. I believe God wants to *eradicate* sin from His universe, and He will do it not by destroying sinners but by transforming them. He is fully able to bring about the complete restoration of His entire creation to a state better than if we had never fallen in the first place. Satan will not have the success of getting billions of people on his side against God—I don't think he'll manage to get even one soul on his side forever. God's victory will be absolutely complete!

Some say this is too good to be true, but I've come to the conclusion that, if anything, my vision of what God will accomplish is *too small*. He is able to do exceedingly abundantly beyond all we can ask or imagine; we can't even conceive of what He has in store for those who love Him, so how could I or anyone else even think up a scenario that is better than what He is actually going to do? The challenge is to use our sanctified imagination to trust Him to go beyond what we can even dream up. Some will say, "Yes, but..." and quote passages that seem to teach eternal damnation—that the wicked are hopelessly lost. But I believe those passages need to be understood in light of the foundational truth that God purposed to send His Son to save the world, and *He will do it.*

# 50

# WHAT ARE THE FRUITS?
# PART 1

One way (though not the only way and not a fool-proof way) to determine whether a doctrine is of God is to examine its fruits. A doctrine that is of God should produce godly fruit. If a teaching itself (not just the sinful, imperfect implementation of it) produces rotten fruit, its validity should be questioned.

Consider, for example, the fruits of the belief that the Bible supports slavery. In the Appendix to his *Narrative of the Life of Frederick Douglass, an American Slave*, Douglass writes about the stark contrast between "the Christianity of this land" and "the Christianity of Christ":

> I find, since reading over the foregoing Narrative, that I have, in several instances, spoken in such a tone and manner, respecting religion, as may possibly lead those unacquainted with my religious views to suppose me an opponent of all religion. To remove the liability of such misapprehension, I deem it proper to append the following brief explanation. What I have said respecting and against religion, I mean strictly to apply to the *slaveholding religion* of this land, and with no possible reference to Christianity proper; for, between the Christianity of this land, and the Christianity of Christ, I recognize the widest possible difference—so wide, that to receive the one as good, pure, and holy, is of necessity to reject the other as bad, corrupt, and wicked. To be the friend of the one, is of necessity to be the enemy of the other. I love the

pure, peaceable, and impartial Christianity of Christ: I therefore hate the corrupt,... partial and hypocritical Christianity of this land.

Where he speaks of the "slaveholding religion" of this land, we can substitute any aspect of our religion that is at odds with what he calls "Christianity proper." These deviations from true Christianity produce bad fruit, revealing themselves as impostors.

So what are the fruits of the different views of life after death and heaven and hell? While I cannot prove a definite cause-and-effect relationship, I believe that there is evidence to suggest that a belief in eternal damnation tends to produce bad fruit. Believing that God imposes extreme punishment on unbelievers, some Christians have found justification for executing similar judgment themselves. They have also reasoned that torturing the body is worth it to try to save the soul. In the past this mentality has resulted in hunting down unbelievers, torturing heretics, and killing those judged guilty of apostasy. We are horrified when Muslims act on their belief that Islam is the only true religion and that infidels deserve death, but there is much to be ashamed of in our own church history. (See "Religious Cruelty," #52.) And although twenty-first-century Christians do not behead unbelievers and heretics or burn them at the stake, we can be quite vicious toward those we consider God's enemies, which damages our witness and destroys our unity. If the proponents of a certain belief exhibit ugly actions, then we need to consider the words of Amartya Sen:

> If you're disturbed that your beliefs seem to attract some rather nasty company, it's worth figuring out whether they are, at core, rather nasty beliefs.

What are the results on a family level? Parents tend to reflect the character of the God they believe in. A father who believes that divine judgment is retributive in nature will tend to carry out the same kind of punishment on his children. He may truly want to model God's character for his children, and he may also want to instill enough fear that his children will be motivated to trust Christ and escape hell. But if he believes that God is harsh and punitive and if he portrays Him that way, the result may be that the child is driven away from the harsh father and away from God Himself. As Rita Swan[1] notes, "Fundamentalists are more likely than others to hold images of God stressing punishment and judgment," which can lead to treating their own children the same way.

Let me be quick to say that I know many lovely Christians who hold the traditional view of eternal damnation. They can be wonderful parents and kind and faithful people. But to some degree there is a disconnect between their view of the character of God and their understanding of what He is calling them to be. They know they should love their neighbors and even their enemies, but it appears that He does not love *His* enemies. It is almost as if they are more loving and more forgiving than He is, which is a disquieting thought.

And what are the results of believing in ultimate restoration? There can be a danger of not feeling enough urgency about sharing the gospel, but generally the fruits are much more positive and healthy. Knowing that every individual is loved by God and eventually will be in His kingdom softens our heart toward those who are now in rebellion and makes us want them to come into the kingdom now. It makes sharing the gospel much more joyful—we have truly *good* news not only for those who hear but also for their loved ones. We can share the gospel more freely because we don't have to worry about somebody asking the sticky questions, like "How could God be so cruel?" "Your religion says that most of humanity is damned—why are you so intolerant and exclusive?" "How can God be fair if He creates people, makes them suffer on earth, and then sends them to hell for not believing in Him?"

When God's judgment is understood correctly, man's innate sense of justice is satisfied: God does not let the Hitlers and hypocrites and Pol Pots and pedophiles off scot-free; He brings severe consequences on those who violate His laws and harm other people. At the same time, He understands that we are all like lost sheep, and He offers Himself as the Good Shepherd and the Savior of the world. He does judge sin, but the judgment is not eternal and hopeless. The wicked and the wayward will receive justice *and* mercy. Evildoers will feel the full impact of how much they have done to hurt others. Wandering children will understand the grief they have caused. But nobody will be left to rot in hell forever; ultimately, all will be restored to the perfection and unity that God designed. This view satisfies our sense of justice and gives us a gospel that produces truly good fruit—compassion toward unbelievers, urgency but not desperation about their salvation, a beautiful picture of a holy and loving God to present to the world, overflowing joy in His wonderful plan, and true hope for the future for every human being.

------

[1]Swan, Rita. "Religious Attitudes on Corporal Punishment." A version of this article appears in *Encyclopedia of Domestic Violence* edited by Nicky Ali Jackson and published by Routledge. Swan is a child advocate who for decades has been working to protect children from harmful religious and cultural practices. Her website, childrenshealthcare.org, contains extensive documentation of the dangers to children of authoritarian religions, including Christian fundamentalism, with its view of God the Father as a punitive judge who brings condemnation on wrong-doers.

# 51

# WHAT ARE THE FRUITS?
# PART 2

Second Peter 3 contains Peter's last written words to us. He speaks of the last days, when the heavens and earth as we know them will be destroyed to make way for "a new heaven and new earth, where righteousness dwells." Since the time is coming when all that is corrupt will be destroyed and Christ's reign of righteousness will be ushered in, we ought to be living godly lives now, as we look forward to that day.

One factor that can make it challenging to live godly lives and can cause conflict among Christians is that the Bible is not always clear. As Peter says of Paul, "His letters contain some things that are hard to understand, which ignorant and unstable people distort, as they do the other Scriptures, to their own destruction" (3:16). In fact, things that are hard to understand are found throughout the Bible, as Peter indicates when he says that people distort Paul's hard-to-understand teachings "as they do the other Scriptures."

The consequences of this problem are enormous. The fact that some ideas in Scripture are *not* plain to see means that good Christians can be at odds over the meaning of a passage. The failure to recognize that some passages are not easy to understand and therefore can have different legitimate interpretations leads to unnecessary hostility and suspicion among believers. Those who say there is only one way to interpret a text usually mean that *their* way is the only way, and anybody who doesn't agree with the *obviously* correct understanding is wrong. Unfortunately, as we well know from church history, wars of all sizes have been fought over the interpretation of the Bible. My plea is that we *not* allow our sacred book to become the source of conflict and fighting among believers.

So what *should* we do? First, I would encourage all Christians to be gracious in the way they treat others in the body of Christ with whom they disagree. What good does it do for the hand to poke out the eye? Or for the teeth to bite the tongue? Or for one foot to stomp on the other? The body functions best when the members build one another up, not tear each other down. We will never see eye to eye about everything with anybody, but we can be respectful toward others with different ideas.

The hand cannot say to the head, "I have no need of you."

We also need discernment to know which matters of interpretation are critical and which ones don't really matter. Some beliefs are at the core of our faith—the ones that constitute the definition of "Christian" and identify us as believers in Christ. Individuals should not make their own definitions of the essentials of the faith; that was done for us very capably in the Nicene Creed, a statement that embodies the essence of what it means to be a Christian and has stood the test of time.

Then there are issues that may have a right or wrong interpretation, but they are not critical to our salvation or our Christian walk. Is our salvation or sanctification really affected by whether we were dunked or sprinkled? By whether we worship on the seventh day or the first day? By whether our church has a Presbyterian or Congregational form of government? These matters can be debated, and in some cases one way may be better than another, but differences in interpretation in these issues should not be cause for breaking fellowship.

But the interpretation of some disputable issues *does* matter. You can make the Bible say pretty much whatever you want it to say, but obviously not all interpretations are good and right. As I have suggested, one way to assess different interpretations is to ask, "What are the fruits of that teaching?" An interpretation that produces good fruit is more likely to be correct than one that produces bad fruit.

Peter says that some people distort the Scriptures "to their own destruction" (3:16). Are the consequences of an interpretation destructive in some way? Then we should question whether the interpretation is correct. As I mentioned in Part 1, an example that comes to mind is slavery. The Bible has been used to justify slavery, but the evil results of enslaving other human beings should tell us that God never intended His Word to be used to legitimize such a system. The Bible has also been used to promote anti-Semitism. Again, it is clear from the fruits of such thinking that God's Word should not be interpreted to justify hatred toward the Jews. In fact, the Bible has been used in support of all kinds of violence against non-Christians and even against other Christians who don't line up in some way. When the fruits of interpretations are in violation of clear principles of Scripture, we should take the hint—the interpretation is *wrong.*

We don't need to look to such extreme examples to find Scripture being misinterpreted and misused. I doubt that any of my present readers would support slavery, anti-Semitism, or violence, but we all need to ask ourselves if any of our interpretations have negative consequences. What kind of fruit do your interpretations produce in your life? What effect do they have on other people and your relationships with them? In light of this test, do any of your interpretations need to be re-examined?

In his book *The End of Faith: Religion, Terror, and the Future of Reason,* Sam Harris gives a brutal assessment of all religions. He makes the case that religion is devoid of reason and is the source of great evil in the world. I agree with much of what he says, with one gigantic exception—that the Christian faith, *rightly understood and practiced,* is the antidote to all that is wrong with religion. We need to be practicing what Paul calls "sincere and pure devotion to Christ" (2 Cor. 11:3), which will produce good fruit in our lives.

As Peter acknowledges, some parts of Scripture are hard to understand, but most of it is crystal clear with regard to "what kind of people [we] ought to be" (2 Pet. 3:11). We are to develop Sermon on the Mount attitudes and fruit of the Spirit qualities. We are to cultivate the characteristics that should identify the people of God. Here are a few examples:

> Therefore, as God's chosen people, holy and dearly loved, clothe yourselves with compassion, kindness, humility, gentleness and patience. Bear with each other and forgive one another if any of you has a grievance against someone. Forgive as the Lord forgave you. And over all these virtues put on love, which binds them all together in perfect unity. Let the peace of Christ rule in your hearts, since as members of one body you were called to peace. And be thankful. Let the message of Christ dwell among you richly as you teach and admonish one another with all wisdom through psalms, hymns, and songs from the Spirit, singing to God with gratitude in your hearts. And whatever you do, whether in word or deed, do it all in the name of the Lord Jesus, giving thanks to God the Father through him (Col. 3:12–17)

> Finally, all of you, be like-minded, be sympathetic, love one another, be compassionate and humble. Do not repay evil with evil or insult with insult. On the contrary, repay evil with blessing, because to this you were called so that you may inherit a blessing. (1 Pet. 3:8–9).

> Dear friends, let us love one another, for love comes from God. Everyone who loves has been born of God and knows God. Whoever does not love does not know God, because God is love. This is how God showed his love among us: He sent his one and only Son into the world that we might live through him. This is love: not that we loved God, but that he loved

us and sent his Son as an atoning sacrifice for our sins. Dear friends, since God so loved us, we also ought to love one another. No one has ever seen God; but if we love one another, God lives in us and his love is made complete in us (1 Jn. 4:7–12).

Yes, there are parts of Scripture that are hard to understand. But what kind of people we ought to be—that's not a mystery!

# 52

# RELIGIOUS CRUELTY

Thomas B. Thayer's 1855 book *The Origin and History of the Doctrine of Endless Punishment*[1] includes a chapter about religious cruelty, in which he argued that believing in a harsh God makes a man similarly harsh in his own character. He may have overstated his premise in rather absolute terms, but as you read these excerpts, consider whether he has a valid point and what are the implications for the way we represent the nature of our God.

At the beginning of the chapter Thayer states his thesis that belief in a cruel religion makes a man cruel:

> If the Christian believe in a cruel religion, believe in it with all his heart, it will make him cruel; it will certainly harden his heart. If he believe in and worship a God of a merciless and ferocious character, this will eventually be, visibly or invisibly, his own character. If he believe the God of the Bible hates any portion of mankind, or regards them with any dislike or displeasure, he also will come to hate them, and to entertain towards them the same feelings which he supposes reside in the bosom of God. If he believe that God will, in expression of those feelings, or for any reason, devote them to flame and torture hereafter, it is natural and necessary that he should infer it would be, for the same reason, acceptable to God that he should devote them to flame and torture here. And if the degree of civilization and the condition of society shall permit; or, in other words, if no power from without prevent, he will assuredly do this, as a

most acceptable offering to Heaven; and to the utmost of his power will conform to what he believes to be the disposition and wishes of God in this respect.

Our society does not permit such torture of others, but if it did, would we practice it? Before giving an automatic answer, consider that our Christian forefathers, without such societal restraints, did indeed "devote them to flame and torture here," in what they believed was obedience to God. As evidence for his thesis, Thayer speaks of the often-dismal history of Christianity in that respect:

> And this is not said without ample means for proving the correctness of the statement. The history of Christianity, so called, in all ages and among every people, and in every form which it has taken, will abundantly establish the truth of the position, that the temper and practice of a people is determined by the spirit of their religion and their gods.

> It is not necessary to enter into a labored description of the doctrines of the Christian church in the days of its darkness and corruption, nor of the awful and revolting views entertained of God, of His disposition towards man, of His government, laws and punishments. It is enough that Paganism in its worst forms has never surpassed, if it has equaled, the savage and terrible descriptions which have been given by Christians of their God. The character ascribed to Him; the dreadful wrath and vengeance with which He is moved; the cold and malignant purpose of creation in regard to millions of souls; the stern severity and gloom of His government; the horrible and never-ceasing tortures which He will inflict on His helpless children—all this, and much more of like character, defies the power of language to set it forth in its true light, or to present it in a manner adequate to its shocking and revolting reality. I give a single example:

Dr. Benson, an eminent English minister, in a sermon on "The Future Misery of the Wicked," says, "God is present in hell, in his infinite justice and almighty wrath, as an unfathomable sea of liquid fire, where the wicked must drink in everlasting torture...." He then adds, "God is, therefore, himself present in hell, to see the punishment of these rebels against his government, that it may be adequate to the infinity of their guilt: his fiery indignation kindles, and his incensed fury feeds the flame of their torment, while his powerful presence and operation maintain their being, and render all their powers most acutely sensible; thus setting the keenest edge upon their pain, and making it cut most intolerably deep. He will exert all his divine attributes to make them as wretched as the capacity of their nature will admit."

After this he goes on to describe the duration of this work of God, and calls to his aid all the stars, sand, and drops of water, and makes each one tell a million of ages; and when all those ages have rolled away, he goes over the same number again, and again, and so on forever.

Dr. Benson's description is quite graphic and extreme but not so very different from what many Christians have believed for centuries:

Christians have believed all this; have believed that God is the enemy of the sinner and unbeliever; that He regards with a fierce displeasure those of a wrong faith or a wrong life; that heretics and the impenitent are an abomination in His sight; and that upon these wretched victims the vials of His wrath will finally be broken, and overwhelm them in endless and irre-trievable ruin.

Thayer goes on to consider what such a view of God does to the one who believes it:

301

A more important question is that which regards the influence of this savage creed upon the believer. To this let us give some attention, and we shall find, what we may expect, that its tendency in all ages, when believed in right earnest, has been to harden the heart, to brutalize the affections, and render those receiving it, under any of its forms, cruel, and ferocious in disposition, and, so far as circumstances would allow, in practice.

He presents Tertullian (c. AD 155–240), a Christian apologist from Carthage in North Africa, as an example of cruelty:

Take as a worthy example the celebrated passage of Tertullian, "How shall I admire, how laugh, how rejoice, how exult, when I behold so many kings and false gods, together with Jove himself, groaning in the lowest abyss of darkness! so many magistrates who persecuted the name of the Lord, liquefying in fiercer flames than they ever kindled against Christians; so many sage philosophers, with their deluded scholars, blushing in raging fire!"

Without doubt, Tertullian was of a fierce and bitter spirit, independently of his religious faith; but this fiery ebullition of hate and ferocity serves to show how perfectly fitted that faith was to add fuel to the flame, and what an ample field and congenial scenes it furnished for his savage nature to revel in. Under the influence of such a belief, his wild temper gathered new vigor, his revengeful feelings were cultivated and strengthened to a frightful degree, till at last he comes to rejoice and exult in the agonies of the damned with a relish that a devil might envy. One cannot but see that it only needed the power to have engaged this ferocious man in the work of torture on earth, the prospect of which in hell he contemplated with such fiendish delight.

Another example of religious cruelty is the Albigensian Crusade (1209–1229):

> A further illustration may be found in the crusades against the Albigenses in the thirteenth century, one of the darkest and bloodiest pages in the history of any religion, Christian or Pagan. The sacrifices of the Goth and Mexican, and the revolting cruelties of the Polynesian and the negro of Dahomy, are scarcely equal to the savage butcheries and the shocking barbarities inflicted by the Catholic crusader, in the name of his God, upon this gentle and virtuous people. No passage in the history of man is more to the purpose of our argument, or more conclusive of the direct influence of religious faith upon the temper and character, than that in which are recorded the persecutions and sufferings of these unhappy reformers. Throughout the whole of this merciless crusade, and amid all its scenes of burning and desolation, of murder and torture, the cry of the ruthless priest was heard, "It is for the glory of God!" And the brutal multitude, believing that they were doing God a service, and securing their own salvation by the slaughter of heretics, rushed forward to the bloody work with the ferocity of tigers and the joy of a Tertullian.

Thayer quotes from *History of Crusades against the Albigenses* by the Swiss historian Sismondi, who accused the monks of inciting the people to "this diabolical work":

> Sismondi says, speaking of the deliberate savageness of the monks who occupied the pulpits and urged on the people to this diabolical work, they "showed how every vice might be expiated by crime; how remorse might be expelled by the flames of their piles; how the soul, polluted with every shameful passion, might become pure and spotless by bathing in the blood of

heretics. By continuing to preach the crusade, they impelled, each year, waves of new fanatics upon those miserable provinces; and they compelled their chiefs to recommence the war, in order to profit by the fervor of those who still demanded human victims, and required blood to effect their salvation." They represented this inoffensive people as the outcasts of the human race, and the especial objects of divine hatred and vengeance; and no devotional exercise, no prayer or praise, no act of charity or mercy, was half so acceptable to God as the murder of a heretic.

[Sismondi continued] "The more zealous, therefore, the multitude were for the glory of God, the more ardently they labored for the destruction of heretics, the better Christians they thought themselves. And if at any time they felt a movement of pity or terror, whilst assisting at their punishment, they thought it a revolt of the flesh, which they confessed at the tribunal of penitence; nor could they get quit of their remorse till their priests had given them absolution.... Amongst them all not a heart could be found accessible to pity. Equally inspired by fanaticism and the love of war, they believed that the sure way to salvation was through the field of carnage. Seven bishops, who followed the army, had blessed their standards and their arms, and would be engaged in prayer for them while they were attacking the heretics. Thus did they advance, indifferent whether to victory or martyrdom, certain that either would issue in the reward which God himself had destined for them."

The zeal of these religious fanatics led them to commit unimaginable acts of savagery:

And most frightfully did they do the work of religious butchery and cruelty. Like the Scandinavian pirates, wherever they went they desolated with fire and sword, sparing neither age, nor sex, nor condition. They even wreaked their furious vengeance on inanimate objects, destroying houses, trees, vines, and every useful thing they could reach, leaving all behind a wide and blackened waste, marked by smoldering and smoking ruins, and the dead and putrefying bodies of murdered men, women, and children.

At the taking of Beziers the wretched sufferers fled to the churches for protection, but their savage enemies slaughtered them on the very altars, and filled the sanctuaries with their mangled bodies. And when the last living creature within the walls had been slain, and the houses plundered, the crusaders set fire to the city in all directions at once, and so made of it one huge funeral pile. Not a soul was left alive, nor a house left standing! During the slaughter one of the knights inquired of a fierce priest how they should distinguish between Catholics and heretics.

"Kill them all!" was his reply, "the Lord will know his own." In this one affair from twenty to thirty thousand human beings perished, because the religion of their butchers assured them that such bloody sacrifices would be acceptable to God.

The atrocities committed by the crusaders included not just murder but torture. Simon de Montfort was a French nobleman who was appointed leader of the Crusader army during the Albigensian Crusade:

But the priests and crusaders were not content with simple murder. It was often preceded by the most exquisite cruelties. De Montfort on one occasion seized a hundred prisoners, cut off their noses, tore out their eyes, and sent them with a one-eyed man as a guide to the neighboring castles to announce to the inhabitants what they might expect when taken. And often, as matter of amusement, so hardened had they become, they subjected their victims to the most dreadful tortures, and rejoiced in their wild cries of agony, and manifested the highest delight at the writhings and contortions of the dying wretches. So perfectly fiendish had these fanatics grown through the influence of their religious belief! And what can more clearly show the connection between faith and practice, or more conclusively demonstrate the truth that the worshiper will be like his god, than the revolting barbarities inflicted upon these humble and innocent people, on the ground that they were hated of the Deity, and devoted by Him to the flames and torments of an endless hell! Verily, the Christian is but a man, and that which makes the Pagan ferocious and bloodthirsty will produce the same effect upon him.

The St. Bartholomew's Day Massacre took place in 1572, starting on the eve of the feast of St. Bartholomew. Over the next several weeks, thousands of French Huguenots were murdered:

> The massacre of St. Bartholomew is another terrible proof of the power of religious faith to convert man into a fiend. As a single exhibition of slaughter and cruelty in the name of God and religion, this is perhaps the most monstrous, and on a more fearful scale, than any before or since. Probably thirty or forty thousand[2] victims perished in Paris and in the provinces in this one butchery! And it would be almost impossible to describe the variety of forms in murder, or to give a catalogue of the cruelties practiced. Even children of ten or twelve years engaged in the work of blood, and were seen cutting the throats of heretic infants!

But what is the most impious of all is the manner in which the news of this massacre was received at Rome by the Church and its head. The courier was welcomed with lively transports, and received a large reward for his joyful news. The pope and his cardinals marched in solemn procession to the church of St. Mark to acknowledge the special providence; high mass was celebrated; and a jubilee was published, that the whole Christian world might return thanks to God(!) for this destruction of the enemies of the church in France. In the evening, the cannon of castle St. Angelo were fired, and the whole city illuminated with bonfires, in expression of the general joy for this dreadful slaughter.[3]

And when we remember that all this was done in the name of Christianity and the church, that it was deemed a grateful offering to God, who, it is supposed, hates heretics, and will give them over to torments infinitely greater than these, and endless, we shudder to think how terrible an engine is superstition, and how nearly it has turned the Christian church into a slaughter-house!

The Inquisition was the supreme example of religious cruelty:

To complete the picture of depravity and cruelty, and confirm the argument for the influence of religion on the heart and life, we need only refer to that thrice-accursed institution, the INQUISITION! In this was concentrated all that was monstrous and revolting. It were impossible to put into words sufficiently expressive the abominable principles upon which its ministers proceeded in their persecutions, or the cold, deliberate, malignant ferocity with which they tortured their miserable victims. Every species of torment was invented that the united talents of the inquisitors could devise; and the protracting of life under the most excruciating agonies, so that the poor wretch might endure to the last degree, was reduced to a perfect system. The annals of Pagan sacrifice, with all its horrors, furnish no parallel to the atrocities of the Romish Inquisition. The blackest and bloodiest page in the history of superstition is that which bears the record of inquisitorial bigotry and ferocity. One would think that even hell itself might applaud the refinement of cruelty, were not the devils kept silent through envy of the superior skill and savageness of their earthly rivals.

This twisted and sadistic view spread from the religious leaders to the people:

But this terrible influence was not confined to the priests of this religion; the cruel and ferocious spirit of it was diffused abroad among all its believers; and its pestilential breath spread over the whole social life of the people. Informers were encouraged, heretics were hunted, private hatred took its revenge, and the most malignant passions of the corrupt heart were roused into action in the service of God and the church. Even the most tender ties of affection, and the most holy relations of life, were crushed beneath the iron heel of religious zeal. Husbands betrayed their wives, and parents their children, and sisters their brothers, and gave them up to the cruelties of the holy office, and to the flames of the auto-da-fe; and, so doing, congratulated themselves upon their fidelity to God, measured by their triumph over the loveliest attributes of humanity. So mighty, in this case also, was the power of a savage religion to crush every kindly feeling, every emotion of love and pity, and to train its followers to cruelty and blood.

Thayer points out that it is not only the Catholic Church and not only Christians of the distant past who are guilty of misrepresenting God and inflicting cruelty in His name:

But this influence is not confined to Catholics beliefs; it is found wherever the doctrines of which it is the

offspring are found. The history of Calvin and Servetus shows the same savage faith, having the power,
doing the same infernal work....

The cruel butcheries of the past, the dungeon, the
rack, the fagot, the bloody scourge falling upon the
back of the meekly suffering Quaker, the cry of
agony, the unheeded prayer for mercy—all these in
the past; —and the exceeding bitterness, the fierce
clamor and unblushing falsehoods of controversy in
the present; the refusal of the common courtesies of
life, or the stern hate that often lurks beneath outward
civility; the malignant sneer at the labors of those who
seek to unfold the truth of God's saving love for all;
the half exultation at any seeming proof of the final
triumph of evil and the ceaseless torments of the
wicked; the hardness of heart with which this result is
sometimes contemplated, and the indifference with
which one sect devotes another to this awful doom—
all these show clearly that the Christian is subject to
the same law which governs other men; show with a
painful distinctness that, so far as the refining
influences of literature and civilization would permit,
the belief in a ferocious god and an endless hell have
done their legitimate work upon his heart. Like the
Aztec of America, and the Norseman of Europe, he
has partaken of the spirit of his deity, and, supposing
it a duty and a most acceptable service, he begins, so
far as he can in this world, the work of torment which
he believes his unforgiving god will make infinite and
endless in the next.

As the words of Queen Mary reveal, belief in a savage
deity leads logically to cruelty toward others:

Queen Mary of England was right when, as Bp.
Burnet says, she defended her bloody persecutions by
appealing to the supposed example of the Deity: "As

the souls of heretics are hereafter to be eternally burning in hell, there can be nothing more proper than for me to imitate the divine vengeance by burning them on earth." This is legitimate and logical reasoning, and exhibits the natural fruits of the doctrine.

Thayer remarks that this savage faith has been somewhat "shorn of its power, to be sure, by the progress of society and civil institutions," but the destructive effects of it are still evident. Is there any hope for truly transforming our culture? The first step is knowing the true character of the One we worship. Thayer's statement quoted in "Should We Love Everybody? Part 2" bears repeating:

> **If, then, we would make mankind what they should be, we must begin with the object of their worship**; we must first make their religion what it should be. We must cast out from the holy place all the dark and ferocious superstitions of the past and the present, whether Pagan or Christian, and in the place of these set up, in all its divine beauty and simplicity, the merciful and loving religion of Jesus Christ. The views which this unfolds of God the Father, of His government and its final issues, can alone be favorable to the spiritual progress of humanity, can alone form the heart of man to gentleness and goodness, and recreate it in the image of heaven.

Thayer quotes from the Biblical Repository for April, 1843:

> "National religions," says a celebrated German, "will not become the friends of virtue and happiness until they teach that the Deity is not only an inconceivably powerful, but also an inconceivably wise and good being; that for this reason He gives way neither to anger nor revenge, and never punishes capriciously; that we owe to His favor alone all the good that we possess and enjoy; that even our sufferings contribute

to our highest good, and death is a bitter but salutary change; in fine, that the sacrifice most acceptable to God consists in a mind that seeks for truth, and a pure heart. Religions which announce these exalted truths offer to man the strongest preservatives from vice, and the strongest motives to virtue, exalt and ennoble his joys, console and guide him in all kinds of misfortunes, and inspire him with forbearance, patience, and active benevolence toward his brethren."

It was Thayer's desire that all people, particularly Christians, would recognize the true character of God and live accordingly. True Christianity would provide humans with powerful motives to virtue and inspire them with "forbearance, patience, and active benevolence":

Even so; let this be the religion of the nations, and soon the world shall be getting forward toward heaven. And it was to reveal these truths, and to bring them near to the heart of humanity, that Jesus gave His life, and labored with all the earnestness of His loving heart.

Let this, then, be the religion of the Christian, and he will be a Christian indeed. Let him believe in God as the parent of all, as the dispenser of life and good to all; let him see Him as Christ saw Him, clothed in robes of light and mercy, and he will love as Christ loved, and, so far as he may, will live as Christ lived. Let him believe that God always blesses, and he will not dare, he will not wish, to curse whom God hath blessed. Let him believe that God never hates, is never angry; and, that he may be like Him, and approved of Him, he will diligently seek to expel all hatred and passion from his own heart. Let him believe that all men are brethren, journeying home-ward to the presence of the Father, where, delivered from all evil, we shall be as the angels; and that it is the earnest entreaty of this Father that we should not fall out by the way, but bear each other's burdens, and love one another as He loves us, loves the world: let these be the Christian's views of God, and he shall indeed be born again from above. Let this be the religion of the nations, and

"Earth shall be paradise again,
And man, O God, thine image here."[5]

---

[1] *The Origin and History of the Doctrine of Endless Punishment* by Thomas B. Thayer; published in 1855. New and enlarged edition; Boston; no. 37 Cornwill; Entered according to Act of Congress, in the year 1855, by James M. Usher in the Clerk's Office of the District Court of the District of Massachusetts; Stereotyped by Hobart & Robbins, New England Type and Stereotype Foundry; Entered into electronic format by Matt Thomas, 1997.

[2] According to the Encyclopedia Britannica, estimates for the number of dead in the St. Bartholomew's Day Massacre vary widely: "Estimates of the number that perished in the disturbances, which lasted to the beginning of October, have varied from 2,000 by a Roman Catholic apologist to 70,000 by the contemporary Huguenot Maximilien de Béthune, duc de Sully, who himself barely escaped death. Modern writers put the number at 3,000 in Paris alone."

[3] Thayer recommends that the reader see "the fiendish letter of the pope to the French king on this occasion, in Smedley's *History of the Reformed Religion in France,* chap. ix."

[4] Thayer says regarding *Fanaticism*, sect. vi by Isaac Taylor, "I would recommend this work to the perusal and study of every clergyman, and every individual, in the land. It is the production of an original thinker, and an eloquent writer. The comparison of the Roman soldier and the Christian monk, in the sixth section, is seldom surpassed simply as a piece of composition, aside from its graphic truth and power."

[5] From "The Lord of Hosts is with us" by J. Montgomery.

# 53

# THE THREE WITNESSES

When you share the gospel, do you tell people about how much God loves them? Do you also warn them of the terrible fate that awaits them in hell if they refuse to repent and turn to Christ?

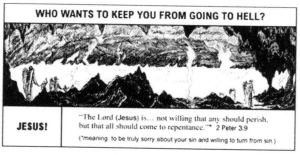

**WHO WANTS TO KEEP YOU FROM GOING TO HELL?**

**JESUS!**

"The Lord (Jesus) is... not willing that any should perish, but that all should come to repentance."* 2 Peter 3:9

(*meaning, to be truly sorry about your sin and willing to turn from sin.)

A Love Story c2002 by Jack T. Chick LLC

If your answer to both questions is "Yes," let me ask another question: Do you ever feel at all conflicted about declaring that this God who loves people so much that He gave His Son for them will allow people to suffer endlessly for failing to trust Him? How do you explain the seeming conflict to anyone who might ask?

1) There is no conflict; it is only our limited human reasoning that sees a conflict.

2) God's ways are higher than our ways (Is. 55:8–9); we cannot comprehend the wisdom of His ways.

3) God is infinitely holy; sin against an infinite God requires infinite punishment.

4) God's love demands that He punish sin; He does it to provide justice for His loved ones.

5) We all deserve condemnation; it is only by God's grace that anyone is saved.

6) God does not force anyone to go to hell; it is their own choice.

7) God is sovereign; He chooses whom He will save and we are not to question Him.

8) All that happens is to the glory of God; defeating and punishing sin brings glory to Him.

9) I do not concern myself with great matters; I have quieted myself like a weaned child with its mother (Ps. 131:1–2).

10) Other: Fill in the blank.

Which of these explanations make the most sense to you? Which are satisfying to your heart and mind? Or do you feel a nagging uneasiness that none really satisfy your soul?

I used to struggle with this dilemma. I thought that you *had* to accept eternal damnation if you wanted to be a good Bible-believing Christian. I used a variety of explanations like these to justify it in my own mind and try to convince others. As I wrestled with this problem, the best I could do was keep coming back to #9:

> O LORD, my heart is not lifted up;
>> my eyes are not raised too high;
> I do not occupy myself with things
>> too great and too marvelous for me.
> But I have calmed and quieted my soul,
>> like a weaned child with its mother;
>> like a weaned child is my soul within me.
> (Ps. 131:1–2)

None of the explanations gave real rest to my soul, so I tried to stop reasoning it out and just trust.

As a young Christian, I figured that a big part of my problem was immaturity; I thought that as I matured in the faith and came to know God better, my heart would be more in tune with His heart, and I would be better able to accept His ways. However, my uneasiness with eternal conscious torment (ECT) did not diminish over the years but rather increased. As I got to know more intimately the character of God and understand more deeply the work of Christ on the cross, the idea that billions of human beings would be lost forever and would suffer endlessly seemed more and more incompatible with God's nature and purposes.

Gradually I came to realize that my resistance to eternal hellfire did not spring from immaturity or from rebellion against God's truth. Rather, it was the work of three witnesses: my conscience, the Holy Spirit, and the Word of God.

Some will say that our **conscience** cannot be trusted, that it is just human feeling. And yet, the Bible says that even unbelievers have a God-given sense of right and wrong:

> When Gentiles, who do not have the law, by nature do what the law requires, they are a law to themselves, even though they do not have the law. They show that *the work of the law is written on their hearts, while their conscience also bears witness,* and their conflicting thoughts accuse or even excuse them (Rom. 2:14–15).

Although it is marred by sin, all people have an innate sense of good and evil. Even in the absence of any law, those inner moral principles help us distinguish right from wrong. Our conscience is not infallible and not the final authority, but if it tells us that something is desperately wrong with the idea that people will be tormented endlessly with no hope of relief, we should pay attention. If no halfway-decent human father would dream of allowing his children to suffer forever, then we have to wonder if the God who implanted basic morals in us would do such a thing.

In addition to our conscience, believers have the **Holy Spirit** to guide us into all truth (Jn. 16:12). The Spirit of truth lives with us and in us and teaches us all things and reminds us of what Jesus said (Jn. 14:17, 26). Beyond the general revelation given to all, Christians have the laws of God placed on our hearts and minds and illuminated by the Holy Spirit:

> The Holy Spirit also bears witness to us… "This is the covenant that I will make with them after those days, declares the Lord: I will put my laws on their hearts, and write them on their minds" (Heb. 10:15–16).

The Holy Spirit helps us to know the character of God as revealed by Jesus. He develops in us the fruit of the Spirit, which is the essence of God's own nature: love, joy, peace, patience, kindness, goodness, faithfulness, gentleness, and self-control. If something is incompatible with these qualities, it is not of God. We should be asking, "Is eternal damnation consistent with the nature of God as exemplified by Jesus Christ and expressed by the Holy Spirit?"

Finally, we have the witness of the **Word of God**. Although believers in ECT find support for their doctrine in Scripture, the witness of the conscience and of the Holy Spirit should alert us to the fact that such an interpretation is mistaken. It violates clear teachings of the Bible, and passages that *seem* to support it should be re-examined in light of clear revelation about the character of God. For example, God Himself declares that the idea of burning people in fire never even occurred to Him; it was the work of Baal worshippers:

> For the children of Israel and the children of Judah have done nothing but evil in my sight from their youth.…They built the high places of Baal in the Valley of the Son of Hinnom, to offer up their sons and daughters to Molech, though I did not command them, *nor did it enter into my mind, that they should do this abomination*, to cause Judah to sin (Jer. 32:30–35).

The true God says He never dreamed of burning human beings even temporarily, never mind endlessly—such a thing is an abomination to Him!

There is abundant evidence in Scripture, from Genesis to Revelation, that God's ultimate purpose is not to abandon most of humanity to endless torment but rather to redeem and restore all of creation. If the witness of your conscience and the Holy Spirit and the Word of God makes you at all uneasy about ECT, please pay attention and keep searching for the truth!

# 54

# THE UNPARDONABLE SIN

People sometimes ask me, "How can you believe that all people will eventually be saved if the Bible says there is at least one sin that will never be forgiven?"[1]

> [T]he blasphemy against the Spirit will not be forgiven.... [W]hoever speaks against the Holy Spirit will not be forgiven, either in this age or in the age to come (Mt. 12:32b, ESV).

> [W]hoever blasphemes against the Holy Spirit never has forgiveness, but is guilty of an eternal sin (Mk. 3:29)

> [T]he one who blasphemes against the Holy Spirit will not be forgiven (Lk. 12:10).

Some see an open-and-shut case here that those who have committed the sin called "blasphemy against the Holy Spirit" can never be forgiven, and that therefore not all people are saved. But there is no consensus about what this sin is, what the results of it are, and what "the age to come" is. In fact, you can find a variety of interpretations, both within a framework of eternal damnation and within a framework of ultimate restoration. Let me suggest one interpretation:

Salvation requires repentance from sin and submission to the convicting and saving work of the Holy Spirit. A person can be guilty of all kinds of sins and still come to Christ for forgiveness and salvation, but he *cannot* be forgiven if he is rejecting God's forgiveness as applied by the Holy Spirit. *As long as* he remains in a state of resistance against the conviction and forgiveness of the Holy Spirit, he *cannot* be saved.

In other words, *you cannot reject the saving work of the Holy Spirit and simultaneously receive the saving work of the Holy Spirit.* Anyone who "speaks against the Holy Spirit"—denies or rejects His work of regeneration—cannot be regenerated.

*No* sin is beyond hope of forgiveness! Even the most heinous sins can be forgiven, because Jesus died as the atoning sacrifice for those sins. But as long as a person refuses to allow the Holy Spirit to work in his heart, he cannot receive that forgiveness. These principles apply in "this age" and in "the age to come," whatever those ages refer to. However, the Holy Spirit is not powerless in the face of a person's present rejection of His work. It is His job to convict of sin, and He will continue to do so until the job is done. Ultimately He is able to bring every knee to bow and every tongue to confess Jesus as Lord.

Every explanation of the unpardonable sin that I have ever read tries to assure you that if you are afraid you have committed the unpardonable sin—you haven't. I would add my reassurance that, whatever your condition, it is not beyond hope. I do believe that you can be guilty of this sin— guilty of blaspheming against the Holy Spirit in the sense of standing in defiance of His convicting and redeeming work. However, you are not hopelessly lost—you can *stop* resisting and allow the Holy Spirit to bring you to repentance and draw you to the cross, where you will be freely pardoned.

---

[1] It should be noted that these passages indicate that other sins *will* be forgiven, even in the age to come:

> "Therefore I tell you, every sin and blasphemy will be forgiven people, but the blasphemy against the Spirit will not be forgiven. And whoever speaks a word against the Son of Man will be forgiven, but whoever speaks against the Holy Spirit will not be forgiven, either in this age or in the age to come" (Mt. 12:31-32).

> "Truly, I say to you, all sins will be forgiven the children of man, and whatever blasphemies they utter..." (Mk. 3:28).

> "And everyone who speaks a word against the Son of Man will be forgiven..." (Lk. 12:10).

# 55

# NOT THEM!

When God called Jonah to go and preach to the Ninevites, Jonah turned and ran the other way as fast and as far as he could. He was horrified that God would give those evil people a chance to repent. When they did, in fact, turn to the Lord, he was angry. He said, in effect, "Lord, I told you so. I knew they would repent, and I knew you would be merciful to them, even though they don't deserve it. So just kill me now. I'd rather be dead than have to be in the family of God with those guys" (Jon. 4:1–3).

When Jesus spoke of how Elijah and Elisha ministered to Gentiles, the Jews instantly turned on Him; they went from speaking well of Him to wanting to kill Him (Lk. 4:22–30). When the laborers in the vineyard went to receive their pay, those who had been working all day (had "borne the burden of the day and the scorching heat") were annoyed that the ones who came at the eleventh hour received the same pay (Mt. 20:12). They begrudged the fact that "those guys" were rewarded in the same measure. Similarly, the disciples were irritated because someone who was not part of their group was doing miracles in Jesus' name. The disciples told him to stop, because "he was not one of us" (Mk. 9:38).

Peter would have had nothing to do with Cornelius if God had not shown him "that [he] should not call any man unholy or unclean" (Acts 10:28) And when he reported back to Jerusalem about his visit with Cornelius, "those who were circumcised took issue with him," complaining that he had eaten with uncircumcised men (Acts 11:2). They couldn't grasp that God would welcome *Gentiles* into their fellowship.

Humans have a way of clustering in clans and cliques and shutting out others who don't fit or aren't considered deserving enough. *Not so with God!* He cared about the Ninevites and told Jonah, "And should not I pity Nineveh, that great city, in which there are more than 120,000 persons who do not know their right hand from their left, and also much cattle?" (Jon. 4:11). God cared about the widow of Zarephath and Naaman the Syrian (Lk. 4). The master told the laborers in the vineyard who complained about others coming in at the last hour, "Do you begrudge my generosity?" (Mt. 20:15). When the disciples grumbled about someone who was not one of them, Jesus said, "Whoever is not against us is for us" (Mk. 9:40). The Lord had to show Peter that God accepts all kinds of people: "God is not one to show partiality, but in every nation the man who fears Him and does what is right is welcome to Him" (Acts 10:34–35).

Jesus *welcomes* all who come to Him, including the Gentiles, who were despised by the Jews:

"Behold, my servant whom I have chosen,
    my beloved with whom my soul is well pleased.
I will put my Spirit upon him,
    and he will proclaim justice to the Gentiles.
He will not quarrel or cry aloud,
    nor will anyone hear his voice in the streets;
a bruised reed he will not break,
    and a smoldering wick he will not quench,
until he brings justice to victory;
    and in his name the Gentiles will hope" (Mt. 12:18–21).

Over and over, the New Testament shouts that God's family is to include Jews *and* Gentiles, that is, Jews and non-Jews—no one is excluded! Simeon recognized the baby Jesus as the one who would bring salvation to Gentiles *and* Jews:

For my eyes have seen your salvation,
    which you have prepared in the sight of all nations:

a light for revelation to the Gentiles,
and the glory of your people Israel" (Lk 2:29–32).

Paul's missionary journeys were to the Gentiles, and he declared that the gospel was for them:

For so the Lord has commanded us, saying, "I have made you a light for the Gentiles, that you may bring salvation to the ends of the earth" (Acts 13:47).

By being the first to rise from the dead, [the Christ] would proclaim light both to our people and to the Gentiles (Acts 26:23).

Or is God the God of Jews only? Is he not the God of Gentiles also? Yes, of Gentiles also (Rom. 3:29).

And the Scripture, foreseeing that God would justify the Gentiles by faith, preached the gospel beforehand to Abraham, saying, "In you shall all the nations be blessed" (Gal. 3:8).

This mystery is that the Gentiles are fellow heirs, members of the same body, and partakers of the promise in Christ Jesus through the gospel (Eph. 3:6).

It is no longer a mystery! God is calling all people into His family. The early Church was learning that former enemies were to be incorporated into the Body of Christ. Do you have any "Gentiles" in your life—people you don't really like and don't want to be part of your fellowship? Any person— or class of people—you think should not be in the Kingdom? Then you are at cross-purposes with the Cross purpose:

For he himself is our peace, who has made the two groups one and has destroyed the barrier, the dividing wall of hostility.... His purpose was to create in himself one new humanity out of the two, thus making peace, and in one body to reconcile both of them to God through the cross (Eph 2:14–16).

# 56

# FROM MOURNING TO JOY

A voice is heard in Ramah,
lamentation and bitter weeping.
Rachel is weeping for her children;
she refuses to be comforted for her children,
because they are no more.
Jeremiah 31:15

In 2012, there were no joyous homecomings for the families whose loved ones were lost in the Sandy Hook tragedy. The victims would not be coming home, and their places at the table would be empty that Christmas and every Christmas to come. The whole nation wept with those who were weeping. Even those of us who did not know the children looked into their innocent faces and refused to be comforted, because they were no more.

Is there anything that we as Christians can offer to families facing such devastating loss? We are the bearers of the gospel—the *good news*. Do we have any good news for them? Our go-to verse for inexplicable affliction—Romans 8:28—can ring hollow; what possible good could ever make up for such horrific evil? And even if some good for somebody does come about, the families of the victims know that their lives will never be right again.

And yet...we know from God's Word that He is good and righteous and sovereign and just. How will He show His goodness and righteousness and sovereignty and justice? Can *He* ever make things right again? By faith we affirm that He *will* right all wrongs and bring about His perfect justice. But what will His justice look like?

As I wrote in "Let Justice Roll On Like a River" (#45), true justice involves both punishing the wrongdoers and making restitution to those who have been wronged. In the case of robbery, for example, justice is not served unless the thief is punished and the goods are returned to their rightful owner. God's justice will certainly include judging and punishing the offenders and restoring what was lost to the victims.

Clearly this perfect justice can never come about through our human justice system in this life. Our hope has to be in God's ability to bring it about in the end. Because Adam Lanza, the Sandy Hook shooter, took his own life, he will never even be dealt with by the human justice system. But rest assured that he faces a far more terrifying judgment—standing before the Judge of all the Earth. He will have to answer to God Himself. He will not get away with anything.

And what about his victims? Our justice system is utterly unable to bring them back to life and restore them to their families. As I wrote earlier,

> Our human justice system is absolutely powerless to bring about full justice in the sense of restoring the lives of those who have been murdered. We can take another life to even the score, but we can't achieve real equity.

> But God can! He is fully able to bring about complete restitution for all losses, including bringing murder victims back from the dead to be reunited with their loved ones.... I believe that His infinite wisdom and infinite power and infinite righteousness will be able to achieve perfect justice.... Only God could weave together the infinite number of factors in the lives of all humanity to bring about perfect justice for all.

Even Adam Lanza will be judged with complete justice. I'm sure there are many who think he should burn in hell forever. But we can't forget that this young man who was barely out of his teens was once a lost and lonely little boy himself. Only God knows all the circumstances of his life and is able to make right whatever may have happened to him. The fact that there is hope for Adam Lanza means there is hope for all of us and hope that one day everything will be made right and there will truly be peace on earth.

The thought of judgment and restoration at some distant, unknown future time may seem small comfort to those who want someone to pay now and who live with the daily reality of a hole in their heart that nothing can fill. But we have to hang on to the reality that God will fulfill His promises, even if we don't understand how or when. He will be the "one God and Father of all, who is over all and through all and in all" (Eph. 4:6). And as He promises in Revelation,

> Behold, the dwelling place of God is with man. He will dwell with them, and they will be his people, and God himself will be with them as their God. He will wipe away every tear from their eyes, and death shall be no more, neither shall there be mourning, nor crying, nor pain anymore, for the former things have passed away (Rev. 21:3–4).

We cannot promise that everything will be made right in this life. The hole in the heart will not go away, the tears will keep coming, the empty place at the table will not be filled. But we can help those who are grieving to know the God who is near to the brokenhearted. We can reach out to other lost and lonely children and adults and introduce them to the One who loved them so much that He laid down His own life for them. We can try to reflect the character of God in our lives so that others will know what He is really like and be drawn to Him, the One who binds up the brokenhearted and comforts those who mourn. In the words of Handel's *Messiah*, taken from Isaiah 40:1, "Comfort ye, comfort ye, my people, saith your God." We can help people hang on to the blessed hope that God will reconcile all to Himself (Col. 1:19–20) and bring about the restoration of everything (Acts 3:21). We can help each other cling to the conviction that God will not fail to bring about the glorious future He has promised. One day death will be reversed and "swallowed up in victory" (1 Cor. 15:54). There will be a stupendous homecoming, and all those who have been snatched away by death will be restored to those who love them. All tears will be wiped away, and there will be no more mourning or crying or pain. As Peter says, "Though you do not now see him, you believe in him and rejoice with joy that is inexpressible and filled with glory" (1 Pet. 1:8). God has promised and He will do it: one day all our sorrow will be overwhelmed with inexpressible joy.

I will turn their mourning into joy;
I will comfort them, and give them gladness for sorrow.
Jeremiah 31:13

# 57

# CALLED FOR A PURPOSE

My friend Beth and I have been doing summer Bible studies together for several years. The first year we did it, I felt lost trying to choose what materials to use, so I went to the Christian Book Distributors (CBD) website in hopes of getting some ideas. There were thousands of options, but one title featured on the main page of the Bible studies section caught my eye: *Calm My Anxious Heart: A Woman's Guide to Finding Contentment,*[1] by Linda Dillow. Not only was the topic perfect for Beth and me; the author was a special person in my life—she and her husband, Jody, were the leaders of the campus ministry through which I committed my life to Christ.

The title of one of the chapters of Linda's book was "A Faulty Focus," about defining your life purpose. As we studied that chapter, it seemed to be a good time to put into writing the thoughts I had been having about my own life purpose. The result was what you are about to read.

As stated in the Westminster Shorter Catechism, "Man's chief end is to glorify God and to enjoy Him forever." The primary purpose of every believer is to glorify the Triune God—to honor the Father, to know Christ, to walk in the Spirit—and in so doing we will find our greatest delight in Him. In addition, I believe that God also has a unique purpose for each of His children. If we understand the reason He put us on earth, we can live each day purposefully, as Jesus did:

> My food is to do the will of him who sent me and to accomplish his work (Jn. 4:34).

When we come to the end of our life we can say with Jesus,

> I glorified you on earth, having accomplished the
> work that you gave me to do (Jn. 17:4).

Defining your life purpose is one of those tasks that author Stephen Covey would identify as "important but not urgent." We tend to spend much of our time on activities that may be urgent but not necessarily important. Those who have truly learned to manage their time—in other words, to manage their lives—know that it is essential to make time for important but non-pressing activities, like determining what God is calling you to accomplish with your life.

Covey urges readers to "begin with the end in mind"—to visualize what it will be like to come to the end of your life and look back on what you have achieved. Knowing where you want to head will help you to take daily steps in the right direction. He advocates writing a "personal mission statement" to express your values and what you want to be and to do. We can learn much about God's will for our lives from His Word, and we can also ask Him for discernment to know His unique purpose for us individually.

> I cry out to God Most High, to God who fulfills his
> purpose for me (Ps. 57:2).

Discovering God's purpose for me has been a process involving a lot of stumbling around, often not even being conscious of anything beyond getting through the daily demands of life. After losing my job a few years ago, I was somewhat at a loss to know how to spend my days. For 30+ years my life had been defined by kids and/or work, and suddenly I wasn't quite sure what I was supposed to do with myself. So I tried to become more intentional about figuring out how God wants me to spend the rest of my life. As part of that discernment process, I spent a day at a seminary to explore how I might use the resources there. That day—and in particular, one class that I attended—proved to be pivotal in helping me see God's purpose for the rest of my days.

When I had the opportunity to visit classes at the seminary, I chose a Pastoral Ministry class because I figured it was related to my interest in counseling and personal ministry. God has given me a ministry to hurting women, and I wanted to learn how to better serve them. I had no idea what that day's topic for the class would be, but it turned out to be a theme that I have a passion for—reconciliation. Just days before, I had written "Reconciliation: The Heart of God's Grand Plan for Creation" (#7), and I was thrilled that the professor spoke about this topic using many of the same passages that I had used (Col. 1, Eph. 2, Rom. 5, and 2 Cor. 5). His emphasis was on the pastoral aspect of reconciliation while mine was on the theological doctrine of reconciliation, but his class helped me to see the direct connection between the two. It provided the link between my two passions, one practical and one theological: my desire to minister to people's emotional and spiritual needs and my interest in the theological question of reconciliation, particularly what it means that God will "reconcile to Himself all things."[1]

In his notes for the class, the professor identified reconciliation as "*the* great work of God":

From Gen. 3 forward, God undertakes the work of reconciling all things to Himself. This is *the* great work of God (Eph. 1:10), which God Himself is ever engaged in (John 5:17).... God's work of reconciling "all things, in heaven and on earth" to Himself, has an *already*—focused on the finished work of Christ at the cross and resurrection (Col. 1:15–23; 2 Co. 5:18a, 19a; Eph. 2:11–22), a *not yet*—which will involve the final defeat of every enemy, principality and power that currently is in defiance of God (1 Cor. 15:20–28), and an *even now* (2 Co. 5:18b, 19b–20).

He showed that Christian ministry *must* involve reconciliation:

It is clear that the reconciling work of Christ includes reconciling humanity back to God (Eph. 2:1–10; Rom.

5:8–10; Col. 1:15–23, etc.) and reconciling humans to one another (Eph. 2:11–22; Gal. 3:28; Col. 3:11; 1 Cor. 12:13). These, then, *must* mark pastoral work.

He named the areas of enmity where God is working to bring about reconciliation and where we can cooperate with Him in that work:

> To fully consider what our current ministry of reconciliation should involve, we need to consider the aspects of enmity that have marked us since the Fall. These include enmity between:

- God v. human
- human v. human
- human v. oneself
- human v. creation (nature)
- human v. creatures
- creature v. creature

My particular interest is in the second and third (restoring relationships between human beings and helping people deal with inner conflict in order to become whole psychologically and emotionally), both of which, of course, also involve the first—being in right relationship with God. I am very thankful that God used this class to bring into focus His great purpose and the need for us to be actively cooperating with Him to bring it about. In partial fulfillment of His purposes for me, the book you are now reading is my effort to share the theology of reconciliation. My first book shows what it looks like to live out the principles of reconciliation—to value all people and help them find wholeness in Christ.

I believe the cross will fully accomplish the reconciliation of the world, and we will be blessed and be a blessing to others as we work to give a foretaste of God's final victory. We can do so by being on board with Jesus in His work of restoration and righteousness as described in Isaiah 61:1–3:

The Spirit of the Lord GOD is upon me,
 because the LORD has anointed me
to bring good news to the poor;
 he has sent me to bind up the brokenhearted,
to proclaim liberty to the captives, and the opening
 of the prison to those who are bound;
to proclaim the year of the LORD's favor,
 and the day of vengeance of our God;
 to comfort all who mourn;
to grant to those who mourn in Zion—to give
 them a beautiful headdress instead of ashes,
the oil of gladness instead of mourning,
 the garment of praise instead of a faint spirit;
that they may be called oaks of righteousness,
 the planting of the LORD, that he may be glorified.

God's purpose for you will include those aspects of His will that apply to all believers, and also a special calling to the unique work He has planned for you, which will be different from mine and everyone else's. I would encourage you to search the Scriptures to find God's will and ask Him to show you His particular purpose for your life. As Paul puts it,

Live life, then, with a due sense of responsibility, not as men who do not know the meaning and purpose of life but as those who do. Make the best use of your time, despite all the difficulties of these days. Don't be vague but firmly grasp what you know to be the will of God (Eph. 5:15–17, Phillips).

---

[1] Sharing the good news of Jesus' complete victory over sin and death—and what it means both theologically and practically—has become my passion. I have found the evidence to be so compelling that I could no more deny it than I could deny the truth of the resurrection. I have to say with Martin Luther, "Here I stand. I can do no other." And I resonate with Jeremiah, who was driven to proclaim the message God had given him: "If I say, 'I will not mention him or speak any more in his name,' there is in my heart as it were a burning fire shut up in my bones, and I am weary with holding it in, and I cannot" (Jer. 20:9).

# 58

# A WORD TO THE CURIOUS: CAUTION, IT'S COSTLY

Very early on in my exploration of Christian Universalism, I came across the stories of some nineteenth-century believers who came under fire for even entertaining the idea of the salvation of all. Pastors lost their pastorates, men and women were abandoned by their friends, church members were ostracized and excommunicated, and many were labeled as heretics or false teachers. I remember thinking, "I'm sure glad that wouldn't happen today!"

How utterly naïve I was! I never imagined how incredibly staunch the resistance would be to the idea that Jesus will save the world. I anticipated that Christians would be rightly cautious about a belief that challenged the status quo, but I was completely blindsided by the vehement opposition to the salvation of all. Even for those who are just exploring universal salvation, I give you fair warning that it may be a rocky road.

As in the nineteenth century, opposition to Christian Universalism is alive and well today. On one online forum for Evangelical Universalism, there was an Introduction section where participants could tell a little about their journey. Nearly everyone who had embraced UR or even considered it had a story of rejection or suspicion from family and friends or from the evangelical community, some even losing their livelihood in Christian ministries.

Becoming a Christian Universalist has been costly for me personally. Online critics have accused me of heresy, false teaching, operating in the flesh, psychological manipulation, abusing Scripture, and cult-like behavior.[1] My salvation has

been called into question, I have been grilled on my orthodoxy, derogatory remarks have been made about my spiritual
condition, and my motives have been attacked.

People I know personally have not been so hostile, but I
have come under suspicion in the local Christian community,
and some friendships have become tense. My beliefs are
suspect in my church, and I am limited in how I can serve
there. I have experienced the loss of trust and respect and the
loss of ministry and the fellowship that went with it. After
two of my online critics contacted the national office of the
ministry I had been part of for more than a quarter-century, I
was dismissed from leadership in that organization. Although
I was no longer a leader, I remained in the organization as a
participant for two and a half more years, until it became
clear that it was time for me to move on. The image that
sticks with me from the nearly thirty years I dedicated to that
ministry is of me walking away on my last day, alone, with no
one saying goodbye.

I tell you these facts not to dissuade you from examining
your faith and considering Christian Universalism; please
*do* put your beliefs to the test! As Eugene Peterson says, "The
reason many of us do not ardently believe in the gospel is that
we have never given it a rigorous testing, thrown our hard
questions at it, faced it with our most prickly doubts."[2] So go
ahead and give the gospel a rigorous testing and throw your
hard questions at it and face it with your most prickly doubts.
I just want to urge you to count the cost and to be aware of
what you may face if you embrace Universal Restoration. I'm
confident that one day Restoration will again be the dominant
view in the Church, but for now it is a lonely road. I always
assumed that I would be part of the ministry from which I
was dismissed until I died, but I'm learning not to make
assumptions about God's will. The memory of the day I was
told I could no longer be a leader is clear—it was my birthday! I remember thinking that getting kicked out was a
strange birthday present, but I know God has His purposes.
Now that I am not an official representative of the organi-

zation, I have freedom to openly proclaim the truly Good News of Jesus' complete victory over sin and death on the cross. If I had stayed in the ministry, this book would not have happened. From time to time God may need to shake us out of a comfortable rut and open our eyes to the path *He* has chosen for us. Our responsibility is to remain faithful, follow the leading of the Holy Spirit, and choose joy instead of bitterness.

---

[1]From direct statements and from verses quoted in reference to me, I have been told by online accusers:

You are an ungodly person.
You are spiritually sick.
You deny Jesus Christ.
You are a heretic/false prophet/false teacher.
You are a hypocrite.
You do wicked works.
You pervert the grace of God.
You were long ago designated for this condemnation.
You believe a different gospel.
You are clearly apostate.
You went out from among the true believers so you are not one of them.
You were probably never saved in the first place.
You have a heart of rebellion.
You have been deceived.
You reject the words of Christ in favor of your carnal thinking.
You are warped and sinning and self-condemned.
You disguise yourself as a servant of righteousness.
Your ignorance in how language works is beyond mind-blowing.

You are dangerous to those who are young in their faith.
You have ruined the gospel.
You deny Christ daily.
You are spiritually dead in your sins.
You are utterly ignorant that you undercut the gospel every time you speak.
You are a savage wolf and your fangs are showing.
You are willfully ignorant.
God sent you a strong delusion, that you should believe a lie.
You are damned because you don't believe the truth but have pleasure in unrighteousness.
UR is the product of your flesh that will have disastrous effects in your life if you don't repent.
You speak perverse things.
You have a Christless ministry.
You don't care about what God says.
You are a liar.
You are a murderer.
You are a child of Satan.

[2]Peterson, Eugene. *A Long Obedience in the Same Direction,* IVP Books, 2000.

# 59

# A WORD TO THE CRITICS: CAUTION, IT'S CRUCIAL

The Church of Jesus Christ has a huge problem on its hands: a large and growing number of Christians worldwide believe that God is ultimately going to save everyone. This belief represents a serious threat to the traditional orthodoxy that has held sway for centuries. If the belief in universal salvation is false, then the Church is in danger of being corrupted by an insidious heresy. On the other hand, if the belief is true, then the Church has been misrepresenting God for centuries by saying that He created billions of people only to have them end up going out of existence or else being forever banished from Him and subjected to endless conscious torment.

So either way—whether ultimate restoration is false or true—the Church faces an enormous challenge. The whole matter of heaven and hell and who goes where and why and for how long is one of the most critical issues confronting the Church, if not *the* most crucial. What is more essential than presenting the truth about who God is and how He determines the eternal destiny of mankind? We *must* get it right so that we accurately present God's truth to a lost world. If we proclaim universal restoration and it is not true, people may be lulled into complacency, thinking they will make it in the end while in reality they are headed for never-ending horror. On the other hand, if we preach hellfire-and-brimstone and *it* is not true, then we drive away people who are put off by what they see as the brutality and the exclusivity of Christianity, which can be huge deterrents to coming to faith.

If you are alarmed about the rise of universalism and want to defend the traditional position, I commend your desire to be faithful to the Word of God. I understand that you want to be cautious about any teaching that might go against Scripture. You want to rightly divide the word of truth and accurately represent God and His purposes. You don't want to be guilty of preaching a weak God who's soft on sin. You don't want to suggest that the cross isn't really necessary because everybody gets saved anyway.

I get it. I'm the same way. And I hope you maintain your commitment to the authority of Scripture. I would just ask that you be willing to consider looking at the Bible with fresh eyes. Take courage to remove the lenses through which all input you receive is filtered. Try looking at the Word through the framework of redemption, which is a theme that runs strong and deep through all of Scripture. Give Christian Universalism an honest hearing. If you don't like what you see or are not convinced by it, you can always go back to believing in annihilation or eternal damnation, and in fact you will come away better equipped to defend your position.

You may be feeling resistance to ideas that seem to challenge what you have believed for years or perhaps decades. The resistance may be particularly strong if you are a pastor or teacher or evangelist because you are afraid that if universal restoration were true, it would somehow threaten to invalidate what you have been preaching and teaching all along. Not at all! Universal salvation is not a *negation* of the fundamental truths of the gospel but rather an affirmation and *amplification* of them. You have been teaching that God did a wonderful thing by sending His Son to be our Savior; it's actually even *more* wonderful than you ever imagined! Believing that Jesus' death on the cross will fully accomplish its purpose of saving all would not discredit your past ministry but rather make your future ministry more powerful.

I chose the title of this chapter deliberately; this subject is *crucial* in the sense that it is supremely important and that it goes to the heart of the matter—the *crux*, the *cross*. What is the purpose of the cross? How powerful is it really? Will Jesus' work on the cross rescue *some* or *all* of His creation from the grip of sin and death?

All sides of this discussion would do well to listen to the words of the British Quaker Book of Faith and Practice:

> When words are strange or disturbing to you, try to sense where they come from and what has nourished the lives of others. Listen patiently and seek the truth which other people's opinions may contain for you. Avoid hurtful criticism and provocative language. Do not allow the strength of your convictions to betray you into making statements that are unfair or untrue. Think it possible that you may be mistaken.

And before trying to silence the voices of restoration, consider the words of Gamaliel, speaking to the people who wanted to kill Peter and the other apostles. In Acts 5 he reminded them of two different leaders who had appeared "claiming to be somebody" and had rallied others to their cause. They died, their followers were scattered, and their movements came to nothing. "Therefore," Gamaliel cautioned his hearers, "in the present case I advise you: Leave these men alone! Let them go! For if their purpose or activity is of human origin, it will fail. But if it is from God, you will not be able to stop these men; you will only find yourselves fighting against God" (Acts 5:38–39).

# 60

# THE HEART OF THE LAW

Now that we are coming to the conclusion of this book, I want to circle back to the theme of love that runs through both of my books. If we could really grasp that "God is love" and

> **GOD IS LOVE.**
> **LOVE ONE**
> **ANOTHER.**

that everything He does is driven by love, we would be able to see Him in all His holiness and compassion. His love, in turn, is the model and impetus for us to "Love one another."

Jesus Himself taught that love is the foundation of our relationship with God and with one another. According to rabbinical Judaism, there are 613 *mitzvoh*, or commandments, in the Torah, the five books of Moses. The commandments are divided into two categories: 248 positive and 365 negative. With so many dos and don'ts, it's virtually impossible to know them all and completely impossible to obey them all. Thankfully, the New Testament gives us the key that enables us to understand God's law in a manageable way and to obey it in a realistic way. When asked "which is the great commandment in the Law," Jesus replied,

> "You shall love the Lord your God with all your heart and with all your soul and with all your mind. This is the great and first commandment. And a second is like it: You shall love your neighbor as yourself. **On these two commandments depend all the Law and the Prophets**" (Mt. 22:37–40).

Our first responsibility, then, is to love God. If you're not sure exactly what that looks like, then consider that our love for God is expressed and demonstrated by loving others. And *that*, my friends, is spelled out very clearly throughout the New Testament.

Let's begin with the book of James—a very practical guide about how to live out our faith. In a Bible study on the book of James, the memory verse for chapter 2 was verse 8:

If you really **fulfill the royal law** according to the Scripture, "You shall love your neighbor as yourself," you are doing well.

This verse is central to chapter 2, and indeed to the entire book of James. *Fulfilling the royal law* means loving your neighbor. James is quoting from the Old Testament, "You shall love your neighbor as yourself: I am the Lord" (Lev. 19:18). Micah echoes the simplicity of this command:

He has told you, O man, what is good;
   and what does the LORD require of you
but to do justice, and to love kindness,
   and to walk humbly with your God? (6:8)

Walking with God means exercising justice, kindness, and humility.

Jesus often reiterates the principle of loving one another as the foundation of following Him. In the Sermon on the Mount, He extends the law of loving our neighbor to loving even our enemies:

"You have heard that it was said, You shall love your neighbor and hate your enemy.' But I say to you, **Love your enemies** and pray for those who persecute you, **so that you may be sons of your Father who is in heaven**.... For if you love those who love you, what reward do you have? Do not even the tax collectors do the same?... You therefore must be perfect, as your heavenly Father is perfect (Mt. 5:43–48).

Loving people who love you back is no big deal—even pagans do that much. What really sets us apart as children of our heavenly Father is loving our enemies. Why? Because God loves *His* enemies, so when we do the same, we are becoming like Him:

> "But I say to you who hear, **Love your enemies**, do good to those who hate you, bless those who curse you, pray for those who abuse you. To one who strikes you on the cheek, offer the other also.... And as you wish that others would do to you, do so to them. If you love those who love you, what benefit is that to you? For even sinners love those who love them. And if you do good to those who do good to you, what benefit is that to you? For even sinners do the same.... But **love your enemies**, and do good, and lend, expecting nothing in return, and your reward will be great, and **you will be sons of the Most High, for he is kind to the ungrateful and the evil**. Be merciful, even as your Father is merciful" (Lk. 6:27–37).

The Golden Rule is in the Luke 6 passage above and also in Matthew 7:12, where Jesus emphasizes that following it is the way to fulfill the Law:

> "So whatever you wish that others would do to you, do also to them, for this is the Law and the Prophets."

As Jesus' ministry was drawing to a close, He wanted to be sure His disciples understood the paramount importance of loving one another as a reflection and demonstration of His love:

> "A new commandment I give to you, that you love one another: **just as I have loved you**, you also are to love one another" (Jn. 13:34).

> "This is my commandment, that you love one another **as I have loved you**" (Jn. 15:12).

"I made known to them your name, and I will continue to make it known, **that the love with which you have loved me may be in them**, and I in them" (Jn. 17:26).

The epistle writers have loads of instructions about how to love one another, even our enemies. In Romans 12:9–21, Paul gives some 30 ways to show genuine love:

Let love be genuine. Abhor what is evil; hold fast to what is good. Love one another with brotherly affection. Outdo one another in showing honor. Do not be slothful in zeal, be fervent in spirit, serve the Lord. Rejoice in hope, be patient in tribulation, be constant in prayer. Contribute to the needs of the saints and seek to show hospitality. Bless those who persecute you; bless and do not curse them. Rejoice with those who rejoice, weep with those who weep. Live in harmony with one another. Do not be haughty, but associate with the lowly. Never be wise in your own sight. Repay no one evil for evil, but give thought to do what is honorable in the sight of all. If possible, so far as it depends on you, live peaceably with all. Beloved, never avenge yourselves.... If your enemy is hungry, feed him; if he is thirsty, give him something to drink.... Do not be overcome by evil, but overcome evil with good.

In Romans 13 Paul emphasizes that love is the fulfillment of the law:

Owe no one anything, except to love each other, for **the one who loves another has fulfilled the law**. For the commandments, "You shall not commit adultery, You shall not murder, You shall not steal, You shall not covet," and any other commandment, are summed up in this word: "You shall love your neighbor as yourself." Love does no wrong to a neighbor; therefore **love is the fulfilling of the law** (Rom. 13:8–10).

The whole of chapter 13 of 1 Corinthians is a description of love, the quality that is greater even than faith or hope. And the prison epistles keep reiterating that love is the fulfillment of the law and a reflection of the character of God in Jesus Christ:

> Through love serve one another. For **the whole law is fulfilled in one word**: "You shall love your neighbor as yourself" (Gal. 5:13–14).

> Be kind to one another, tenderhearted, forgiving one another, **as God in Christ forgave you** (Eph. 4:32).

> Therefore **be imitators of God**, as beloved children. And walk in love, as Christ loved us and gave himself up for us, a fragrant offering and sacrifice to God (Eph. 5:1–2).

> And it is my prayer **that your love may abound** more and more, with knowledge and all discernment, so that you may approve what is excellent, and so be pure and blameless for the day of Christ, filled with the fruit of righteousness that comes through Jesus Christ, to the glory and praise of God (Phil. 1:9–11).

> You have put off the old self with its practices and have put on the new self, which is being renewed in knowledge **after the image of its creator**.... Put on then, as God's chosen ones, holy and beloved, compassionate hearts, kindness, humility, meekness, and patience, bearing with one another and, if one has a complaint against another, forgiving each other; as the Lord has forgiven you, so you also must forgive. And **above all these put on love**, which binds everything together in perfect harmony (Col. 3:9–14).

If you need more specifics about how to love your neighbor, consider the rest of the "one another" passages in the epistles. Here are some more of the dozens of verses that tell us how to treat one another:

Accept one another, then, just as Christ accepted you
(Rom. 15:7).

Bear one another's burdens (Gal. 6:2).

Be patient, bearing with one another in love (Eph.
4:2).

Submit to one another (Eph. 5:21)

In humility consider others better than yourselves
(Phil. 2:3)

Encourage one another (1 Th. 4:18; 5:11; Heb. 10:25).

Build one another up (I Th. 5:11)

Always seek to do good to one another (1 Th. 5:15)

Spur one another on toward love and good deeds
(Heb. 10:24).

Pray for one another (Js. 5:16).

Live in harmony with one another (1 Pet. 3:8)

Offer hospitality to one another (1 Pet. 4:9).

Clothe yourselves with humility toward one another
(1 Pet. 5:5)

In chapter 3 of his first epistle, John says that the one
who does not love his brother is *not* a child of God (v. 10).
Chapter 4 is all about love; in verses 7–21 alone, the word *love*
appears 27 times. The key is that God is love, and because He
loves us, we ought to love one another:

Beloved, let us **love one another**, for **love is from
God**, and whoever loves has been born of God and
knows God. Anyone who does not love does not
know God, because **God is love**.... Beloved, if **God
so loved us**, we also ought to **love one another**....
And this commandment we have from him: whoever
loves God must also **love his brother** (1 John 4:7–8,
11, 21).

Looking at all these verses might seem as overwhelming
as the 613 commands in the Torah. But when you boil it all
down to love, it becomes simple. Not easy to do—obedience
can be really hard—and not always easy to figure out, but at

least we have one key principle through which to evaluate all our actions. So try putting your decisions to the love test: Are they reflections of the love of Jesus? The more our new self is renewed in knowledge after the true image of its Creator, the more we will look like Him, and the more the world will see Him as He really is—the loving Father who cares for every single human being He has created and will one day reconcile them all to Himself and to one another.

I pray that you, being rooted and established in love,
may have power, together with all the Lord's holy people,
to grasp how wide and long and high and deep is the love
of Christ, and to know this love that surpasses knowledge—
that you may be filled to the measure of all the fullness of God.
Ephesians 3:17−19

# ABOUT THE AUTHOR

Diane Perkins Castro was born in Syracuse, New York, the first of five children. In 1972, she married an astrophysicist from a city due south of Syracuse on the other side of the equator—Juan Antonio (Tony) Castro from Lima, Peru. Their three daughters were born in the Midwest and their three sons on the North Shore of Massachusetts, where they have made their home for more than 35 years.

Diane spent the better part of 18 years as a stay-at-home mom and then entered the field of educational publishing. Working first for a small development house and later for a large publishing company, she wrote and edited print and on-line materials for math and language arts instruction. Free-lancing in recent years has allowed her the flexibility to spend more time with family—visiting aging parents, caring for Tony when he developed cancer, and traveling to be with scattered children and grandchildren, now numbering one grandson and seven granddaughters. She enjoys playing volleyball (three seasons on the beach this year), trying (and mostly failing) to beat her sons in Ping-Pong, hiking, biking, snowboarding, and occasionally running obstacle races and in a throwback to her childhood, playing dodgeball.

Diane's first book, *Reflections of a Tomboy Grandma,* centers on the theme that every human being is created by God in His image and has great worth. The book was wildly success-ful, earning the coveted 1,769,317[th] spot on Amazon's best-seller list and selling 66 copies the first month alone (mostly to her very supportive mother and other family members).

# APPENDIX A:
# QUICK QUESTIONS

*In any discussion of universal salvation, certain questions and objections are likely to arise. The whole topic is so massive that it's difficult to pursue one train of thought without getting sidetracked by another equally compelling one. Here are very brief answers to some of the usual questions, many of which are discussed in greater detail in the essays in the body of this book. Use this Appendix to find short answers to questions you may have, and read the chapters suggested in parentheses (#) or use the Index to find more information on each topic.*

**Q:** Does ultimate restoration mean all paths lead to heaven?

**A:** No! The only way to become fit for heaven is through Jesus Christ by way of the cross. We must come to Him in humility and repentance and He must cleanse us through His blood shed for our sins. (#7, 19, 22, 24, 44)

**Q:** Doesn't universalism downplay the seriousness of sin?

**A:** No! Biblical universalism has a very strong view of the seriousness of sin. In fact, God hates sin so much that He will do everything in His power to *eradicate* it from His creation. No one will get away with anything; the consequences of sin are severe, but the discipline will be purposeful—to bring about repentance and salvation. (#32, 45)

**Q:** Does universalism do away with hell and judgment?

**A:** Not at all. Judgment is very much a part of the belief, but its purpose is redemptive, not just retributive. Judgment is necessary to deal with sin and drive it out and purify the sinner to be fit for heaven. Whatever form "hell" actually takes, it will be awful. "It is a fearful thing to fall into the hands of the living God." But it is not hopeless. (#41, 42)

**Q:** Doesn't a belief in ultimate restoration reduce the incentive to share the gospel?

**A:** By no means! Suppose you know that your child will be in a terrible fire and suffer horrible burns, but you know he will not die. Within twenty years he will recover completely and be fine. Does the knowledge that he will not die take away the incentive to warn him about the fire? Not at all! You still feel great urgency, just not absolute desperation and hopelessness. Similarly, those who do not come to Christ in this life will face judgment for their sins, and although they will not suffer forever, those who love them feel the urgency to warn them about the judgment to come and to offer them joy and peace now. Moreover, the gospel of ultimate restoration truly is *good news!* The traditional gospel might be good news for those who have opportunity to respond to it, but it is the worst possible news for their loved ones who have already died without Christ. Sharing the traditional gospel means eventually revealing the dark secret that all the non-elect/unrepentant ones are being tormented forever (or else are annihilated and go into oblivion), with no possibility of being reunited with believers—which is a serious deterrent to those who might otherwise accept the gospel. How much more joyous it is to be able to share with people the good news that Jesus died for them *and* that He is offering the same gift to their loved ones who have died! (#14, 31, 35, 50)

**Q:** Is *universalism* the right word to describe this belief?

**A:** Yes and no. I love the word *universal.* It speaks of an expansiveness that we can't begin to comprehend and so is the perfect word to describe God's all-encompassing grace. However, the word has been co-opted by Unitarians and others to the point that most evangelicals automatically assume it is heretical. We need to take back the word, so I use it, but judiciously, so I am not misunderstood. (Intro)

**Q:** Most Christians throughout most of church history have believed in eternal damnation. Doesn't that mean it's true?

**A:** No. The doctrine of eternal conscious torment (ECT) has been a long-standing tradition—the majority view for about 1,600 years—but the fact that a majority of people believe something does *not* make it true. There were many Christians in the early centuries of the church who believed in ultimate restoration, as shown in J. W. Hanson's 1899 book, *Universalism: The Prevailing Doctrine of the Christian Church During Its First Five Hundred Years* and in Thomas Allin's *Christ Triumphant*. For a modern treatment of ultimate restoration in the early Church, see *The Christian Doctrine of Apokatastasis: A Critical Assessment from the New Testament to Eriugena* (2013), by church history scholar Ilaria Ramelli. It is unlikely that you will purchase or wade through her book ($350 and more than 900 pages!), but you can find a very accessible explanation of this question in George Sarris's *Heaven's Doors*.

**Q:** Is it heresy to believe in ultimate restoration?

**A:** Technically speaking, perhaps. The dictionary definition of *heresy* is "an opinion or doctrine at variance with established religious beliefs." Although ultimate restoration was the dominant view in the early centuries of the church, it runs counter to what the majority of Christians have believed since then, so in that sense it is "at variance with established religious beliefs." However, the term *heresy* is a loaded word, implying opposition to the fundamental tenets of the faith, like those regarding the person of Christ or His work on the cross. A person can believe absolutely in the authority of Scripture, the virgin birth, the deity of Christ, the atonement, and every word of the Apostles' Creed and the Nicene Creed, and also believe in ultimate restoration. Such a person is not a heretic. (#37)

**Q:** Do Jesus and Paul contradict one another in their views of heaven and hell?

**A:** No. Their views are from different angles but not contradictory. In His teaching Jesus often used parables, which make a specific point in a somewhat veiled way and should not be pressed to the limit on every detail. He frequently employed hyperbole, a figure of speech that exaggerates in order to make a point. Not everything He said is to be taken literally (e.g. "If your eye causes you to sin, gouge it out and throw it away"). His teaching is to be understood by knowing the context, His audience, and the meaning of the words in that language and culture. Paul wrote an extensive systematic theology, teaching explicitly about what was accomplished on the cross. To interpret the words of Paul and Jesus, keep in mind that the teaching of one complements—not contradicts—that of the other.

**Q:** Isn't ultimate restoration just an accommodation to the twenty-first-century mindset that rejects absolutes and finds Christianity narrow-minded and offensive?

**A:** No. It is true that the contemporary mentality denounces anything it perceives as exclusive or intolerant. However, belief in ultimate restoration is not at all a new phenomenon; it has been around since the New Testament and throughout church history. It is not acquiescence to modern philosophy and psychology but rather an honest attempt to look at all of Scripture and find the truth, regardless of how it might be received by our culture or by the religious authorities. Furthermore, you could make a case that belief in eternal damnation fit quite nicely with the mentality of Egyptian or Babylonian or medieval culture. Perhaps *that* view took root in response to prevailing ideas in the culture. (#4)

**Q:** Matthew 25:46 says, "And these [the goats] will go away into eternal punishment, but the righteous into eternal life." Since the life of the righteous is everlasting, the punishment of the wicked is also everlasting (same word). Or as Moses Stuart put it, "We must either admit the endless misery of hell, or give up the endless happiness of heaven." Case closed, right?

**A:** No. An entire chapter or more could be devoted to this question, but the short answer is that the word translated "eternal" is *aionios*, meaning "of the age" or "age-abiding." The word translated "punishment" is *kolasis*, which is remedial correction. The verse could be better translated, "The wicked will go away into restorative chastisement in the age to come, and the righteous will enter into the life of the age to come." (See George Sarris's *Heaven's Doors*.)

**Q:** By saying that a loving God wouldn't allow people to suffer forever, aren't you relying on human wisdom to try to make God in your own image?

**A:** No, just the opposite. God created *us* in *His* image, and our concepts of love and justice are derived from His. We have a God-given sense of what is right and wrong, fair and unfair, loving and unloving. While human wisdom is not an infallible guide to good and evil, if it tells us that something is terribly wrong, we should *pay attention*. If our conscience says it would be monstrous to make people suffer forever with no hope of relief, then we should not ascribe such a thing to God. To do so makes the words *love* and *justice* meaningless; to call endless torture "loving" and "just" strips the words of any intelligible meaning. We are not trying to tell God what to do to suit our own notions of loving and fair; He has shown us what it means to be loving and just, and we're simply relaying what He has revealed as His purposes. (#4, 7, 12, 19)

**Q:** Don't you want people like Hitler to pay for their crimes? Do you really want to see Hitler in heaven?

**A:** Yes and yes! I want justice. I don't want tyrants and evil men to get away with anything; I want them to suffer the consequences of their actions and to feel the pain they have inflicted on others. But it would give me no satisfaction to see them suffer forever. Whenever I hear the testimony of a murderer or drug dealer or slave trader or prostitute or self-righteous Pharisee who has been transformed by the grace of God, I marvel again at how awesome He is. I look forward to hearing billions of those stories. I eagerly anticipate Hitler's humbling and his reconciliation with the millions of people he hurt. To see forgiveness requested, granted, and received countless times in perfect fullness will be glorious indeed. And relative to God, Hitler's salvation is not much different from my own; we're both just sinners standing before God pleading the blood of Jesus. (#8, 30, 45, 50, 56)

**Q:** Isn't the desire for the final salvation of everyone just wishful thinking? Don't people latch on to the idea of ultimate restoration just because they're worried about their loved ones who don't know Christ?

**A:** No and no. Almost everyone who is presented with the idea says, "I wish it were true"; there is a longing for complete restoration of the universe as it was intended to be and, of course, for the salvation of all our loved ones, and in the case of compassionate people, even for the salvation of our enemies. But wishful thinking doesn't make something true, and it is stupid to believe something just because it makes you feel better. For my own part, yes, I want it to be true, but no, I don't want to be deceived if it's not true. Even if all of my own family and friends came into God's family, it wouldn't change the fact that billions of other people have lost their loved ones. Obviously the personal element makes it more important to know the truth in this regard, but my pursuit is for truth above comfort. Praise God if I get both! (#1, 4, 31, 32)

**Q:** It's better for people to think there is an eternal hell and then be pleasantly surprised to find out there's not, than to think there is no eternal hell and then find themselves in it. Aren't the consequences of being wrong much graver if you proclaim universal salvation?

**A:** No. Consider that if you proclaim eternal damnation and it is *not* true, you have completely misrepresented the character of God and wrongly portrayed Him as one who allows the torture of billions of people—an extremely serious offense against Him. Is it even possible to err in portraying God as *more* merciful or *more* loving than He really is? The fear of hell can produce converts, but it does not lead people into a loving, trusting relationship with God. And the preaching of hellfire and damnation has driven many people *away* from God. (#15, 52, 59)

**Q:** Don't we just have to live with the tension that God is good and loving but in His infinite wisdom, which we humans can't understand, He allows billions of His creatures to go to hell?

**A:** No. God gave us a mind, a heart, and a conscience, which He expects us to use to the best of our ability. He does ask us to believe things that are difficult to comprehend, that are paradoxical or even seem contradictory, but He doesn't want us to abandon our reason and accept something abhorrent with the rationalization that God is good and He knows what He's doing and we, the clay, just have to accept it by faith and His ways are higher than our ways, etc., etc. Does He really want us to "believe"—and teach others to believe—something that violates every sense of reason, compassion, and justice in our being? We have to go through all kinds of mental contortions just in order to be able to live with the idea. It's not wrong to try to make sense of it and try to understand God's mind and grasp His purposes. If we just can't make any sense of how a good and loving Father could annihilate most of His children or allow them to suffer ad infinitum, maybe the reason is because it's nonsense—not because God has some sublime, inscrutable purpose in it. (#12)

**Q:** Isn't it true that if a person rebels against God throughout his lifetime, then he'll just continue to harden his heart after he dies?

**A:** No. In order to accept the idea that some people will be punished forever, we have to convince ourselves that somehow they deserve it and they wouldn't repent even if they had the chance. (Because if they *would* repent if given the chance, then it would seem awfully unfair not to give them the chance.) We all get varying degrees of revelation about God here on earth, but no mortal has seen God in all His holiness, splendor, love, and mercy; at best, we have distorted images of who He is. Many people reject not God Himself, but the twisted image they have of Him. It is actually quite far-fetched to believe that no one would ever change his mind even if he saw Jesus face to face and realized the consequences of his rebellion and understood the fullness of the gospel. (#26, 44)

**Q:** Doesn't the Bible say that there is no opportunity to repent after death?

**A:** No. The verse often quoted to support this idea says nothing of the sort. Hebrews 9:27 says, "Man is destined to die once, and after that to face judgment." It simply says that you die and then you get judged, which universalists believe. Again we have to ask if something makes sense: Will God reach out to a person in mercy until he draws his last breath, and then a split second later set His face against the person with implacable wrath? Here is the only real concession that universalists need: that there is opportunity to receive God's mercy after death. If so, it is completely reasonable to believe that in the eons to come, eventually everyone will be won over. (#22)

**Q:** Doesn't the story of the rich man and Lazarus prove that unbelievers who have died experience eternal torment in hell, with no possibility of crossing over into heaven?

**A:** No. This passage (Lk. 16:19–31) is often cited as proof that the wicked are locked in to their fate, with a great unbridgeable chasm between them and the joys of heaven. Like every other apparent damnation text, this one can be and has been interpreted within a universalist framework. I have not dealt extensively with this passage because many other writers have done it very capably. See for example George Sarris's *Heaven's Doors* (pp. 110ff) and Thomas Talbott's *The Inescapable Love of God* (pp. 86ff). One consideration is that Jesus had not yet died, and He would become the One to bridge the great chasm.

**Q:** Does a belief in ultimate restoration produce good fruit in one's life?

**A:** Yes, it should. You see each person as the object of God's love, not just His wrath, and you reach out to them in that love. Without the terror that a person will be irremediably lost forever, one would never try to use force or threats or manipulation to get him to confess Christ. Perhaps the greatest gift of this belief is joy; it lifts a great weight from your soul and allows you to feel joy in anticipation of heaven, not the dread that people you care about might be permanently separated from you. You also feel peace as you rest in the knowledge that God will not do anything monstrous. You can be more patient, knowing that God has not just our earthly lifetime to accomplish His purposes in people. The other fruits of the Spirit flow more naturally too. (#30, 50, 51, 52)

**Q:** Haven't universalists often gone way off into false doctrines? Doesn't that invalidate their teaching?

**A:** Yes, and No. It is true that some universalists became tangled with false beliefs; for example, some eventually joined with unitarians to become the Unitarian Universalist Association, and several individual universalists have ended up espousing various heresies. But that doesn't prove that universalism is false. Practically every denomination or institution that has ever existed has experienced some corruption. It doesn't mean they were wrong about everything.

**Q:** Some people come to faith because of fear of eternal punishment. If that fear is removed, won't those people lose the motivation to come to faith and fail to respond to the gospel?

**A:** No. Let's examine the logic of this argument. It is questionable whether people come to true saving faith out of fear of eternal damnation. If you encountered a man and feared that he would torture you if you didn't do what he demanded, would you enter into a relationship of love and trust with him? Or would you say and do whatever you thought was necessary to avoid that fate? Fear of eternal condemnation might get people to say the right words or come to church, but it can hardly create the relationship of faith and love that God desires. The universalist position, on the other hand, is far more likely to draw people into a loving relationship with the Father. If the gospel is preached with a balanced view of God's judgment as part of the redemptive process, then people will have a *healthy* fear of punishment, knowing that it is fair and purposeful. Like a good father who disciplines his children as an expression of his love, God intends His judgment for the good of His children. It is severe and should be taken very seriously, but it works with God's love to draw sinners in a way that terrorizing them never could. (#15, 31, 32)

**Q:** Aren't you just thinking up a plan you like and using your human values to call it "better" than God's plan as revealed in the Bible?

**A:** No! I didn't think it up—it's in the Bible, it's totally God's idea, and it is the best possible plan! Again, it's OK to use our minds and hearts. If it's good for one sinner to be saved, isn't it better for two to be saved? If there is rejoicing in heaven over one sinner who repents, won't there be more rejoicing over two, or two million? If someone is left out, won't there be less rejoicing and more sorrow? Some time ago I read an article about heaven, and it encouraged the readers to let their imagination run wild and just try to picture what heaven will be like. As I thought about it, what came to mind was not streets paved with gold and great banquets with sumptuous food, but rather, people. What will give us the most joy is being with all the people we care about and having absolutely perfect relationships with each one and getting to know all of God's other children. By any measure, it is better to have more people there than to have fewer. How could I or anyone else possibly think up or imagine a heaven that is better than what God will actually do? (1 Cor. 2:9). (#4, 7, 13, 15)

**Q:** One of the most prominent images of hell is fire. Isn't fire a symbol of judgment and the wrath of God?

**A:** Yes. But fire also represents purification. God uses the image of fire to show that He will purify each person by burning up every trace of sin in his life. Yes, He will be ruthless—in seeking out sin and destroying it so that it can no longer harm His children. (#39, 40, 41, 42)

**Q:** If people think they will eventually end up in heaven no matter what, won't they just live as they please?

**A:** No. Actually, that is a much greater problem for those who believe you are predestined for either heaven or hell and therefore are locked in to one fate or the other. If people understand the gravity of rebelling against a holy God, they will not try to get away with anything. And if they truly understand the loving character of the One who calls them, they will want to please Him in every way. An anecdote about nineteenth-century universalist Hosea Ballou illustrates this principle:

Ballou was riding the circuit in the New Hampshire hills with a Baptist minister one day, arguing theology as they traveled. At one point, the Baptist looked over and said, "Brother Ballou, if I were a Universalist and feared not the fires of hell, I could hit you over the head, steal your horse and saddle, and ride away, and I'd still go to heaven."

Hosea Ballou looked over at him and said, "If you were a Universalist, the idea would never occur to you."[1] (#35)

**Q:** Will Satan be saved?

**A:** It's not a straightforward yes-or-no question. What I am *confident* about is that God will redeem everyone Jesus died for, that is, all of humanity. Will Satan be "saved" in the same sense that you and I are saved? I cannot answer that question. I believe that God will restore His entire creation to its original perfection. Will Satan be restored along with the rest of creation? The position that seems most consistent with my belief in God's desire and ability to eradicate sin and death from the universe is that yes, Satan will be part of the restoration of all things. (#7)

**Q:** Are the gates of heaven always open?

**A:** Yes. John says of the New Jerusalem, "On no day will its gates ever be shut, for there will be no night there. The glory and honor of the nations will be brought into it" (Rev. 21:25–26). The "nations" are the ones who throughout Scripture and particularly in Revelation have been violently opposed to God. Now they are coming in to receive healing from the tree of life (Rev. 22:1–2). No one will want to *leave* the heavenly city; the gates are open so people can come *in*. As the hymn "For All the Saints" declares, "From earth's wide bounds, from ocean's farthest coast, Through gates of pearl streams in the countless host, Singing to Father, Son and Holy Ghost. Alleluia! Alleluia!"

---

[1] Recounted on www.christianheretic.com

# APPENDIX B:
# BELL'S HELLS:
## SEVEN MYTHS ABOUT UNIVERSALISM
## BY ROBIN PARRY

*Robin Parry's "Bell's Hells" is the best concise explanation of Christian Universalism I have seen. I have given it to many people in hopes of clarifying misconceptions, and I wanted to include it in my book as a ready reference for readers. It was originally published in The Baptist Times on 17 March 2011 and is reprinted here by permission.*

On Tuesday February 22 2011, Rob Bell—the influential pastor of Mars Hill Bible Church in Grand Rapids, Michigan—posted the promotional video for his new book, *Love Wins*.

Rumours started spreading almost immediately that Bell's forthcoming book advocated universalism and, unsurprisingly, the Internet went white-hot. On Saturday February 26 Justin Taylor, a well-known neo-Calvinist, posted his provisional reflections about Bell as a universalist on The Gospel Coalition blog and, reportedly, by that evening about 12,000 people had recommended his post on Facebook.

That same day Rob Bell was in the top 10 trending topics on Twitter. And from there the number of blog posts exploded. Overnight, universalism went from being a marginal issue that most evangelicals felt that they could ignore to being the next big debate.

Feelings are running high at the moment and a lot of strong language is being used. I think that if the church is to have a fruitful discussion on this matter (rather than a bad tempered battle-to-the-death) then it is essential that we have a clear understanding of what Christian universalists actually believe. A lot of myths about universalism are informing the current debate and I want to explore seven of them very briefly below.

To begin it will be helpful to have a quick definition of Christian universalism. Christian universalists are (mostly) orthodox, Trinitarian, Christ-centred, gospel-focused, Bible-affirming, missional Christians. What makes them universalists is that they believe that God loves all people, wants to save all people, sent Christ to redeem all people, and will achieve that goal.

In a nutshell, it is the view that, in the end, God will redeem all people through Christ. Christian universalists believe that the destiny of humanity is 'written' in the body of the risen Jesus and, as such, the story of humanity will not end with a tomb.

## Myth: Universalists don't believe in hell

Many an online critic of Bell has complained that he, along with his universalist allies, does not believe in hell. Here, for instance, is Todd Pruitt: 'Rob Bell . . . denies the reality of hell.' Mr BH adds, 'To Hell with No Hell. To Hell with what's being sold by Rob Bell.'

Nice rhyming but, alas, this is too simplistic.

Historically all Christian universalists have had a doctrine of hell and that remains the case for most Christian universalists today, including Bell. The Christian debate does not concern whether hell will be a reality (all agree that it will) but, rather, what the nature of that reality will be. Will it be eternal conscious torment? Will it be annihilation? Or will it be a state from which people can be redeemed?

Most universalists believe that hell is not simply retributive punishment but a painful yet corrective/educative state from which people will eventually exit (some, myself included, think it has a retributive dimension, while others do not).

So it is not hell that universalists deny so much as certain views about hell. (To complicate matters a little there have even been a few universalists that believed that hell is an eternal, conscious torment! An unusual view for a universalist but possible—honest.)

## Myth: Universalists don't believe the Bible

One does not have to read Bell's detractors for long before coming across the following sentiments: Universalists are theological 'liberals' that reject the 'clear teaching of the Bible'. Surely all good Bible-believing Christians will believe that some/many/most people are damned forever? 'If indeed Rob Bell denies the existence of hell, this is a betrayal of biblical truth,' says R Albert Mohler. David Cloud, concerned about Bell's questioning classical conceptions of hell, writes, 'It is evil to entertain questions that deny Bible truth.'

So, are universalists really Bible-denying? No.

Historically, Christian universalists have been Bible-affirming believers and that remains the case for many, perhaps the majority, today. The question is not 'Which group believes the Bible?' but, 'How do we interpret the Bible?'

The root issue is this: there are some biblical texts that seem to affirm universalism (eg Romans 5:18; 1 Corinthians 15:22; Colossians 1:20; Philippians 2:11) but there are others that seem to deny it (eg Matthew 25:45; 2 Thessalonians 1:6–9; Revelation 14:11; 20:10–15).

At the heart of the biblical debate is how we hold these two threads together. Do we start with the hell passages and reread the universalist texts in the light of them? That is the traditional route. Or, do we start with universalist passages and reinterpret the hell texts in the light of them? That is what many universalists do.

Or do we try to hold both sets of biblical teachings in some kind of tension (and there are various proposals for how we might do that—some leaning towards traditionalism, others leaning towards universalism)?

There is also the question of wider biblical-theological themes and their relevance. For instance, biblical teaching on God's love, justice, punishment, the cross-resurrection, covenant, etc. How might reflection on those matters influence our theology of hell?

This is not just about finding 'proof texts' to whip your opponent with (both sides are capable of that) but about making best sense of the Bible as a whole. And when we follow the big plotline of the scriptures, which ending to the story has the best 'fit'? Universalists believe that the ending in which God redeems his whole creation makes the most sense of the biblical metanarrative. Traditionalists disagree.

My point is that this debate is not a debate between Bible-believing Christians (traditionalists) and 'liberals' (universalists). It is, to a large extent, a debate between two sets of Bible-believing Christians on how best to understand scripture.

## Myth: Universalists don't think sin is very bad

Blogger Denny Burke thinks that Bell's 'weak' view of hell is based on a 'weak' view of sin which, in turn, is based on a 'weak' view of God: 'Sin will always appear as a trifle to those whose view of God is small.'

Universalists 'obviously' think that sin isn't something to get too worked up about—after all they believe that God's job is to forgive people, right?

Once again we are in the realm of mythology. Propose a view on the seriousness of sin as strong as you wish and you'll find universalists who would affirm it. Does sin affect every aspect of human life? Is it an utter horror that degrades our humanity and warrants divine wrath? Does it deserve eternal punishment?

Universalists could affirm all of these things so long as they believed that God's love, power, grace, and mercy are bigger and stronger than sin. Universalists do not have a low view of sin, they have a high view of grace: 'Where sin abounds, grace abounds all the more.'

## Myth: Universalists believe in God's love but forget his justice and wrath

Here is Britten Taylor's response to Rob Bell: 'God is love. But, He is also just. God pours out His mercy, but He also pours out His wrath.' The implication is that universalists overplay divine love and forget that God is also holy and just. Right? Wrong.

Christian universalists have a lot to say about God's holiness, justice, and even his wrath. Typically they think that God's divine nature cannot be divided up into conflicting parts in such a way that some of God's actions are loving (eg, saving sinners) while others are just and full of anger (eg, hell).

They see all of God's actions as motivated by 'holy love'. Everything God does is holy, completely just, and completely loving.

So whatever hell is about it must be compatible not simply with divine justice but also with divine love. Which means that it must, in some way, have the good of those in hell as part of its rationale.

Universalists feel that one potential danger in traditional theologies of hell is that while they make much of God's justice and anger they appear to be incompatible with his love and, as a result, they divide up the unity of God's nature.

## Myth: Universalists think that all roads lead to God

Here is Kevin Mullins' definition of universalism in his discussion of Bell: 'Universalism—the belief that everyone, regardless of faith or behavior, will be counted as God's people in the end. All roads lead to Him. All religions are just different expressions of the same Truth.'

That idea is what underlies crparke's comment that, 'If Rob Bell denies hell then he denies the need for a "savior" and makes the sacrifice of Jesus irrelevant.'

Here our Internet conversation partners have confused universalism (the view that God will one day save all people through Christ) with pluralism (the view that there are many paths to God and that Jesus is simply one of them). But Christian universalists deny pluralism. They insist that salvation is found only through the atoning work of Christ. Without Jesus nobody would be redeemed!

Now there is a disagreement between Christians about whether one needs to have explicit faith in Jesus to share in the salvation he has bought. Some Christians, called exclusivists, think that only those who put their trust in the gospel can be saved. Others, called inclusivists, think that it is possible to be saved through Christ even without explicit faith in him.

Thus, for inclusivists it is possible to be saved even if, for instance, you have never heard the gospel. Inclusivists would maintain that if someone responds in humility, love, and faith to the truncated divine revelation that they have received then God can unite them to Christ and they may be considered as, perhaps, 'anonymous Christians'.

But we need to be careful not to confuse the discussion between exclusivists and inclusivists with the issue of universalism. Many people make that mistake. The former debate concerns how people can experience the salvation won by Christ while the latter concerns how many people will be saved. Two different questions.

Thus, some universalists are inclusivists (eg, Rob Bell) but others are exclusivists, maintaining that only people who trust in the gospel can be saved. (Obviously exclusivist universalists have to believe that salvation is possible after death.)

But whether one is speaking of exclusivist or inclusivist universalists, neither relegate Jesus to the sidelines.

## Myth: Universalism undermines evangelism

Here is Matt: 'I do think the Scripture is clear that salvation at least has some limits. If it doesn't, then preaching and evangelism are ultimately wasted activities.' And R Albert Mohler worries that, 'If indeed Rob Bell denies the existence of hell, this...has severe...evangelistic consequences.' Why, after all, would anyone bother to go through all the effort and struggle of evangelism if God is going to save everyone in the end anyway?

So must universalism undermine evangelism? Not at all. There are many reasons to engage in mission and evangelism, not least that Christ commands it. And it is a huge privilege to join with God in his mission of reconciling the world to himself. The gospel message is God's 'foolish' way of setting the world right so, of course, universalists will want to proclaim it.

Fear of hell is not the only motivation for mission. And, what is more, the majority of universalists do fear hell. Whilst they may not view it as 'the end of the road', they still consider it to be a dreadful state to be avoided.

And historically universalists have not run from mission. Here are the words of an eighteenth century Baptist universalist, Elhanan Winchester, who was himself an evangelist: 'There is no business or labour to which men are called, so important, so arduous, so difficult, and that requires such wisdom to perform it [as that of the soul-winner]. The amazing worth of winning souls, makes the labour so exceeding important, and of such infinite concern' (sermon on the death of John Wesley, 1791).

## Myth: Universalism undermines holy living

Here is Frank: 'Oh thank goodness Rob Bell is here to explain that we can do whatever we want because (drum roll please)…there's no consequence, there's no hell!' And Frank is not alone. During 17th, 18th and 19th centuries many Christians were especially worried that if the fear of hell was reduced people would have little to constrain their sinful behaviour. Thus universalism, they feared, would fuel sin.

But the fear of punishment is not the only motive for avoiding sin and, even if it were, universalism does, as has already been mentioned, have space for some such fear. But far more important for holy living—indeed the only motive for heartfelt holy living—is the positive motivation inspired by love for God.

Who, after all, would reason, 'I know that God created me, seeks to do me good, sent his Son to die for me, and that he will always love me…so I must hate him!'? On the contrary, the revelation of divine love solicits our loving response (1 John 4:19).

Clearly there is an important debate to be had but if we desire more light and less heat we need to start by getting a clearer understanding of the view under discussion.

---

Robin Parry is author of *The Evangelical Universalist* (SPCK) and editor of *Universal Salvation? The Current Debate* (Paternoster) and 'All Shall Be Well': Explorations in Universal Salvation and Christian Theology, from Origen to Moltmann (Cascade/James Clarke).

# APPENDIX C:
# CHRISTIAN BELIEFS ABOUT WHO GOES TO HEAVEN AND WHO GOES TO HELL

The chart on the next page presents some of the major Christian views regarding who ends up in heaven and who ends up in hell. There is some overlap among the positions (for example, Calvinists are probably Exclusivists, Arminians subscribe to Free Will and can believe in the Narrow Gate or Wider Mercy, Universalists can be either Exclusivists or Inclusivists, etc.), but this overview gives you a simplified picture of the various views.

The problem with this scheme, in my opinion, is that the model itself is mistaken. Rather than thinking of the afterlife as two places, with everyone being in one place or the other, we should be thinking in terms of the Kingdom of God. I see life after death as a continuum of the Kingdom of God. I believe that God will have a tailor-made judgment for every individual that will take into account every factor that has a bearing on the person's life. Everyone will experience the presence of God differently: those who are still in rebellion against Him will experience the searing intensity of His holiness and the agonizing torment of guilt and reproach. For those who are in right relationship with God, who have been washed in the blood of Christ and have no unconfessed sin, being in the presence of God will be utterly blissful and blessed.

| | HEAVEN | HELL |
|---|---|---|
| **Calvinist** | The elect | The non-elect (hell = eternal conscious torment) |
| **Arminian** | Those who accept God's offer of salvation | Those who reject God's offer of salvation |
| **Universalist** | All in the long run | None forever (the time of judgment has an end) |
| **Conditional Immortality (Annihilation)** | Those who are given eternal life because of their faith/righteousness | Some temporarily; none forever (the wicked will eventually be destroyed) |
| **Free Will** | Those who choose to trust Christ as Savior before death | Those who choose not to trust Christ as Savior before death |
| **Catholic** | Those who are in full communion with God (believers can pass from purgatory to heaven) | Those who reject God (believers who need purification spend time in purgatory) |
| **Eastern Orthodox** | Saints experience the presence of God as paradise | Unbelievers experience the presence of God as punishment |
| **Exclusivist (Restrictivist)** | Those who have explicit faith (OT—in God; NT—in Christ) | Those who do not have explicit faith in the God of the Bible/in Christ |
| **Inclusivist** | Those who believe the revelation they have received | Those who reject the revelation they have received |
| **Narrow Gate** | Few | Many |
| **Wider Mercy** | Many | Few |
| **Book of Life I** | All whose names are written in the Book of Life | All whose names are not written in the Book of Life |
| **Book of Life II** | All except those whose names are blotted out of the Book of Life by their explicit rejection of God | Those whose names are blotted out of the Book of Life by their explicit rejection of God |

# APPENDIX D:
# HELL SURVEY

For a long time I have wanted to do a survey to test a hypothesis of mine. Several years ago I wrote a short survey and started exploring ways to do it, but I learned that doing it right would be very complicated, time-consuming, and expensive. Since designing and implementing a survey that would produce results with real validity would take a lot more knowledge, time, and money than I have, I tabled the idea for later.

In the meantime, I came across some other studies of a similar nature, with results that were intriguingly consistent with what I had observed anecdotally. I decided that a survey of my own, even if not statistically valid, could yield some food for thought and fodder for discussion, so I am going ahead with my own very informal survey.

The questions for the online survey are shown here. Most of the survey consists of clicking buttons, which will take only a few minutes, but it allows for optional written comments and explanations, which of course I would welcome. In addition to questions about your gender and age, there are four questions for which you mark any of the given answers that apply. If you would like to participate, please go to https://www.surveymonkey.com/r/RP86WHC.

1.  **What is your gender?**
    ○ female
    ○ male

2.  **What is your age:**
    ○ 11–20
    ○ 21–30
    ○ 31–40
    ○ 41–50
    ○ 51–60
    ○ 61–70
    ○ 71–80
    ○ 81–90
    ○ 91–100

3.  **How would you identify yourself with respect to religion? (Please select all that apply.)**
    ○ Agnostic
    ○ Anglican
    ○ Arminian
    ○ Atheist
    ○ Born-again
    ○ Buddhist
    ○ Calvinist
    ○ Charismatic
    ○ Christian
    ○ Eastern Orthodox
    ○ Evangelical

○ Fundamentalist

○ Greek Orthodox

○ Hindu

○ Jewish

○ Muslim

○ New Age

○ Occasional church-goer

○ Pentecostal

○ Protestant

○ Reformed

○ Regular church-goer

○ Roman Catholic

○ Seeker

○ Unitarian

○ Universalist

○ Other (please specify; add denomination if desired)

4. **Which of the following statements best describe your worldview? (Please select all that apply.)**

○ The universe has always existed.

○ The universe was created by God.

○ Life is the product of evolutionary forces.

○ Life is the work of a creator.

○ Human beings are created in the image of God.

○ Human reason sets the standard for moral values.

○ The Bible is the standard for moral values.

○ The Koran is the standard for moral values.

○ The Bible is the Word of God.

○ The Bible is inerrant.

○ Human beings are basically good.

○ Human beings are basically evil.

○ Human beings are a mix of good and evil.

○ Life is an illusion.

○ Life is deterministic; we have little control over our fate.

○ There are absolute moral values.

○ There are no absolutes with respect to moral values.

○ All sentient life has equal value.

○ All human beings have equal value.

○ Other (please specify)

5. **How would you describe the teachings you received and the feelings you experienced about hell and the afterlife when you were growing up? (Please select all that apply.)**

○ There is no hell.

○ There is no afterlife; you die physically and cease to exist.

○ The Bible teaches that there is a literal after-life hell.

○ People who do not go to heaven will be annihilated.

○ Hell is a place of unending physical torment.

○ Hell is separation from God.

○ Hell is a state of mind.

○ God's purposes in judgment are redemptive.

○ Anyone who does not believe in Jesus goes to hell.

○ Hell is a temporary state where sins are punished.

○ People who need cleansing from sin go to purgatory.

○ Hell is the product of a twisted desire to control others.

○ I experienced fear of going to hell myself.

○ I experienced fear that my loved ones would go to hell.

○ I was emotionally unstable because of fear of hell.

○ Other (please specify)

6. **How would you describe your present beliefs and feelings about hell and the afterlife? (Please select all that apply.)**

○ There is no hell.

○ There is no afterlife; you die physically and cease to exist.

○ Hell is a place of unending physical torment.

○ Hell is a state of mind.

○ God's purposes in judgment are redemptive.

○ Anyone who does not believe in Jesus goes to hell.

○ Hell is a temporary state where sins are punished.

○ People who need cleansing from sin go to purgatory.

○ Hell is the product of a twisted desire to control others.

○ I experience fear of going to hell myself.

○ I experience fear that my loved ones will go to hell.

○ I am emotionally unstable because of fear of hell.

○ Other (please specify)

# OTHER RESOURCES

Not so long ago, believers in Ultimate Restoration were relatively few and far between. There are now countless books, articles, blogs, websites, and online groups dedicated to sharing the news of God's full victory in Christ. It's not far-fetched to say that the Internet is serving a similar function for the spread of the truly Good News as the printing press served for spreading the Bible. Believers around the globe are connecting with each other and supporting one another in what can be a difficult struggle against the tide of traditional belief in hell. Here are some of the many resources that can help you go deeper in understanding about eternal destinies.

## Books about Ultimate Restoration

### *Heaven's Doors: Wider Than You Ever Believed!*
### By George W. Sarris

I have not always believed in ultimate restoration. Like most of my pastors and teachers and Christian friends, I accepted the idea that unbelievers would spend eternity in hell. Back in the mid-80s I learned that my friend George Sarris had some crazy notion that everybody would be saved and I thought, "Well, *obviously* that's wrong."

Another two decades passed before I gave the idea any consideration. By then George and his family had moved out of state, but we stayed in touch and occasionally saw each other. At the wedding of the son of some mutual friends, I asked George about it out of curiosity, and he offered to send me a paper he had written for a seminary class. Reading that paper did not convince me that God is going to redeem everyone, but it did give me permission to explore the idea without fear that I would be at risk of falling into heresy.

As I began to consider that maybe, just maybe, Jesus actually would save the world, I felt hope rising in me—hope that God was really more loving and more powerful than I knew and that His purposes were bigger and better than I ever imagined. I started reading everything I could find on the subject, including going back and reading the Bible with new eyes and with a willingness to recognize that I might have been wrong. Little by little I became thoroughly convinced that Jesus is indeed the Savior of the world and will accomplish the salvation of the world.

The paper that George wrote for that seminary class in 1978 became the foundation for *Heaven's Doors*. The basic information that launched me on my journey has been greatly expanded, with more documentation as well as stories to illustrate the truths. For decades George thought he was alone in believing that Jesus would save the world, but now there is a growing worldwide community of believers in ultimate restoration, and his book is helping to spread the Good News.

## Hope Beyond Hell: The Righteous Purpose of God's Judgment
### By Gerald Beauchemin

One of the first books I read on the topic of Universal Restoration was *Hope Beyond Hell* by Gerry Beauchemin, a missionary dentist. It is packed with Scripture and is thoroughly sound theologically and also very accessible for lay people. The book is available for a small donation or can be downloaded for free on hopebeyondhell.net. I found that it made a good study guide for a Bible study on Ultimate Redemption. (If anyone would like to host a Bible study on this topic, I would be happy to share with you the materials I prepared, including study questions for each chapter/lesson and follow-up emails for each session, with a recap of the session, suggestions for further reading, and often a light-hearted anecdote, joke, cartoon, or youtube video.)

### *The Inescapable Love of God*
### By Thomas Talbott, Sr.

Another book that was instrumental in shaping my thinking was Tom Talbott's *The Inescapable Love of God,* first published in 1999, with a new revised version in 2014. You will see its influence throughout my book. From it I learned that God's love is more powerful than all sin, more than able to overcome all our resistance and rebellion and draw every single human being to bow the knee and acknowledge Jesus Christ as Lord. Dr. Talbott is a committed Christian and a wise philosopher who thoroughly understands both the Scriptural foundation and the philosophical arguments for universal restoration. If you are already leaning toward ultimate redemption, this book will solidify your convictions. If you are skeptical or have never considered it or are dead-set against it, please read it with an open mind, open Bible, and open heart!

### *The Inescapable Love of God: 2nd Edition, Audiobook*
### By Thomas Talbott, Sr., narrated by George W. Sarris

I'm delighted that two key mentors in my life—one a personal friend and one a friend through his writing—have teamed up to produce a resource that will get the word out about this wonderful Good News and be a blessing to many. The audio version of the second edition of *The Inescapable Love of God* is narrated by George Sarris, a professional actor and speaker who is also the narrator of the entire NIV, produced by Zondervan. If you are an audio learner, listen to George as he narrates Tom's book.

### *The Evangelical Universalist*
### By Gregory MacDonald

Theologian Robin Parry wrote *The Evangelical Universalist* under the pseudonym Gregory MacDonald. He answers the question "Can an orthodox Christian, committed to the historic faith of the Church and the authority of the Bible, be a universalist?" with a resounding "Yes." He uses Scripture to build a biblical case for Christian Universalism, including tackling the passages that are problematic for Bible-believing Universalists. A must-read book for those who want a solid biblical foundation for believing in the salvation of all. (For a briefer answer to the question of whether biblical Christianity and Universalism are compatible, see the article by Robin Parry in Appendix B.)

### *Love Wins: A Book about Heaven, Hell, and the Fate of Every Person Who Ever Lived*
**By Rob Bell**

Rob Bell's 2011 book set off a firestorm, with Christians lining up to denounce him before the book even hit the shelves. Bell asks incisive questions that strike at the heart of traditional evangelical concepts of hell, and many found the book threatening to orthodox Christianity, even though Bell does not label himself a universalist, and he doesn't even really answer many of the questions he raises. I don't align myself with Rob Bell, partly because I find him a little fuzzy so I don't know exactly what he does believe, but I'm grateful that he sparked the conversation that continues to this day.

### *Christ Triumphant: Universalism Asserted as the Hope of the Gospel on the Authority of Reason, the Fathers, and Holy Scripture,* **Annotated Edition**
**By Thomas Allin, edited by Robin Parry**

Allin first published *Christ Triumphant* in 1885 in order to "plead for the acceptance of this central truth as the great hope of the gospel, that the victory of Jesus Christ must be final and complete, i.e., that nothing can impair the power of his cross and passion to save the entire human race." Robin Parry has given us a new (2015) edition of Allin's work with a foreword by Thomas Talbott and an introduction giving the historical context. The addition of subtitles and annotations greatly helps the reader follow Allin's reasoning.

I read *Christ Triumphant* after writing most of my own book, and I was gratified to find much in common in our writings. While we all learn from those who have gone before us, God also leads people to the same truths independently. And I like to think that God smiles with me at the author's name: ALL IN!

### Universalism: The Prevailing Doctrine of the Christian Church During Its First Five-Hundred Years
### By J. W. Hanson

Hanson's book is from the same time period as Allin's. He argues that Universal Restoration was widely accepted in the early Church and by the Church Fathers. He identifies Augustine (AD 354–430) as a driving force in the shift to a belief in hell as eternal conscious punishment.

### The Christian Doctrine of Apokatastasis: A Critical Assessment from the New Testament to Eriugena
### By Ilaria Ramelli

At about $350 and almost 900 pages, this book is not likely to be purchased and read cover to cover by the average Christian. But you could do what I did and check it out of a seminary library and use it as a resource. Ilaria Ramelli is a highly respected scholar and professor who specializes in Early Christianity. Her book demonstrates that *apokatastasis* (the doctrine of the restoration of all things) was grounded in the New Testament and held to be true by many Church Fathers. As Robin Parry writes, "This deeply impressive study is the fruit of sixteen years of research into the history of early Christian belief in universal salvation. In almost 900 pages of carefully argued analysis, Ramelli leaves no stone unturned in her attempt to recover a story that has never before been told with anything like this much attention to the range and depth of evidence.... This work will unquestionably be the go-to book on the doctrine of *apokatastasis* for many years to come."

## *Universal Salvation? The Current Debate*
## Edited by Robin A. Parry and Christopher H. Partridge

This book opens with three chapters in which Thomas Talbott presents a case for Christian Universalism. Then the other contributors give biblical responses, philosophical responses, theological responses, and historical responses, followed by Talbott's reply to his critics. Obviously not all the facets of the question can be addressed and refuted in one book, but the major points are covered intelligently and respectfully. And all the contributors are committed to a high view of Scripture. As Gabriel Fackre explains in the Foreword, "On matters of authority, the primacy of Scripture is given its due, tradition is taken seriously and reason is honoured in the development of points of view, pro or con."

## *Four Views on Hell, 2ⁿᵈ Edition*
## Edited by Preston Sprinkle

In the first edition of this book (1996), the four views of hell were literal, metaphorical, purgatorial, and conditional. At that time, universal salvation was not even in the running. Significantly, the second edition (2016) includes Ultimate Reconciliation as one of the views, defended by Robin Parry, with the other contributors being Denny Burk (Eternal Conscious Torment), John Stackhouse (Conditional Immortality), and Jerry Walls (Purgatory). Each contributor presents his case and then the others have an opportunity to respond, which makes this book a good way to compare the different views side by side.

## *Sinners in the Hands of a Loving God: The Scandalous Truth of the Very Good News*
## By Brian Zahnd

Jonathan Edwards' 1741 sermon "Sinners in the Hands of an Angry God," was intended to awaken his hearers to the dreadful reality of hell and thus to draw them to Christ. Brian Zahnd draws sinners to Christ by revealing the Father's love for all His wayward children. As one reviewer expresses it, "With the heart of a pastor and the skill of a poet, Brian Zahnd cuts through all the fear and fundamentalism to reveal a gospel that is indeed good news."

## *Her Gates Will Never Be Shut: Hope, Hell, and the New Jerusalem*
## By Bradley Jersak

Brad Jersak neither accepts the standard evangelical doctrine of hell nor dogmatically affirms that all will be saved. He humbly lays out the various possibilities for final judgment, using Scripture as the authority on these matters but recognizing that the Bible is not entirely clear and can be interpreted in a variety of ways. He stops short of certainty but gives plenty of reason to hope that all will respond to the invitation to enter the eternal city whose gates will never be shut.

## *Raising Hell: Christianity's Most Controversial Doctrine Put under Fire*
## By Julie Ferwerda

The product description for Julie's book begins, "Have you ever considered the apparent injustices, inconsistencies, and even contradictions of the doctrine of hell? For starters, do earthly parents love their children more than God? Does God ask you to forgive your enemies when He is not willing to do the same?"

Julie is not afraid to ask the questions that many Christians have on their minds but perhaps are reluctant to ask for fear of being judged by others. She digs deep in the Bible for the answers, and she also uses God-given common sense.

In my opinion, in her subsequent writings Julie has gone a little too far in her resistance to traditional doctrines in some areas. But her book chronicles her own journey of discovery as she honestly wrestled with Scripture and delved into the tough questions about eternal destinies, and it can serve to stimulate your thinking as you forge your own path.

# Books that Support the Traditional View of Hell

When exploring any controversial topic, it is important to read not just material that supports what you believe, but material that challenges your beliefs. Doing so will force you to articulate what you believe and perhaps reconsider your position. Even though I want readers to embrace restoration, I advocate reading books that argue against it. Here are a few:

## *Hell Under Fire: Modern Scholarship Reinvents Eternal Punishment*
### Edited by Christopher W. Morgan and Robert A. Peterson

This book contains contributions from an impressive list of Christian scholars, including Gregory K. Beale, Daniel I. Block, Sinclair B. Ferguson, R. Albert Mohler Jr., Douglas J. Moo, J. I. Packer, and Robert W. Yarbrough, as well as the two editors. It is one of the better defenses of a traditional hell, but my copy of the book is riddled with sticky notes, comments, and highlighting where I feel the argument falls short or contains logical fallacies or is blatantly wrong.

In the first chapter, Al Mohler laments the disappearance of the doctrine of hell, which he says was once "centrally enshrined in the system of theology." But the real question is whether it is centrally enshrined in *Scripture*. The second chapter opens with the question "What does the Old Testament teach about hell?" to which Daniel Block answers, "Very little." And although Jesus speaks of something translated as "hell" in many of our English Bibles, He was not speaking of a fiery place of torture in the afterlife. Why should a doctrine be centrally enshrined in our theology if the whole Old Testament barely alludes to it and the New Testament is not referring to our common conception of it? So right off the bat, this book has a fundamental problem, and there are many more.

Reading this book will help you understand the doctrine of eternal damnation and better equip you to defend or refute it. Perhaps you will be persuaded that it is true or be reinforced in your conviction that it is a biblical doctrine that should be vigorously maintained. Or maybe you will have the same experience I did—becoming more convinced that it is a *good* thing that the traditional doctrine of hell is under fire and that it needs to be abandoned in favor of a more biblical view. In his opening sentence, Al Mohler states that hell was "a fixture of Christian theology for over sixteen centuries," which is true. IMO, it's time to go back to the predominant view of the first four centuries of the church—*apokatastasis.*

### God Wins: Heaven, Hell, and Why the Good News Is Better than Love Wins
### By Mark Galli

*God Wins* was one of a number of books that came out to refute Rob Bell's *Love Wins* (and it has the feel of a knee-jerk reaction to a challenge that made traditionalists very uncomfortable). Managing Editor for *Christianity Today* Mark Galli "maintains that 'love wins' isn't deep or rich enough—and that there is even better news for humanity. God wins" (yet it's not entirely clear what that means or how it's better).

### Erasing Hell: What God Said about Eternity, and the Things We've Made Up
### By Francis Chan and Preston Sprinkle

*Erasing Hell* also came out after *Love Wins*, in an attempt to defend the traditional view of hell. Unlike some books on the subject, it is pastoral as well as theological. What I really appreciate about Francis Chan is his pastor's heart in dealing with people who have lost unsaved loved ones. I don't think he has particularly good answers for them, but he is sensitive and sympathetic.

It is interesting to note that, since writing this book, Chan's co-author, Preston Sprinkle, has evolved somewhat in his thinking on the subject. He has come to see more biblical evidence for annihilation, and he no longer considers ultimate reconciliation to be outside the bounds of orthodoxy.

## *The Fire that Consumes: A Biblical and Historical Study of the Doctrine of the Final Punishment*
### By Edward Fudge

I include this book here because it takes the traditional position that hell is a place of everlasting destruction, but it does not advocate eternal conscious torment. Edward Fudge, who passed away in November 2017, believed that there will be judgment for each unbelieving individual, culminating in total annihilation rather than going on forever.

## Websites

### tentmaker.org

This website, hosted by Gary and Michelle Amirault, is a leading source for materials about Universal Salvation. It contains a wealth of information, including articles, books, tracts, and videos.

### evangelicaluniversalist.com

This site is another rich source of information, with discussion threads on hundreds of different topics related to Evangelical Universalism. At some point this forum will be migrated to another engine, at which time the content will be frozen, but as of this printing there are still new posts.

### Evangelical Universalism (Invitation & Debate)

This Facebook group "is a place where brothers and sisters in Christ (of every stripe) can discuss and/or debate what we call 'Evangelical Universalism' (the Christian doctrine of Universal Reconciliation) with gentleness and respect." It is a closed group but you can just ask to be added as a member.

### auburn.edu/~allenkc/culinks.html

This webpage from Auburn University has an extensive list of dozens of Universal Reconciliation websites.

## Films

### *Hellbound?*
### Directed by Kevin Miller

In this provocative documentary, Kevin Miller has assembled a variety of voices all across the spectrum to discuss the question of hell. Interviewees include pastors Greg Boyd, Kevin DeYoung, and Mark Driscoll, authors Sharon Baker, Brad Jersak, Robert McKee, Brian McLaren, Robin Parry, Frank Schaeffer, Jerry Walls, and William Paul Young, radio host Hank Hanegraaf, exorcist Bob Larson, Bible scholar Jaime Clark-Soles, Archbishop Lazar Puhalo, Jonathan and Margie Phelps of the Westboro Baptist Church, Mike Bickle of the International House of Prayer, evangelist Ray Comfort, and Catholic apologist Peter Kreeft.

The film asks, "Does hell exist? If so, who goes there, and why? More importantly, what do our views about hell say about us and our understanding of God? And how do our beliefs about these issues affect the kind of world we create, the kind of people we become?"

As a follow-up to the movie, Kevin Miller wrote the book *Hellrazed* five years later, in 2017. He spoke with some of the original contributors and other people who have spoken out on the issue to get their input on how the debate has changed and how it has remained the same.

### *Hell and Mr. Fudge*
### LLT Productions

The film follows the life of Edward Fudge (*The Fire that Consumes*) in his pursuit of the truth about hell, which started when he lost a childhood friend in a car accident. It continued and intensified when he became a Bible-belt preacher in Alabama in the 70s. The film chronicles this humble and intense man's wrestling with truth, at great personal cost, until he comes to rest in the belief that God does not send unbelievers to never-ending torture, but rather puts them out of existence.

# BIBLIOGRAPHY

Allin, Thomas. Edited by Robin A Parry. *Christ Triumphant: Universalism Asserted as the Hope of the Gospel on the Authority of Reason, the Fathers, and Holy Scripture.* Eugene, OR: Wipf & Stock, 2015 (orig. 1891).

*Analytical Greek Lexicon, The.* Grand Rapids, MI: Zondervan Publishing House, 1974.

Barker, Kenneth, ed. *The NIV Study Bible.* Grand Rapids, MI: Zondervan Publishing House, 1985.

Bauer, Walter. Revised and augmented by William F. Arndt, F. Wilbur Gingrich, and Frederick W. Danker (BDAG). *A Greek-English Lexicon of the New Testament and Other Early Christian Literature.* Chicago: University of Chicago Press, 1979 (orig. 1957).

Beale, Gregory K. *We Become What We Worship: A Biblical Theology of Idolatry.* Downers Grove, IL: InterVarsity Press, 2008.

Beauchemin, Gerry. *Hope Beyond Hell: The Righteous Purpose of God's Judgment.* Olmito, TX: Malista Press, 2007, 2010.

Beecher, Edward. *History of Opinions on the Scriptural Doctrine of Retribution.* New York: D. Appleton and Company, 1878.

Bell, Rob. *Love Wins: A Book about Heaven, Hell, and the Fate of Every Person Who Ever Lived.* New York: HarperOne, 2011.

Berry, George Ricker. *Interlinear Greek-English New Testament.* Grand Rapids, MI: Baker Books, 1999.

Brontë, Anne. "A Word to the 'Elect'" from *Poems by Currer, Ellis, and Acton Bell.* London: Smith, Elder & Co., 1846.

Carroll, Lewis, edited by Stuart Dodgson Collingwood. "Eternal Punishment," from *The Lewis Carroll Picture Book*. London: T. F. Unwin, 1899.

Castro, Diane Perkins. *Reflections of a Tomboy Grandma: On the Immeasurable Worth of Every Human Being*. Beverly, MA: ID Publishing House, 2017.

Chan, Francis and Preston Sprinkle. *Erasing Hell: What God Said about Eternity, and the Things We've Made Up*. Colorado Springs, CO: David C. Cook, 2011.

Covey, Stephen R.. *The 7 Habits of Highly Effective People*. New York: Free Press, 1989.

Dillow, Linda. *Calm My Anxious Heart: A Woman's Guide to Finding Contentment*. Colorado Springs, CO: NavPress, 1998, 2007.

Douglass, Frederick. *Narrative of the Life of Frederick Douglass, an American Slave*. Boston, 1843.

Eby, J. Preston. *Savior of the World*. El Paso, TX: CreateSpace, 2014.

Edwards, Jonathan. "The Eternity of Hell Torments." Sermon XI from *Sermons of Jonathan Edwards*, 1780.

Ferwerda, Julie. *Raising Hell: Christianity's Most Controversial Doctrine Put under Fire*. Vagabond Group, 2011.

Fudge, Edward. *The Fire that Consumes: A Biblical and Historical Study of the Doctrine of the Final Punishment*. Eugene, OR: Cascade Books, 2011.

Galli, Mark. *God Wins: Heaven, Hell, and Why the Good News Is Better than Love Wins*. Carol Stream, IL: Tyndale House Publishers, Inc., 2011.

Grudem, Wayne. *Systematic Theology: An Introduction to Biblical Doctrine*. Leicester, Great Britain: InterVarsity Press and Grand Rapids, MI: Zondervan Publishing House, 1994.

Hanson, J. W. *Universalism: The Prevailing Doctrine of the Christian Church During Its First Five-Hundred Years.* Boston and Chicago: Universalist Publishing House, 1899.

Harris, Sam. *The End of Faith: Religion, Terror, and the Future of Reason.* New York, London: W. W. Norton & Company, 2004.

Jersak, Bradley. *Her Gates Will Never Be Shut: Hope, Hell, and the New Jerusalem.* Eugene, OR: Wipf & Stock, 2009.

Jones, Brian. *Hell Is Real (But I Hate to Admit It).* Colorado Springs, CO: David C. Cook, 2011.

Kalomiros, Alexandre. "The River of Fire." Seattle, WA: St. Nectarios Press, 1980.

Lewis, C. S. *The Great Divorce.* London: Geoffrey Bles, 1945.

————. *The Problem of Pain.* New York: Macmillan, 1940.

MacDonald, Gregory. *The Evangelical Universalist.* Eugene, OR: Cascade Books, 2006.

Morgan, Christopher W. and Robert A. Peterson, eds. *Hell Under Fire: Modern Scholarship Reinvents Eternal Punishment.* Grand Rapids, MI: Zondervan, 2004.

Noe, John. *Hell Yes / Hell No.* Indianapolis, IN: East2West Press, 2011.

Papanikolaou, Aristotle and Elizabeth H. Prodromou. *Thinking Through Faith: New Perspectives from Orthodox Christian Scholars.* Crestwood, NY: St. Vladimir's Seminary Press, 2008.

Parry, Robin A. and Christopher H. Partridge, eds. *Universal Salvation? The Current Debate.* Grand Rapids, MI: William B. Eerdmans Publishing Company, 2003.

Perschbacher, Wesley J., ed. *The New Analytical Greek Lexicon.* Peabody, MA: Hendrickson Publishers, Inc., 1999.

Peterson, Eugene. *A Long Obedience in the Same Direction: Discipleship in an Instant Society.* Downers Grove, IL: InterVarsity Press, 2000 (orig. 1980).

Ramelli, Ilaria. *The Christian Doctrine of Apokatastasis: A Critical Assessment from the New Testament to Eriugena.* Leiden, The Netherlands: Brill, 2013.

Ramelli, Ilaria and David Konstan. *Terms for Eternity: Aiōnios and Aïdios in Classical and Christian Texts.* Piscataway, NJ: Gorgias Press, 2011.

Sarris, George W. *Heaven's Doors: Wider Than You Ever Believed!* Trumbull, CT: GWS Publishing, 2017.

Shedd, William G. T. *Dogmatic Theology.* Phillipsburg, NJ: Presbyterian and Reformed Publishing Company, 2003 (orig. 1888).

Sprinkle, Preston, ed. *Four Views on Hell: Second Edition.* Grand Rapids, MI: Zondervan, 2016.

Spurgeon, Charles H. "Profit and Loss." Sermon #92, 1856.

Talbott, Thomas. *The Inescapable Love of God.* Eugene, OR: Cascade Books, 2014, (orig. 1999).

Thayer, Joseph H. *Thayer's Greek-English Lexicon of the New Testament.* Peabody, MA: Hendrickson Publishers, Inc., 1996 (orig. 1885).

Thayer, Thomas. *The Origin and History of the Doctrine of Endless Punishment.* Boston: Universalist Publishing House, 1855.

Zahnd, Brian. *Sinners in the Hands of a Loving God: The Scandalous Truth of the Very Good News.* New York: Waterbrook, 2017.

# SCRIPTURE INDEX

The locations of Scripture references mentioned in the text are identified by chapter number. Chapter 5 ("Presuppositions and Interpretations") is divided into sections dealing with specific passages. Since the chapter is long, the locations of the Scripture references are identified by Passage number (P1, P2, etc.). With thanks to my mom, Phyllis Perkins, for suggesting the idea of including a Scripture index.

# INDEX

# Index

# Index

Ramelli, Ilaria, 14, 236, 251, 349, 378

ransom, 19, 53

Real Men Read Pink, 157

Reardon, Paul, 57

reason, 13, 128, 143, 208, 353

reconciliation, 20, 24, 30, 76, 248, 329–30

redemption, 75, 117, 129, 189

Rees, Timothy, 108

refiner's fire, 229, 246

*Reflections of a Tomboy Grandma,* by Diane Perkins Castro, 1, 345

Reformation, 139, 261

Reformed Theology, 41, 111, 201, 202, 207, 209

regeneration, 41

religion, 296, 299

repentance, 31, 52, 76, 120, 134, 354

restoration, 2, 7, 30, 51, 72, 141, 142, 144

resurrection, 4, 54, 73

reunion, 72, 282

rich man and Lazarus, 354

river of fire, 241, 247

"Rock of Ages," by Augustus Toplady, 151

Rodman for Kids, 57

royal law, 339

## S

salvation, loss of, 136

salvation, post-mortem, 120, 164

sanctification, 181

Sandy Hook, 323

Sarris, George W., ix, 237, 349, 351, 355, 374, 376

Satan, 283, 284, 358

Savior of the world, 29

Scientology, 99

semantics, 188, 191

Sen, Amartya, 291

separation from God, 233

Servetus, Michael, 309

*7 Habits of Highly Effective People, The,* by Stephen Covey, 17

Shadrach, Meshach, and Abednego, 239

Shedd, W. G. T., vi, 186–200

sheep and goats, 139, 177, 350

Sheol, 33, 237, 238, 242

Simeon, 321

sin, 134, 347, 362

*Sinners in the Hands of a Loving God,* by Brian Zahnd, 379

"Sinners in the Hands of an Angry God," by Jonathan Edwards, 167, 379

Sismondi, 303

Six Star Finisher, 58

slavery, 290, 296

Slick, Matt, 41, 253

Smedley, 312

Smith, Timothy Dudley, 111

Snitzelhoff, 113

Sodom, 138, 258

Solomon's temple, 240

Sorting Hat, 258

sovereignty of God, 38, 40, 41, 85, 128, 159, 206, 254, 287

Spaulding Hospital, 57

53668272R00232

Made in the
USA
Lexington, KY